Printed at the Mathematical Centre, 49, 2e Boerhaavestraat, Amsterdam.

The Mathematical Centre, founded the 11-th of February 1946, is a non-profit institution aiming at the promotion of pure mathematics and its applications. It is sponsored by the Netherlands Government through the Netherlands Organization for the Advancement of Pure Research (Z.W.O), by the Municipality of Amsterdam, by the University of Amsterdam, by the Free University at Amsterdam, and by industries.

MATHEMATICAL CENTRE TRACTS 52

P.C. BAAYEN (ed.)

TOPOLOGICAL STRUCTURES

Proceedings of a Symposium, organized by the Wiskundig Genootschap of the Netherlands on November 7, 1973, in honour of J. de Groot (1914-1972)

MATHEMATISCH CENTRUM AMSTERDAM 1974

AMS (MOS) subject classification scheme (1970): 00A10, 01A70, 54A00, 54H99, 54C10, 54A05, 05C10, 18A20, 57A20

ISBN: 90 6196 096 7

Prof. dr. J. de GROOT

born May 7, 1914

died September 11, 1972

CONTENTS

PREFACE

When the Board of the "WISKUNDIG GENOOTSCHAP" decided to select General Topology as the theme of the 1973 Fall Symposium, it did so to honor the memory of J. DE GROOT, member of the "Genootschap" from 1937 till his sudden and untimely death on September 11, 1972.

The Board feels it was fortunate in finding M.A. MAURICE of the Vrije Universiteit in Amsterdam willing to organize the symposium, which was held in Amsterdam on November 7, 1973.

Apart from a memorial lecture on the topological work of DE GROOT, lectures were given by J.M. AARTS (Delft), H. HERRLICH (Bremen) and E.A. MICHAEL (Seattle, Wash.; temporarily Zürich). In addition a few close associates and friends of DE GROOT, who had helped in providing material for the memorial lecture, were invited to contribute a paper by title. Of those invited, R.D. ANDERSON and miss N.S. KROONENBERG (Baton Rouge, Lafayette) and G. STRECKER (Manhattan, Kansas) responded positively.

In addition, these Proceedings contain notes of a lecture given by DE GROOT (in a Summer course of the Mathematical Centre) a few weeks before he died. In this lecture he described a new idea for using graphs in topology, and it is clear from notes left by him, and from some of his last conversations, that he intended to prepare a paper on the subject that was to contain much more that what we can reconstruct now. Two of his students, W.J. BLOK and J. BRUIJNING, using the notes left by DE GROOT, reconstructed his lecture, worked out the proofs and added some examples. Also, BRUIJNING used these ideas to obtain a new and simple proof of DE GROOT's internal characterization of the cubes I^n and I^∞. We are grateful that BLOK and BRUIJNING permitted us to add their reports to these Proceedings.

On behalf of the Board of the "WISKUNDIG GENOOTSCHAP" I sincerely thank Prof. MAURICE for organizing this symposium, and the lecturers for their indispensable and vital assistance in making the symposium a success. Also, I want to express my gratitude both to the lecturers and to those who otherwise contributed papers to these Proceedings for their congenial cooperation.

Thanks are due also to the Dutch Government, which financially supported the Symposium, and to the Mathematical Centre, which made it possible to publish these Proceedings.

P.C. Baayen.

TOPOLOGICAL STRUCTURES

SOME CLASSES OF QUOTIENT MAPS by E. MICHAEL

TOPOLOGICAL STRUCTURES by H. HERRLICH

COMPONENT PROPERTIES AND FACTORIZATIONS by G.E. STRECKER

OPEN PROBLEMS IN INFINITE-DIMENSIONAL TOPOLOGY

by R.D. ANDERSON and NELLY KROONENBERG

MATHEMATICAL CENTRE TRACTS 52, 1974, 1-28

THE TOPOLOGICAL WORKS OF J. DE GROOT

P.C. BAAYEN *)

1. The decease of JOHANNES DE GROOT on September 11, 1972 put an end to an active and productive life. At this symposium, organized in part to honor the memory of DE GROOT, I may ask your attention for a survey of his work as a topologist. The interesting contributions of DE GROOT outside the domain of topology (such as his papers on algebra or analysis) will not be touched upon in this lecture; neither will DE GROOT's papers dealing with subjects of a philosophical nature be discussed. A more comprehensive treatment of the complete scientific work of DE GROOT is to be found in the paper *In memoriam J. de Groot, 1914-1972* in: Nieuw Archief voor Wiskunde (3), 21 (1973) 1-36 (in Dutch), or in the obituary paper *Johannes de Groot 1914-1972* in: General Topology and its Applications, 3 (1973) 3-32. These papers were used extensively in the preparation of the present lecture.

A restriction to the activities of DE GROOT in the field of topology does not imply, however, a reduction to a discussion of those sixty-odd among his papers dealing with topological themes: the importance of DE GROOT as a topologist derives at least as much from his influence as teacher, as colleague and as friend on the scientific activities of the mathematicians around him. That influence has been large; for an explanation, one should take into account not only the qualities of the mathematician DE GROOT, but also those of the teacher and of the man.

---

*) Free University at Amsterdam & Mathematical Centre, Amsterdam
The Netherlands

Professor DE GROOT was an inspiring teacher. His lectures always were prepared carefully, and they were of great suggestiveness. But most of all his regularly conducted "discussions of progress" with assistants, co-workers and others interested in his kind of mathematics, have been of great importance to those who participated. DE GROOT always was full of ideas and suggestions which others could put to use or might elaborate upon. A colleague in the USA wrote to me about such meetings: "Han would sit there with ideas and suggestions shooting from him like sparks! Indeed, so many good ideas would come out of these sessions that it was a little frustrating that one could hope to follow through on only a few of them until the next meeting."

DE GROOT knew how to put his students to work, and he got them to tell him and each other regularly about their approach, their results and frustrations. His criticism then was without exception both to the point and kind. The stimulating interest of DE GROOT in the work of his students and his continuous encouragement resulted in several publications (some of them jointly with him). Under his supervision twelve doctoral theses were completed [*)] (eleven of these deal with topological subjects).

Please permit me to add a few remarks about the man HAN DE GROOT, as I have known him. DE GROOT was a man of great sensitivity, hiding his vulnerability behind a behavior of great charm and courteousness, at the same time remaining somewhat detached. He worked hard, and took scientific endeavour -especially mathematics- very seriously; he asked much of his coworkers, but required most of himself. DE GROOT had a strict sense of justice; when confronted with unfairness in his direct environment, he could not remain inactive. He was not easily persuaded to accept a compromise.

As a consequence of this combination of traits his life -especially during his last years- was not always easy. Again and again, however, the work with his students afforded him comfort and consolation.

2. In the scientific activities of DE GROOT, two periods are to be discerned. From 1940 to 1964 he was involved with a great number of diverse -but often interconnected- problems (although almost from the start some dominant themes can be recognized). From 1964 -in which year he suffered a serious illness- the creation of new, "global" topological theories came

---

[*)] A list of these doctoral theses is appended at the end of this paper (p.26).

to the fore.

Among the fields in which DE GROOT published results before 1964, the most important ones are the following:

(i) extension of topological or continuous maps; theory of compactifications;
(ii) non-archimedean topology; theory of dimension;
(iii) groups of autohomeomorphisms; rigid spaces;
(iv) linearization of maps;
(v) cardinal invariants of topological spaces.

Subjects on which DE GROOT worked since 1964, are

(vi) cotopology;
(vii) characterization of complete regularity as a separation axiom, and, originating from this, the study of "GA-compactifications";
(viii) antispaces; connectedly generated spaces;
(ix) superextensions; supercompactness;
(x) topological manifolds, and infinite-dimensional topology.

In this lecture it will not be possible to treat adequately DE GROOT's contributions to each of these subjects. Some will be skipped altogether, others will be touched upon much too concisely. However, I hope the topics selected for more extensive discussion will give you some idea of the diversity and the originality of the topological works of DE GROOT.

3. From the introduction to DE GROOT's thesis [7] (from 1942) *) I quote the first four sentences:
"Studying some domain of science, one tries at first to obtain a global overview of the terrain to be investigated. In doing so, one usually selects "the course of least resistance", avoiding for the time being those regions which offer special difficulties.

Thus it happened in topology. One of the domains, offering particular difficulties even now, although investigations have already made considerable progress, is that to which belongs the theory of non-compact, respectively non-bicompact spaces."

---

*) The following system of references is used throughout this article. Publications of DE GROOT -of which a list is added- are referred to by means of arabic numbers between square brackets. Roman numbers are used to refer to theses prepared under his supervision. All additional references are identified by bracketed lower-case letters.

DE GROOT continues, saying that after the compact spaces first locally compact spaces were studied, and that another important abstraction was introduced by ZIPPIN, namely, his concept of *semicompactness* or *rimcompactness* (a topological space is rimcompact if every point has arbitrary small neighborhoods with compact boundary). Then he suggests:
"Subsequent to the introduction of the concepts compact (...) and semicompact it becomes natural to continue in this way and consider spaces, in which every point has arbitrary small neighborhoods with (...) rimcompact boundaries; etc. etc. If one persists in this way, there exists a reasonable chance that after some time one will gain knowledge of the properties of very general non-compact spaces".

In a later chapter of his thesis DE GROOT amplifies these ideas, defining the *compactness degree* $\mathrm{cmp}\ X$ of a space X in the following way:

$\mathrm{cmp}\ X = -1$	$\Leftrightarrow$	X is compact;
$\mathrm{cmp}\ X \le n+1$	$\Leftrightarrow$	every $p \in X$ has arbitrary small neighborhoods U such that cmp (boundary U) $\le n$;
$\mathrm{cmp}\ X = n$	$\Leftrightarrow$	$\mathrm{cmp}\ X \le n+1$ and $\mathrm{cmp}\ X \not\le n$.

It is clear that the rimcompact spaces are exactly those spaces X for which $\mathrm{cmp}\ X \le 0$.

We need a few more definitions. If (Y,j) is a compactification of X -i.e., j is a topological map of X on a dense subset of Y, and Y is compact- we will call $Y\setminus j[X]$ the *remainder* of X in this compactification. The *compactness deficiency* $\mathrm{def}\ X$ of a space X is the least number n such that X has a compactification with a remainder of dimension n.

In his thesis DE GROOT proves the following theorem:

If X *is a separable metrizable space, then:* $\mathrm{cmp}\ X = 0 \Leftrightarrow \mathrm{def}\ X = 0$.

(Later on, FREUDENTHAL [g] obtained the equivalence of $\mathrm{cmp}\ X = 0$ and $\mathrm{def}\ X = 0$ for Hausdorff spaces X).

One can easily prove that for separable metrizable spaces X always $\mathrm{cmp}\ X \le \mathrm{def}\ X$. DE GROOT conjectured that $\mathrm{cmp}\ X = \mathrm{def}\ X$ for all such spaces. In [65], DE GROOT & NISHIURA proved the validity of this conjecture for some classes of spaces, such as the extremely disconnected spaces; cf. also [57]. Several mathematicians have investigated this challenging problem. One line of attack might start from a determination of internal, necessary and sufficient conditions for $\mathit{def}\ X \leq n$. Such conditions have been given by AARTS [IX] and SMIRNOV [u],[v]; their respective characterizations are of a completely different nature, however; and DE GROOT's conjecture remains unproved.

Another result in DE GROOT's thesis dealing with rimcompact spaces is the following one:

Among the separable metrizable spaces the ideally compactifiable ones are exactly the rimcompact spaces with a compact space of quasicomponents.

(An *ideal compactification* of a separable metrizable space X is a metric compactification (Y,j) of X with a zero-dimensional remainder, which is maximal among all such compactifications, in the usual sense: if (Z,k) is another metric compactification of X with zero-dimensional remainder, then $k = f \circ j$ for a unique continuous map $f: Y \to Z$; cf. FREUDENTHAL's *endpoint-compactifications*).

DE GROOT calls a set A in a topological space X *quasiconnected* at a point $p \in X \backslash A$, if p has arbitrary small neighborhoods U such that at most one quasicomponent of $U \cap A$ has p as an adherence point. If A is quasiconnected at every $p \in B \subset X \backslash A$, then A is called quasiconnected about B. One of the extension results in DE GROOT's dissertation now can be formulated in the following manner:

Let X *be a dense subset of a separable metrizable space* Y *and let* $Y \backslash X$ *be zero-dimensional. The two assertions below are equivalent:*

(a) *every topological map* f *of* X *onto a subset of an arbitrary separable metrizable space* Z, *with the property that* $\overline{f[X]} \backslash f[X]$ *is zero-dimensional, can be extended to a continuous map* $\tilde{f}: Y \to Z$;

(b) $Y \backslash X$ *is quasiconnected about* X.

Extension theorems were considered in the very first papers of DE GROOT on topology ([2],[4],[6]); in later papers too he returns again and again to extension and compactification results (cf. [54],[55],[56],[58],[69],[85]). By way of illustration we quote two more theorems, both from papers by DE GROOT and MCDOWELL ([55] and [69]):

Let M *be a separable metrizable space, and* Φ *a countable collection of autohomeomorphisms of* M. *Then* M *has a metric compactification* $\tilde{M}$ *such that every* $\phi \in \Phi$ *can be extended to an autohomeomorphism of* $\tilde{M}$.

A locally connected rimcompact Hausdorff space X *possesses a locally con-*

nected compactification if and only if at most finitely many of its components are compact. If this condition is satisfied, then X *even has a locally connected compactification with zero-dimensional remainder. If in addition* X *is locally compact, the one-point compactification of* X *is already locally connected.*

4. At an early stage already DE GROOT showed his interest in non-archimedean topology. For instance, in 1942 a paper [5] by him and F. LOONSTRA appeared, dealing with the topological properties of fields with a non-trivial non-archimedean valuation. A characterization was given of those fields that are separable (in the topological sense), and it was noted that all these separable fields can be compactified to a Cantor set, with a countable remainder.

In 1955 DE GROOT published again on non-archimedean topology; cf. [42] and [34]. He proved:

A metrizable space is non-archimedeanly metrizable if and only if $\dim X = 0$. *A locally non-archimedeanly metrizable* T_2*-space is non-archimedeanly metrizable if and only if it is paracompact.*

As observed in the remark which was added in proof to [42], both these theorems may be obtained from results of KATĚTOV [k] and of MORITA [n]. (Moreover, NAGATA [o],[p] obtained far-reaching generalizations of these results in [34]).

In a certain sense things like this were rather typical for DE GROOT: he got very good ideas completely on his own and worked on them because they interested him; in such a case he sometimes did not spend much time checking the literature (which, moreover, in some instances was not readily available to him), so once in a while it turned out later that he had been anticipated.

The last-quoted theorem shows a connection between zero-dimensionality of a metrizable space, and the existence of a special metric for that space. For separable metric spaces, a direct generalization to the case of arbitrary dimension n was obtained by DE GROOT in [45] (cf. also [49]). Starting from a (rather complicated) result of NAGATA [o],[p] (which, however, applies to all metric spaces), DE GROOT proved the following result:

A topological space X *is a separable metrizable space of dimension at most* n *if and only if its topology can be generated by a totally bounded metric* ρ *satisfying the following condition:*

for every n+3 *points* $x,y_1,y_2,\ldots,y_{n+2}$ *in* X *there are indices* i, j, k *such that* $i \neq j$ *and* $\rho(y_i,y_j) \leq \rho(x,y_k)$.

Apparently it is still an unsolved problem whether or not one can remove the condition of total-boundedness, thus making this theorem applicable to general metric spaces. Cf. also NAGATA [q] for a related theorem, which indeed applies to arbitrary metric spaces.

5. In this lecture I can not dwell long on DE GROOT's work on groups of autohomeomorphisms and on rigid spaces; I will just mention some results. In [53] DE GROOT proved:

Every group is isomorphic to the autohomeomorphism group of some connected, locally connected complete metric space of any preassigned dimension ≥ 1; *every group is isomorphic to the autohomeomorphism group of a compact connected Hausdorff space.*

As an immediate corollary (using the GEL'FAND-KOLMOGOROV theory on rings of continuous functions), he derived the purely algebraic result:

Every group is the automorphism group of some commutative ring.

On the other hand, not every group can be realized as the full autohomeomorphism group of a zero-dimensional Hausdorff space. Cf. also [60].

The special case of the trivial (one-element) group plays a special role. Calling a topological space *rigid* if its autohomeomorphism group consists only of the identity map, DE GROOT & WILLE [50] showed:

There exists a rigid Peano curve in $\mathbb{R}^2$.

In fact, they constructed a Peano curve P (of finite order) with a stronger rigidity property: no topological map of P into P exists, and they also indicate that there are continuously many pairwise topologically distinct rigid Peano curves. In [53] DE GROOT proceeded to prove:

There exists a family of 2^c *zero-dimensional subsets of* $\mathbb{R}$ *such that no member of this family can be mapped into any other member or into itself by means of a locally topological map, nor onto any other member or onto itself by means of a non-constant continuous map. There exists a family of* 2^c *one-dimensional, connected and locally connected subsets of* $\mathbb{R}^2$ *with these properties.*

Generalizations and related results are to be found in [60] and in [71].

6. Through his work (with MCDOWELL) on the simultaneous extension of mappings in metric spaces (cf. section 3 above), DE GROOT became interested in methods to obtain nicer descriptions of such mappings by means of a modified representation of the space. Thus, in [54] he proved the following theorem:

If G *is a locally compact topological group with a countable base, and* G *acts as a topological transformation group on a metric space* M, *the metric in* M *can be replaced by an equivalent one with the result that every* $g \in G$ *becomes uniformly continuous on* M.

Next, DE GROOT investigated the following problem, taking into account that every metric space M can be embedded in a suitable Hilbert space: given a topological transformation group (G,M), with M metrizable, is it possible to embed M into a linear topological space L (preferably a nice one, such as a Hilbert space) in such a way that the mappings $g \in G$ become (restrictions to M of) linear autohomeomorphisms of L? More exactly: do there exist a linear space L, a topological embedding $\tau: M \to L$ and an (algebraic) isomorphism Φ of G into the group $GL(L)$ of all linear autohomeomorphisms of L, such that the diagram

(*)

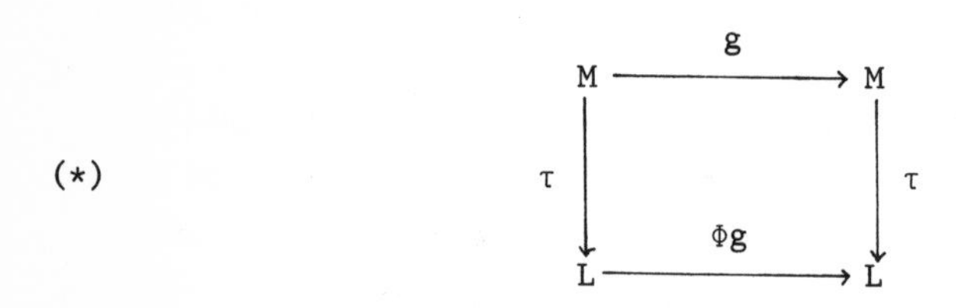

commutes for every $g \in G$? In case the answer is positive, we say that the action of G can be linearized in L.

In [56] he (together with COPELAND, JR.) tackled this problem under the restrictions that M is separable and G is cyclic. It is shown that then the answer is positive, and that for L one may take a separable Hilbert space H. In fact:

There exists a universal linear autohomeomorphism Λ *of* H *such that for any separable metric space* M *and any autohomeomorphism* g_0 *of* M *there exists a topological embedding* $\tau: M \to H$ *with* $g_0 = \tau^{-1} \circ \Lambda \circ \tau$.

Much stronger results can be obtained (as is to be expected) if M is finite-dimensional and G is finite (in fact, in [56] only cyclic G are considered):

Let M *be a separable metric space of dimension* n, *and let* G *be a finite cyclic group of prime order* p. *Then a topological embedding* τ *of* M *into euclidean space* $\mathbb{R}^{3n+3}$ *(even in* $\mathbb{R}^{3n+2}$ *in case* n *is odd or* $p = 2$) *can be found such that the action of* G *is linearized; and these dimensions for the the euclidean spaces are best-possible.*

These results were later taken up and considerably extended by KISTER & MANN [m], who determined the minimal dimension of the euclidean space in the case where G is a compact abelian Lie group with a finite number of distinct isotropy subgroups and M is locally compact, and in the case where G is finite abelian and M is an arbitrary finite-dimensional separable metric space.

In [58], DE GROOT considered topological transformation groups (G,M) where M is an arbitrary metric space and G is compact. He showed that in that case L can be taken to be a (real) Hilbert space, while one can construct Φ in such a way that all linearized maps $\Phi(g)$ are unitary. In the same paper, he also constructed a universal linearization in the much more general case of a completely regular space M of given weight m and a semigroup G of continuous self-maps of M; in this case, naturally, L will no longer be metrizable and is in fact taken to be the topological product of m copies of the reals. DE GROOT also proved (but never published) the following result:

For every transfinite cardinal number m *there exists a denumerable group* Γ *of linear autohomeomorphisms of the real Hilbert space* L *of weight* m *which is universal for all transformation groups* (G,M), *with* M *a metric space of weight* $\leq m$ *and* G *countable.*

This means that for each such (G,M) there exist a topological embedding $\tau: M \to L$ and an isomorphism Φ of G into $GL(L)$, such that not only diagram (*) above commutes, for every $g \in G$, but, moreover, $\Phi[G] = \{\phi : \phi = T \mid \tau M \text{ for some } T \in \Lambda\}$. DE GROOT's construction was first described, and, at the same time, considerably extended, in [VII].

These extended results are treated in the joint paper [73] by BAAYEN & DE GROOT. Let G be a locally compact group. A *weight function* on G is a positive real-valued function f on G with the following properties:

(i) $f(\varepsilon) = 1$, where ε is the unit element of G;

(ii) f is square-summable with respect to Haar measure in G;

(iii) $\sup\{f(\gamma) \cdot f(\gamma\gamma_0)^{-1} : \gamma \in G\} < \infty$ for every $\gamma_0 \in G$.

As shown later by Mrs. PAALMAN-DE MIRANDA [s], such a weight function exists on a locally compact group G if and only if G is in addition σ-compact. Taking this into account, the main result of [73] now is contained in the following theorem:

Let (G,M) *be a topological transformation group, such that* G *is locally compact* σ*-compact, and* M *is metrizable. Then the action of* G *can be linearized in a Hilbert space* H.

One may take H such as to have the same weight as M, except when M is finite. (There are additional results on universal linearizations, and also on linearizations of transformation semigroups).

(It is a natural question to ask whether the isomorphism Φ: G $\to$ GL(H) used in linearizing (G,M) can be taken to be topological. I proved [c] that the Φ constructed in [73] is always an open map, and e.g. is topological if G is compact, provided GL(H) is supplied with the strong operator topology. Modifying (and simplifying) the original proofs, DE VRIES [x] showed that Φ can be taken to be a topological isomorphism in the general case of a locally compact, σ-compact transformation group G.)

7. Skipping the first of DE GROOT's papers on cardinal invariants on topological spaces ([19], dealing with a local cardinal invariant called *quasiorder*, which is related to local-connectedness) I should at least mention a few of his ideas from [64].

DE GROOT introduced the *spread* s(X) of a space X as the supremum of all cardinalities of discrete subspaces of X, and the *height* h(X) as the supremum of all cardinals of well-ordered (by inverse inclusion $\supset$) strictly decreasing families of closed subsets of X. Besides some elementary inequalities, he proved results as the following (where exp m stands for 2^m):

If X *is a Hausdorff space, then* h(X) $\leq$ |X| $\leq$ exp h(X) *and* s(X) $\leq$ |X| $\leq$ $\leq$ exp exp exp s(X). *If* X *is regular, the last inequality may be sharpened to* s(X) $\leq$ |X| $\leq$ exp exp s(X).

Approximately at the same time, similar results (for completely regular spaces) were obtained by ISBELL [i]. Since the appearance of [64], this area has attracted new interest of several mathematicians. A very good source of information is the book of JUHÁSZ [j].

As a matter of fact, such a development is in a certain sense typical for DE GROOT. So to speak he was often present at the beginning of new investigations (frequently his work meant a new impulse); then his attention shifted, and the further developments were left to others.

8. We now come to the second (and last) period in the productive life of DE GROOT. As noted already in section 2, in this period his mathematical activities were mainly devoted to the creation of new topological theories, although he also became interested in, and started to contribute to, infinite-dimensional topology and the theory of topological manifolds.

In this lecture we will only discuss, on the one hand, DE GROOT's ideas on cotopology, and, on the other hand, several results originating from his use of linked systems. In both lines of development, the notion of a subbase plays an important role. (In fact, DE GROOT used to stress the importance of subbases for topology. In [89] he compares a subbase with a set of generators for a group, and writes: "This notion of a subbase is clearly the primitive underlying notion. It is 'algebraically' clear but geometrically 'vague and undetermined'. Although used occasionally -defenition of topological products- it is still -in the author's opinion- neglected to a great extent.")

We will completely leave aside DE GROOT's work on antispaces and compactness as an operator ([68],[70],[72],[79]), his work on connectedly generated spaces ([77]), and his contributions to infinite-dimensional topology ([80],[81]; cf. also [89]).

9. Intrigued (as many before him) by the fact that topologically complete metrizable spaces on the one hand, and locally compact Hausdorff spaces on the other hand, are Baire spaces, DE GROOT set out to find a unifying concept. Of course, such unifications were available already, e.g. both classes of spaces mentioned above are contained in the class of Čech complete spaces, and every Čech complete space is a Baire space. However, an analysis of the standard proof of BAIRE's theorem led DE GROOT first to another unification, the concept of subcompactness [62], and then to a new theory: that of *cotopology* [66],[82],[83].

A centered system $\mathcal{S}$ of open sets in a T_3-space X is called *regular* if for every $U \in \mathcal{S}$ there exists a $V \in \mathcal{S}$ such that $\overline{V} \subset U$. As defined in [62], X is (*countably*) *subcompact* if it has an open base $\mathcal{B}$ such that every (countable) regular centered system $S \subset \mathcal{B}$ has a non-empty intersection.

DE GROOT proved that every locally compact Hausdorff space is subcompact (taking for $\mathcal{B}$ all open sets with compact closure), and that in a metrizable space subcompactness and countable subcompactness are both equivalent to topological completeness. Next, every (countably) subcompact regular space is a Baire space. In fact, every subcompact regular space is an m-Baire space for every infinite cardinal number m, where a space is called *m-Baire* if it is not the union of at most m closed sets none of which contains a non-empty intersection of less than m open sets. As subcompactness is preserved under topological products and unions, while any open continuous image of an m-Baire space is again m-Baire, this leads to a great multitude of Baire spaces.

DE GROOT was not satisfied with the notion of subcompactness because there was no analogue of ALEXANDER's lemma; he kept working on it, and gradually came to cocompactness and cospaces. In some of his earlier lectures on this subject, he used definitions which differ from the one finally adopted in [66],[82] and [83], and which in some cases were used by other authors who came to work in this field, but his final choice amounts to the following:

A topological space X is called *cocompact* if there exists a family $\mathcal{B}$ of closed subsets of X satisfying the following conditions:

(i) for every $p \in X$ and for every neighborhood U of p, there is a $B \in \mathcal{B}$ with $p \in \text{Int } B$ and $B \subset \bar{U}$,

(ii) every centered subsystem of $\mathcal{B}$ has a non-empty intersection.

More generally, a *cotopology* for X is a topology on X generated by an open subbase $\{X \backslash B : B \in \mathcal{B}\}$, where $\mathcal{B}$ is a family of closed subsets of X satisfying (i), and a *cospace* of X is obtained if the underlying set of X is furnished with a cotopology of X. Now, if E is any topological property, X is called *co-E* if it has a cospace satisfying E. In case E is the property of being compact, we get a notion of cocompactness which reduces to the one defined previously, by ALEXANDER's subbase theorem.

We need one more definition: A function $f: X \to Y$ is called *cocontinuous* if X and Y have cospaces $^*X$ and $^*Y$, respectively, such that f considered as a map from $^*X$ into $^*Y$ is continuous. Now, the following holds true:

On metrizable spaces, cocompactness coincides with subcompactness, and hence with topological completeness; all locally compact Hausdorff spaces are cocompact, and every cocompact space is a Baire space. Cocompactness is pre-

served under topological products and unions, and is inherited by open subspaces.

There are many cocompact spaces which are not complete in the sense of ČECH (one easy example is the topological product of uncountably many copies of the real line, as it contains the space of rational numbers -which is not topologically complete- as a closed subset); TALL [w] has given an example in the other direction, which shows that neither class of spaces is a subclass of the other.

Cotopology -the theory of cospaces and of cocontinuous maps- was developed by DE GROOT in close collaboration with AARTS and MCDOWELL. We mention here some of the more interesting results from [82] and [83]. (Most of them are already contained in the seminar notes [66].)

If $^*X$ *is a cospace of* X, *then every compact set in* $^*X$ *is closed in* X.
A separable metric space is cocompact if and only if it is a cocontinuous image of the Cantor discontinuum.
The following spaces all admit compact Hausdorff cospaces: all locally compact Hausdorff spaces; all rim-compact separable complete metric spaces (hence certainly all zero-dimensional separable complete metric spaces); all cocontinuous images of compact Hausdorff spaces.
A space is co-(locally) compact if and only if it is cocompact.

An extensive study of cocompactifications was made by AARTS, who also studied relations between cocompactness and proximity spaces ([a],[b]).

10. We will now discuss those papers of DE GROOT in which superextensions and the property of supercompactness play a prominent role.

The origin of these ideas is to be found in a theorem of DE GROOT and AARTS on complete regularity as a separation axiom. Some definitions are called for.

A family of sets *screens* a pair of disjoint subsets A,B of X if its union is X while each of its members meets at most one of the sets A,B. Let $S \subset P(X)$ be called *normal* (*weakly normal*) if for any two disjoint $A,B \in S$ there exists a subfamily of S consisting of two elements (of a finite number of elements) screening A and B. The family S is called *regular* (*weakly regular*) if for every $x \in X$ and every $A \in S$ such that $x \notin A$, there exists a subfamily of S consisting of two elements (of a finite number of elements) screening $\{x\}$ and A. The family S is called T_1 if for each $x \in X$, $\{x\} =$

$= \cap \{S \in \mathcal{S} : x \in S\}$.

The theorem of AARTS and DE GROOT, referred to above, reads as follows (cf. [67],[75]):

The following three assertions concerning a topological space X *are equivalent:*

(i) X *is completely regular;*

(ii) X *has a base* $\mathcal{S}$ *for the closed sets which is normal and regular;*

(iii) X *has a subbase* $\mathcal{S}$ *for the closed sets which is weakly normal and weakly regular.*

Under the additional assumption that $\mathcal{S}$ is a ring of sets, the characterization (ii) had already been obtained by FRINK [h]. In [66], DE GROOT & AARTS proved the above result under the additional assumption, in assertion (iii), that all finite intersections of members of $\mathcal{S}$ belong to $\mathcal{S}$. In his thesis [IX], AARTS first showed that this additional assumption could be removed (using proximity relations and corresponding compactifications). DE GROOT, however, preferred to work via a Wallman-type compactification, and introduced maximal linked systems and superextensions in order to obtain a proof along these lines. This proof is the one to be found in [75]. Roughly, it runs as follows.

Let $\mathcal{S}$ be a subbase for the closed sets in a T_1-space X such that $\mathcal{S}$ is weakly normal and T_1 (this is certainly the case if $\mathcal{S}$ is weakly normal and weakly regular). Then a compact Hausdorff space $\lambda_{\mathcal{S}}X$, the *superextension* of X relative to $\mathcal{S}$, is defined as follows [74], [76], [78]. The elements of $\lambda_{\mathcal{S}}X$ are maximal linked subsystems of $\mathcal{S}$ (a family of sets is called *linked* if any two of them have a non-empty intersection). The topology of $\lambda_{\mathcal{S}}X$ is obtained by taking as a subbase for the closed sets the collection $\{\{\xi : S \in \xi \in \lambda_{\mathcal{S}}X\} : S \in \mathcal{S}\}$.

The mapping μ: $X \to \lambda_{\mathcal{S}}X$ sending $x \in X$ onto $\{S : x \in S \in \mathcal{S}\}$ is easily seen to be a topological embedding. Let $\beta_{\mathcal{S}}X$ be the closure of $\mu[X]$ in $\lambda_{\mathcal{S}}X$ (in general $\beta_{\mathcal{S}}X \neq \lambda_{\mathcal{S}}X$); $\beta_{\mathcal{S}}X$ is a Hausdorff compactification of X, called in [85] the *GA-compactification of* X *relative to* $\mathcal{S}$. It follows that X is completely regular.

With regard to the notation $\beta_{\mathcal{S}}X$, it should be remarked that $\beta_{\mathcal{S}}X$ is the Cech-Stone compactification βX of X in case $\mathcal{S}$ is the family of all zero-sets of X, and also if X is normal and $\mathcal{S}$ is the family of all closed subsets of X.

It is possible to obtain $\beta_{\mathcal{S}}X$ as a quotient of a Wallman-type compactification $\omega_{\mathcal{S}}X$ (and actually it was obtained in this way in [75]). The quotient map π: $\omega_{\mathcal{S}}X \to \beta_{\mathcal{S}}X$ is studied in [65]. The main result of that paper, however, deals with spaces X in which the collection C of all connected closed subsets is a subbase for the closed sets (i.e. X is connectedly generated). In that case, $\beta_C X$ is connectedly generated too, and if in addition C is weakly regular and weakly normal, then (as is shown in [65] $\beta_C X$ is locally connected.

For a unifying treatment of Wallman-type compactifications and superextensions, see also the extensive paper of CSÁSZÁR [d]. VAN DER SLOT [t] adopted DE GROOT's methods of maximal linked systems to the study of realcompactness.

The defining subbase for the closed sets of $\lambda_S X$, i.e. the collection $\{\{\xi : S \in \xi \in \lambda_S X\} : S \in S\}$, is easily seen to have the property that every linked subcollection has a non-empty intersection. Consequently, the subbase for the open sets of $\lambda_S X$, obtained by going over to complements, is such that any cover by subbase-sets has a subcover consisting of two elements only. Such a subbase is called a *binary subbase*, and a space is called *supercompact* if it has a binary subbase. Therefore, every superextension is supercompact.

In [76], DE GROOT announced that all compact polyhedra are supercompact, and conjectured that the same holds for all compact metric spaces. This conjecture was proven to be true by O'CONNOR [r].

Supercompactness also plays a fundamental role in the results of the joint paper of DE GROOT & SCHNARE [86]. Let an open subbase S of a space X be called *comparable* if whenever $X = S_0 \cup S_1 = S_0 \cup S_2$, with $S_i \in S$ $(i=0,1,2)$, then either $S_1 \subset S_2$ or $S_2 \subset S_1$. Then the main result of [86] is the following theorem:

A topological space X *is homeomorphic to the topological product of totally ordered compact spaces if and only if* X *is a* T_1*-space with a comparable binary subbase for the open sets.*

Using the methods of [86], VAN DALEN & WATTEL [f] obtained a characterization of orderable spaces in terms of subbases. Calling a collection S of sets a *nest* if it is totally ordered under inclusion, and an *interlocking nest* if in addition every $S_0 \in S$ which is an intersection of strictly larger members of S has a representation as a union of strictly smaller members of S, they proved that a T_1-space is orderable if and only if it has an open subbase consisting of two interlocking nests, and that a T_1-space is homeomorphic to a connected ordered space if and only if it has a subbase consisting of two nests L and R such that in every cover of the space by non-empty members of $L \cup R$ there exists an $L \in L$ and an $R \in R$ which intersect. Extending this, VAN DALEN [e] gave a similar characterization of products of orderable spaces.

Comparable binary subbases also turn up in the following truly remarkable characterization of the n-dimensional cubes I^n, to be found in [89]:

A topological space X *is homeomorphic to* I^n *if and only if* X *has the following properties:*

(i) X *is* T_1*;*

(ii) X *is connected;*

(iii) dim X = n;

(iv) X *has a countable, comparable binary subbase.*

A characterization of the Hilbert cube is obtained if condition (iii) is replaced by

(iii*) X *is infinite-dimensional.*

These four conditions (which are quite simple and natural) are independent. Their nicest aspect, of course, is that they are fully intrinsic.

Another characterization of the Hilbert cube K, also intrinsic, was conjectured by DE GROOT, and he tried very hard to prove it: $K = \lambda_G I$ (where I stands for the unit interval, and G denotes the collection of all closed subsets of I). It is still an open problem whether this is true. In this connection another still open conjecture of DE GROOT should be mentioned, namely, that the Hilbert cube is the only homogeneous compactum homeomorphic to its own cone.

Finally, the theory of superextensions can be used to obtain a kind of duality between compact metrizable spaces (with a preferred subbase for the open sets), and countable graphs. DE GROOT was working on this in the weeks before his death. His notes on this subject were studied, arranged and completed by his students W.J. BLOK and J. BRUIJNING. As the publication they prepared [90] is reprinted in the Proceedings of this Symposium (p. 29-37), I will refrain from further treatment here.

11. DE GROOT found much pleasure in his mathematical activities; on the other hand, he took them very seriously, and worked at them quite intensely. For him the creative performance of mathematics was much more than his daily work; it was his high duty. Guided by this sense of responsibility with respect to his scientific work DE GROOT built up many fruitful contacts with

topologists all over the world. He was the main founder of the journal, "General Topology and its Applications."

The productivity of JOHANNES DE GROOT came to an end on September 11, 1972. It is hardly possible to decide, at this moment, how much of his work will turn out to have lasting value. It is not so important either. The integrity and the enthusiasm of his way of practising mathematics will remain a stimulating and influential memory for those who were privileged to know him.

12. LIST OF PUBLICATIONS OF J. DE GROOT

1941

[1] *Mededeeling betreffende het lichaam der rationale functies*, Handelingen 28e Nederl. Natuur- en Geneesk. Congres, Utrecht, 15-17/4/1941 (Boom-Ruijgrok, Haarlem, 1941), pp. 93-94, (in Dutch).

[2] *Sätze über topologische Erweiterung von Abbildungen*, Proc. Kon. Nederl. Akad. Wetensch., 44 (1941) 933-938 (= Indag. Math., 3 (1941) 419-424).

1942

[3] *Bemerkung über die analytische Fortsetzung in bewerteten Körper*, Proc. Kon. Nederl. Akad. Wetensch., 45 (1942) 347-349 (= Indag. Math., 4 (1942) 120-122).

[4] *Bemerkung zum Problem der topologischen Erweiterung von Abbildungen*, Proc. Kon. Nederl. Akad. Wetensch., 45 (1942) 655-657 (= Indag. Math., 4 (1942) 232-234).

[5] *Topologische Eigenschaften bewerteter Körper* (with F. LOONSTRA), Proc. Kon. Nederl. Akad. Wetensch., 45 (1942) 658-664 (= Indag. Math., 4 (1942) 235-241).

[6] *On the extension of continuous functions*, Proc. Kon. Nederl. Akad. Wetensch., 45 (1942) 842-843 (= Indag. Math., 4 (1942) 293-294).

[7] *Topologische Studiën. Compactificatie, voortzetting van afbeeldingen en samenhang*, thesis Univ. of Groningen, (v. Gorcum, Assen, 1942), 109 pp., (in Dutch).

1943

[8] *Ueber die Fortsetzung differenzierbarer Funktionen*, Mathematica (Zutphen) Ser. B, 12 (1943) 15-24.

1945

[9] *Topological classification of all closed countable and continuous classification of all countable pointsets*, Proc. Kon. Nederl. Akad. Wetensch., 48 (1945) 237-248 (= Indag. Math., 7 (1945) 42-53).

1946

[10] *Some topological problems*, Proc. Kon. Nederl. Akad. Wetensch., 49 (1946) 11-17 (= Indag. Math., 8 (1946) 11-17).

[11] *Space groups and their axioms*, Proc. Kon. Nederl. Akad. Wetensch., 49 (1946) 53-58 (= Indag. Math., 8 (1946) 53-58).

[12] *A theorem concerning analytic continuation*, Proc. Kon. Nederl. Akad. Wetensch., 49 (1946) 213-222 (= Indag. Math., 8 (1946) 110-119).

[13] *Continuous classification of all microcompact 0-dimensional spaces*, Proc. Kon. Nederl. Akad. Wetensch., 49 (1946) 518-523 (= Indag. Math., 8 (1946) 337-342).

[14] *A theorem concerning analytic continuation II*, Proc. Kon. Nederl. Akad. Wetensch., 49 (1946) 793-801 (= Indag. Math., 8 (1946) 496-504).

1947

[15] *A note on 0-dimensional spaces*, Proc. Kon. Nederl. Akad. Wetensch., 50 (1947) 131-135 (= Indag. Math., 9 (1947) 94-98).

[16] *Topological characterization of all subsets of the real number system*, Proc. Kon. Nederl. Akad. Wetensch., 50 (1947) 836-844 (= Indag. Math., 9 (1947) 387-395).

[17] *Topologie*, MC report ZC 5 (Mathematisch Centrum, Amsterdam, 1947), iv + 90 pp., (in Dutch).

[18] *Het scheppend vermogen van de wiskundige*, Euclides (Groningen), 22 (1947) 152-167, (in Dutch).

1948

[19] *Local connectedness and quasiorder*, Proc. Kon. Nederl. Akad. Wetensch., 51 (1948) 885-890 (= Indag. Math., 10 (1948) 313-318).

1949

[20] *Fantasie van punt tot punt*, inaugural address at the Technol. Univ. of Delft (Noordhoff, Groningen, 1949), 15 pp., (in Dutch).

[21] *Fantasie van punt tot punt*, Euclides (Groningen), 24 (1949) 243-253, (in Dutch).

1950

[22] *Exemple d'un groupe avec deux générateurs, contenant un sous-groupe commutatif sans un système fini de générateurs*, Nieuw Arch. Wisk. Ser. 2, 23 (1950) 128-130; *erratum*, Nieuw Arch. Wisk. Ser. 2, 23 (1951) 253.

[23] *Realisations under continuous mappings*, Proc. Kon. Nederl. Akad. Wetensch., 53 (1950) 1538-1547 (= Indag. Math., 12 (1950) 483-492).

[24] *Het dimensiebegrip en de nulde dimensie*, in: *Zeven voordrachten over topologie*, Prof. dr. H. FREUDENTHAL & Dr. W. PEREMANS (eds.), Centrumreeks 1 (Noorduijn, Gorinchem, 1950), pp. 26-35, (in Dutch).

1951

[25] *Decomposition spaces I*, Proc. Kon. Nederl. Akad. Wetensch. Ser. A, 54 (= Indag. Math., 13) (1951) 109-115.

1952

[26] *Tijd onder mathematisch aspect*, inaugural address at the Univ. of Amsterdam (Amsterdam, 1952), 20 pp., (in Dutch).

1953

[27] *Handleiding analyse, deel II, met vraagstukken*, Handleidingen bij het onderwijs aan de Technische Hogeschool Delft No. a-3 (D.U.M., Delft, 1953), 160 pp., (in Dutch).

1954

[28] *Het congruentiebegrip*, Faraday, 23 (1954) 1, (in Dutch).

[29] *Free subgroups of the orthogonal group* (with T.J. DEKKER), Compositio Math., 12 (1954) 134-136.

[30] *Decompositions of a sphere* (with T.J. DEKKER), in: Proc. Internat. Congress of Mathematicians 1954, Vol. II (Noordhoff, Groningen & North-Holland Publ. Co., Amsterdam, 1954), p. 209.

[31] *Example of two sets neither of which contains a continuous image of the other*, Proc. Kon. Nederl. Akad. Wetensch. Ser. A, 57 (= Indag. Math., 16) (1954) 525-526.

1955

[32] *On Cohen's topological characterization of sets of real numbers*, Proc. Kon. Nederl. Akad. Wetensch. Ser. A, 58 (= Indag. Math., 17) (1955) 33-35.

[33] *On a compactness criterion of Freudenthal*, Proc. Kon. Nederl. Akad. Wetensch. Ser. A, 58 (= Indag. Math., 17) (1955) 130-131.

[34] *A note on non-Archimedean metrizations* (with H. DE VRIES), Proc. Kon. Nederl. Akad. Wetensch. Ser. A, 58 (= Indag. Math., 17) (1955) 222-224.

[35] *Continuous mappings of a certain family*, Fund. Math., 42 (1955) 203-206.

1956

[36] *A system of continuous, mutually non-differentiable functions*, Math. Z., 64 (1956) 192-194.

[37] *On some problems of Borsuk concerning a hyperspace of compact sets*, Proc. Kon. Nederl. Akad. Wetensch. Ser. A, 59 (= Indag. Math., 18) (1956) 95-103.

[38] *On the axioms of Baer and Kurosh in modular lattices* (with PH. DWINGER), Proc. Kon. Nederl. Akad. Wetensch. Ser. A, 59 (= Indag. Math., 18) (1956) 596-601.

[39] *Orthogonal isomorphic representations of free groups*, Canad. J. Math., 8 (1956) 256-262.

[40] *Decompositions of a sphere* (with T.J. DEKKER), Fund. Math., 43 (1956) 185-194.

[41] *An isomorphism criterion for completely decomposable abelian groups*, Math. Ann., 132 (1956) 328-332.

[42] *Non-archimedean metrics in topology*, Proc. Amer. Math. Soc., 7 (1956) 948-953.

1957

[43] *Indecomposable abelian groups*, Proc. Kon. Nederl. Akad. Wetensch. Ser. A, 60 (= Indag. Math., 19) (1957) 137-145.

[44] *Equivalent abelian groups*, Canad. J. Math., 9 (1957) 291-297.

[45] *On a metric that characterizes dimension*, Canad. J. Math., 9 (1957) 511-514.

[46] *Convex sets in projective space* (with H. DE VRIES), Compositio Math., 13 (1957) 113-118.

[47] *Algemene topologie, Serie voordrachten over Metriseringstheorie*, MC report ZC 42 (Mathematisch Centrum, Amsterdam, 1957), 12 pp., (in Dutch).

1958

[48] *Metrization of a set which is mapped into itself* (with H. DE VRIES), Quart. J. Math. Oxford Ser. 2, 9 (1958) 144-148.

[49] *Some special metrics in general topology*, Colloq. Math., 6 (1958) 283-286.

[50] *Rigid continua and topological group-pictures* (with R.J. WILLE), Arch. Math. (Basel), 9 (1958) 441-446.

[51] *Indecomposable abelian groups with many automorphisms* (with H. DE VRIES), Nieuw Arch. Wisk. Ser. 3, 6 (1958) 55-57.

[52] *Automorphism groups of rings*, in: Internat. Congress of Mathematicians 1958, Abstracts of short comm. and scient. programme, (Edinburgh, 1958), p. 18.

1959

[53] *Groups represented by homeomorphism groups I*, Math. Ann., 138 (1959) 80-102.

[54] *The action of a locally compact group on a metric space*, Nieuw Arch. Wisk. Ser. 3, 7 (1959) 70-74.

1960

[55] *Extension of mappings on metric spaces* (with R.H. MCDOWELL), Fund. Math., 48 (1960) 251-263.

1961

[56] *Linearization of a homeomorphism* (with A.H. COPELAND JR.), Math. Ann., 144 (1961) 80-92.

[57] *Generalisaties van het dimensiebegrip (Seminar notes on compactification and dimension in metric spaces)* (with J.M. AARTS, A.B. DE MIRANDA & H. DE VRIES), MC report ZC 54 (Mathematisch Centrum, Amsterdam, 1961), 29 pp., (in Dutch).

1962

[58] *Linearization of mappings*, in: *General Topology and its Relations to Modern Analysis and Algebra*, Proc. Symp. in Prague, 1-18/9/1961, (Academia, Prague, 1962), pp. 191-193.

1963

[59] *A case of colouration in the four colour problem* (with J.M. AARTS), Nieuw Arch. Wisk. Ser. 3, 11 (1963) 10-18.

[60] *Autohomeomorphism groups of 0-dimensional spaces* (with R.H. MCDOWELL), Compositio Math., 15 (1963) 203-209.

[61] *Almost fixed point theorems for the Euclidean plane* (with H. DE VRIES & T. VAN DER WALT), Proc. Kon. Nederl. Akad. Wetensch. Ser. A, 66 (= Indag. Math., 25) (1963) 606-612.

[62] *Subcompactness and the Baire category theorem*, Proc. Kon. Nederl. Akad. Wetensch. Ser. A, 66 (= Indag. Math., 25) (1963) 761-767.

1964

[63] *Additive groups of integer-valued functions over topological spaces*, in: Proc. Colloq. Abelian Groups, Tihany, 1963 (Akademia Kiado, Budapest, 1964), pp. 77-80.

1965

[64] *Discrete subspaces of Hausdorff spaces*, Bull. Acad. Polon. Sci. Sér. Sci. Math. Astronom. Phys., 13 (1965) 537-544.

1966

[65] *Inductive compactness as a generalization of semicompactness* (with T. NISHIURA), Fund. Math., 58 (1966) 201-218.

[66] *Colloquium cotopologie 1964-1965* (notes by J.M. AARTS, introduction by J. DE GROOT), MC report ZC 65 (Mathematisch Centrum, Amsterdam, 1965), vi + 49 pp., (in Dutch).

[67] *Complete regularity as a separation axiom* (with J.M. AARTS), Internat. Congress of Mathematicians 1966, Abstracts of brief scientific communications, section 8, (Moscow, 1966), p. 31.

1967

[68] *An isomorphism principle in general topology*, Bull. Amer. Math. Soc., 73 (1967) 465-467.

[69] *Locally connected spaces and their compactifications* (with R.H. MCDOWELL), Illinois J. Math., 11 (1967) 353-364.

[70] *The compactness operator in general topology* (with G.E. STRECKER & E. WATTEL), in: *General Topology and its Relations to Modern Analysis and Algebra II*, Proc. Second Prague Topological Symp. 1966 (Academia, Prague, 1967), pp. 161-163.

1968

[71] *On the existence of rigid compact ordered spaces* (with M.A. MAURICE), Proc. Amer. Math. Soc., 19 (1968) 844-846.

[72] *Strengthening Alexander's subbase theorem* (with G.E. STRECKER, E. WATTEL & H. HERRLICH), Duke Math. J., 35 (1968) 671-676.

[73] *Linearization of locally compact transformation groups in Hilbert space* (with P.C. BAAYEN), Math. Systems Theory, 2 (1968) 363-379.

[74] *Superextensions* (with G.A. JENSEN & A. VERBEEK), MC report ZW 1968-017 (Mathematisch Centrum, Amsterdam, 1968), 33 pp.

1969

[75] *Complete regularity as a separation axiom* (with J.M. AARTS), Canad. J. Math., 21 (1969) 96-105.

[76] *Supercompactness and superextensions*, in: *Contributions to Extension Theory of Topological Structures*, Proc. Symp. Berlin 1967 (VEB Deutscher Verlag Wiss., Berlin, 1969), pp. 89-90.

[77] *Connectedly generated spaces*, in: Proc. Internat. Symp. on Topology and its Applications, Herceg-Novi, Yugoslavia, 25-31/8/1968 (Belgrade, 1969), pp. 171-175.

[78] *Superextensions* (with G.A. JENSEN & A. VERBEEK), in: Proc. Internat. Symp. on Topology and its Applications, Herceg-Novi, Yugoslavia, 25-31/8/1968 (Belgrade, 1969), pp. 176-178.

[79] *Compactness as an operator* (with H. HERRLICH, G.E. STRECKER & E. WATTEL), Compositio Math., 21 (1969) 349-375.

[80] *Lectures on dimension theory for infinite dimensional spaces* (with J. NAGATA), mimeographed notes, Univ. of Florida (Gainesville (Fla.), 1969), 27 pp.

[81] *Topological Hilbert space and the dropout effect*, MC report ZW 1969-016 (Mathematisch Centrum, Amsterdam, 1969), 7 pp.

1970

[82] *Cocompactness* (with J.M. AARTS & R.H. MCDOWELL), Nieuw Arch. Wisk. Ser. 3, 18 (1970) 2-15.

[83] *Cotopology for metrizable spaces* (with J.M. AARTS & R.H. MCDOWELL), Duke Math. J., 37 (1970) 291-295.

1971

[84] *Andere modellen voor ruimte en tijd*, Kon. Nederl. Akad. Wetensch., Verslag Afd. Natuurk., 80 (1971) 113-115, (in Dutch).

1972

[85] *Local connectedness and other properties of GA compactifications* (with J.L. HURSCH & G.A. JENSEN), Proc. Kon. Nederl. Akad. Wetensch. Ser. A, 75 (= Indag. Math., 34) (1972) 11-18.

[86] *A topological characterization of products of compact totally ordered spaces* (with P.S. SCHNARE), General Topology and Appl., 2 (1972) 67-73.

[87] *Gekleurde en ongekleurde graphen als hulpmiddel bij algebra en meetkunde*, in: *Vacantiecursus 1972, Grafentheorie en haar toepassingen*, MC report VC 26, (Mathematisch Centrum, Amsterdam, 1972), pp. III.1 - III.6, (in Dutch).

[88] *On the topological characterization of manifolds*, in: *General Topology and its Relations to Modern Analysis and Algebra III*, Proc. Third Prague Topological Symp. 1971, (Academia, Prague, 1972) pp. 155-158.

[89] *Topological characterizations of metrizable cubes*, in: *Theory of sets and topology* (Felix Hausdorff Gedenkband), VEB Deutscher Verlag Wiss., Berlin, 1972, pp. 209-214.

1974

[90] *Graph representations of topological spaces*, notes prepared by W.J. BLOK & J. BRUIJNING, report of the Math. Institute of the Univ. of Amsterdam, 1974; also reproduced in these Proceedings, pp. 29-37.

[91] *The generalized Schoenflies theorem for Euclidean n-space*, in: *Topics in Topology*, in: Coll. Math. Soc. János Bolyai 8, Budapest, 1974, pp. 351-354.

13. DOCTORAL THESES PREPARED UNDER SUPERVISION OF J. DE GROOT

[I] KORTHAGEN, TH. J., *Fundamentaalgroepen voor algemene continua*, thesis Univ. of Amsterdam (Poortpers, Amsterdam, 1955), 55 pp. (in Dutch).

[II] DEKKER, T.J., *Paradoxical decompositions of sets and spaces*, thesis Univ. of Amsterdam (van Soest, Amsterdam, 1958), 46 pp.

[III] BOLAND, J. CH., *Bijdrage tot de topologie der vlakke, continue afbeeldingen*, thesis Univ. of Amsterdam (van Soest, Amsterdam, 1959), 52 pp., (in Dutch).

[IV] VRIES, H. DE, *Compact spaces and compactifications. An algebraic appraoch*, thesis Univ. of Amsterdam (van Gorcum, Assen, 1962), 79 pp.

[V] WALT, T. VAN DER, *Fixed and almost fixed points*, thesis Univ. of Amsterdam (Mathematisch Centrum, Amsterdam, 1963), 131 pp. [also MC Tracts 1, 128 pp.].

[VI] MAURICE, M.A., *Compact ordered spaces*, thesis Univ. of Amsterdam (Mathematisch Centrum, Amsterdam, 1964), 76 pp. [also MC Tracts 6, 76 pp.].

[VII] BAAYEN, P.C., *Universal morphisms*, thesis Univ. of Amsterdam (Mathematisch Centrum, Amsterdam, 1964), 188 pp. [also MC Tracts 9, 182 pp.].

[VIII] PAALMAN-DE MIRANDA, A.B., *Topological semigroups*, thesis Univ. of Amsterdam (Mathematisch Centrum, Amsterdam, 1964), 174 pp. [also MC Tracts 11, 169 pp.].

[IX] AARTS, J.M., *Dimension and deficiency in general topology*, thesis Univ. of Amsterdam (Druk V.R.B, Groningen, 1966), 55 pp.

[X] SLOT, J. VAN DER, *Some properties related to compactness*, thesis Univ. of Amsterdam (Mathematisch Centrum, Amsterdam, 1968), 60 pp. [also MC Tracts 19, 56 pp.].

[XI] WATTEL, E., *The compactness operator in set theory and topology*, thesis Univ. of Amsterdam (Mathematisch Centrum, Amsterdam, 1968), vi + 62 pp. [also MC Tracts 21, viii + 61 pp.].

[XII] VERBEEK, A., *Superextensions of topological spaces*, thesis Univ. of Amsterdam (Mathematisch Centrum, Amsterdam, 1972), xii + 156 pp. [also MC Tracts 41, x + 155 pp.].

REFERENCES

[a] AARTS, J.M., *Cocompactifications*, Nederl. Akad. Wetensch. Proc. Ser. A, 73 (= Indag. Math., 32) (1970) 9-21.

[b] AARTS, J.M., *Semi-proximity spaces and cocompactness I, II*, Nederl. Akad. Wetensch. Proc. Ser. A, 73 (= Indag. Math., 32) (1970) 403-427.

[c] BAAYEN, P.C., *Topologische linearisering*, Report 2, Wiskundig Seminarium, Free University, Amsterdam, 1967 (in Dutch).

[d] CSÁSZÁR, A., *Wallman-type compactifications and superextensions*, Period. Math. Hungar., 1 (1971) 55-80.

[e] DALEN, J. VAN, *A characterization of products of totally ordered spaces*, to appear in General Topology and Appl.

[f] DALEN, J. VAN & E. WATTEL, *A topological characterization of ordered spaces*, to appear in General Topology and Appl.

[g] FREUDENTHAL, H., *Kompaktisierungen und Bikompaktisierungen*, Nederl. Akad. Wetensch. Proc. Ser. A, 54 (= Indag. Math., 13) (1951) 184-192.

[h] FRINK, O., *Compactifications and semi-normal spaces*, Amer. J. Math., 86 (1964) 602-607.

[i] ISBELL, J.R., *Remarks on spaces of large cardinal number*, Czechoslovak Math. J., 14 (89) (1964) 383-385.

[j] JUHÁSZ, I., *Cardinal functions in topology*, Mathematical Centre Tracts 34, Amsterdam, 1971.

[k] KATĚTOV, M., *On the dimension of non-separable spaces I*, Czechoslovak Math. J., 2 (77) (1952) 333-368, (in Russian).

[m] KISTER, J.M. & L.N. MANN, *Equivariant imbeddings of compact abelian Lie-groups of transformations*, Math. Ann., 148 (1962) 89-93.

[n] MORITA, K., *Normal families and dimension theory for metric spaces*, Math. Ann., 128 (1954) 350-362.

[o] NAGATA, J., *On a relation between dimension and metrization*, Proc. Japan Acad., 32 (1956) 237-243.

[p] NAGATA, J., *Note on dimension theory for metric spaces*, Fund. Math., 45 (1958) 143-181.

[q] NAGATA, J., *On a special metric and dimension*, Fund. Math., 55 (1964) 181-194.

[r] O'CONNOR, J.L., *Supercompactness of compact metric spaces*, Nederl. Akad. Wetensch. Proc. Ser. A, 73 (= Indag. Math., 32) (1970) 30-34.

[s] PAALMAN-DE MIRANDA, A.B., *A note on W-groups*, Math. Systems Theory, 5 (1971) 168-171.

[t] SLOT, J. VAN DER, *A survey of realcompactness*, in: *Theory of sets and topology* (Felix Hausdorff Gedenkband), VEB Deutscher Verlag Wiss. Berlin, 1972, pp. 473-494.

[u] SMIRNOV, YU. M., *Ueber die Dimension der Adjunkten bei Kompaktifizierungen*, Monatsber. Deutsch. Akad. Wiss. Berlin, 7 (1965) 230-232.

[v] SMIRNOV, YU M., *On the dimension of remainders in bicompact extensions of proximity and topological spaces*, Mat. Sb., 69 (111) (1969) 141-160, (in Russian).

[w] TALL, F.D., *A counterexample in the theories of compactness and of metrization*, Nederl. Akad. Wetensch. Proc. Ser. A, 76 (= Indag. Math. 35) 471-474.

[x] VRIES, J. DE, *A note on topological linearization of locally compact transformation groups in Hilbert space*, Math. Systems Theory, 6 (1972) 49-59.

MATHEMATICAL CENTRE TRACTS 52, 1974, 29-37

GRAPH REPRESENTATIONS OF TOPOLOGICAL SPACES

J. DE GROOT

Notes prepared by W.J. Blok & J. Bruijning *)

INTRODUCTION

This paper contains a report of a lecture given by the late J. DE GROOT at the *Vacantiecursus (Summerschool) 1972* of the Mathematical Centre, Amsterdam [2]. Use has been made of DE GROOT's own notes. Section 1 contains a survey of the basic theory; in section 2 some examples are discussed.

The graph-theoretical approach developed in this paper was used in 1973 to give an alternative proof for DE GROOT's topological characterization for the interval, finite-dimensional cubes, and the Hilbert cube [1]. This proof, due to J. BRUIJNING, is presented in the appendix following this paper.

1. BASIC THEORY

DEFINITION. Let X be a set and F a collection of subsets of X. Then F is called *linked* iff

$$\forall F_1, F_2 \in F\colon F_1 \cap F_2 \neq \emptyset.$$

DEFINITION. Let X be a topological space and S a subbase for the closed

*) University of Amsterdam, Amsterdam, The Netherlands.

sets of X. Then S is called *binary* iff

$$\forall S' \subset S\colon S' \text{ is linked} \Rightarrow \bigcap S' \neq \emptyset.$$

The space X is called *supercompact* if it has a binary subbase for its closed sets.

DEFINITION. A *graph* is a pair (V,K), where V is a set and K is a collection of two-point subsets of V. The elements of V are called *vertices*, the elements of K *edges*. A graph (V,K) is *complete* (or: a *clique*) if $\{u,v\} \in K$ for all $u,v \in V$ with $u \neq v$. If $V' \subset V$, the induced graph structure will make V' a *subgraph* (V',K') of (V,K).

We will make use of the following theorem [3].

THEOREM (J. O'CONNOR). *If* X *is a compact metric space, then* X *has a binary subbase for the closed sets (i.e.,* X *is supercompact).*

Let X be a supercompact T_1-space, and S a binary subbase for the closed sets. To the pair (X,S) we assign a graph $(V,K) = \Gamma(X,S)$ as follows:

$$V = S;$$

$$K = \{\{S_1,S_2\} \mid S_1 \in S,\ S_2 \in S,\ S_1 \neq S_2 \text{ and } S_1 \cap S_2 \neq \emptyset\}.$$

Conversely, to each graph (V,K) we assign a pair $(X,S) = \Delta(V,K)$, where X is a supercompact T_1-space and S a binary subbase for its closed sets, in the following manner: first we put

$$X = \{W \mid W \text{ is a maximal clique (m.c.) in } V\};$$

next, if $v \in V$ we define $v^+ = \{W \mid v \in W \in X\}$, and we put

$$S = \{v^+ \mid v \in V\}.$$

We now proceed to show that indeed X is a supercompact T_1-space with S as a binary subbase for the closed sets. First, X is T_1: suppose $x,y \in X$, $x \neq y$. Recall that x and y are m.c.'s in (V,K). By the maximality of x, there exists a $v \in V$ such that $v \in x \backslash y$. It follows that $x \in v^+$ and $y \notin v^+$.

Next, S is binary: suppose $S' \subset S$ is linked, say $S' = \{w^+ \mid w \in V' \subset V\}$. Now $w_1^+ \cap w_2^+ \neq \emptyset$ means: there exists an m.c. x with $w_1 \in x$ and $w_2 \in x$. So $\{w_1, w_2\} \in K$. Consequently, V' is a complete subgraph of (V,K). Let x_0 be an m.c. with $V' \subset x_0 \in X$. It then follows that $x_0 \in \bigcap\{w^+ \mid w \in V'\} = \bigcap S'$.

We write $(X,S) \approx (X',S')$ if there exists a bijection from X onto X' which takes S onto S'. We write $(V,K) \approx (V',K')$ if there exists a bijection from V onto V' which takes K onto K'.

THEOREM 1. $\Delta \circ \Gamma\ (X,S) \approx (X,S)$.

PROOF. Write $\Delta \circ \Gamma\ (X,S) = (X',S')$. Define $\phi\colon X \to X'$ as follows.

$$\phi\colon x \longmapsto \{S \in S \mid x \in S\}.$$

Note that $\phi(x)$ is an m.c. in $\Gamma(X,S)$ and therefore a point of X'.

Now ϕ is onto: if $x' \in X'$, i.e. x' is an m.c. of $\Gamma(X,S)$, we take x to be the unique point in $\bigcap\{S \in S \mid S \in x'\}$ (since s' is maximal complete, it is maximal linked and $\bigcap x'$ indeed consists of one point). It follows that $x' = \phi(x)$. Also, ϕ is one-to-one: let $x,y \in X$, $x \neq y$. Then $\exists S \in S\colon x \in S$ and $y \notin S$. Therefore, $S \in \phi(x)$ and $S \notin \phi(y)$, so that $\phi(x) \neq \phi(y)$.

Finally, let $S \in S$. Then $\phi(S) = \{S'' \subset S \mid S''$ is a maximal linked family in S and $S \in S''\} = S^+ \in S'$. Conversely, if $S' \in S'$, then there exists a vertex v of $\Gamma(X,S)$ with $S' = v^+$. But v belongs to S, hence it follows that $S' = \phi(v)$. This completes the proof. □

In general, it is not true that $\Gamma \circ \Delta(V,K) \approx (V,K)$, as can be seen from the following example:

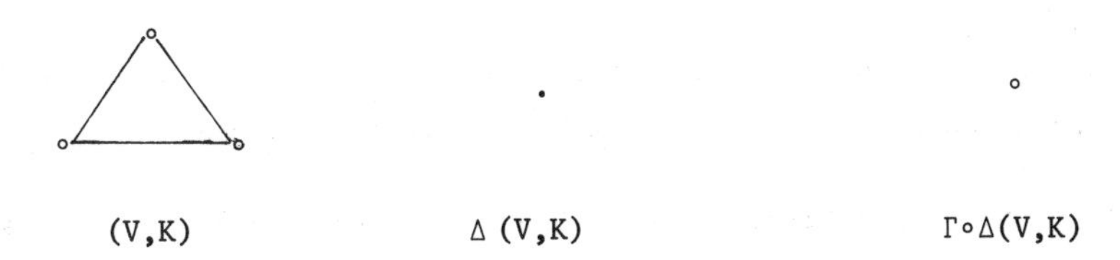

DEFINITION. A graph (V,K) is a *space graph* if for all $v,v' \in V$ such that $v \neq v'$ there exists an m.c. $x \subset V$ such that

$$(v \in x \text{ and } v' \notin x) \quad \text{or} \quad (v' \in x \text{ and } v \notin x).$$

<u>THEOREM 2</u>. *If* (V,K) *is a space graph, then* $\Gamma\circ\Delta(V,K) \approx (V,K)$.

<u>PROOF</u>. Write $\Gamma\circ\Delta(V,K) = (V',K')$. Define $\phi\colon V \to V'$ by

$$\phi\colon v \longmapsto \{x \mid x \text{ is an m.c. of } V \text{ and } v \in x\}.$$

(Note that $\phi(v) = v^{+}$, hence $\phi(v)$ is a subbase element of $\Delta(V,K)$ and therefore a vertex of V'.)

We show that ϕ is surjective: a vertex of V' is a subbase set in $\Delta(V,K)$, hence it is of the form v^{+} with $v \in V$. Also ϕ is injective: if $v_1 \neq v_2$ $(v_1,v_2 \in V)$ then there exists an m.c. $x \subset V$ such that, say, $v_i \in x$ and $v_2 \notin x$. It follows that $v_1^{+} \neq v_2^{+}$.

Next, ϕ takes K onto K': if $\{v_1,v_2\} \in K$, there exists an m.c. x which contains both v_1 and v_2. It follows that $v_1^{+} \cap v_2^{+} \neq \emptyset$, and that $\{v_1^{+},v_2^{+}\} \in K'$. Finally, if $v_1',v_2' \in V'$ are such that $\{v_1',v_2'\} \in K'$, and if $v_i' = v_i^{+}$ with $v_i \in V$ $(i=1,2)$, then apparently $v_1^{+} \cap v_2^{+} \neq \emptyset$; so there exists an m.c. x in V which contains both v_1 and v_2, implying that $\{v_1,v_2\} \in K$. □

<u>REMARK</u>. If X is any supercompact T_1-space, and $\mathcal{S}$ a binary subbase for the closed sets of X, then $\Gamma(X,\mathcal{S})$ is a space graph: if $S_1 \neq S_2$ $(S_1,S_2 \in \mathcal{S})$ there exists, say, a point $x \in S_1 \setminus S_2$. Then $W = \{S \in \mathcal{S} \mid x \in S\}$ is an m.c. with $S_1 \in W$ and $S_2 \notin W$.

Thus we have established a one-to-one correspondence (up to $\approx$-equivalence) between pairs $(X,\mathcal{S})$ (where X is a supercompact T_1-space, and $\mathcal{S}$ a binary subbase for the closed sets) and space graphs (V,K).

<u>DEFINITION</u>. Let (V,K) be a graph. Then $A \subset V$ is called neighbouring if $A \cap M \neq \emptyset$ for every m.c. $M \subset V$.

<u>DEFINITION</u>. Let (V,K) be a graph. A *small clique* (s.c.) is a clique $U \subset V$ which is contained in at least two different maximal cliques.

<u>REMARK</u>. If $(X,\mathcal{S})$ is non-trivial, and $\Gamma(X,\mathcal{S}) = (V,K)$, then $\emptyset \subset V$ is an s.c.

<u>THEOREM 3</u>. *Let* X *be compact* T_1, $\mathcal{S}$ *a binary subbase for the closed sets of* X *and* $\Gamma(X,\mathcal{S}) = (V,K)$. *Then the following conditions are equivalent:*

(i) X *is* T_2;

(ii) *for every s.c.* $U \subset V$ *an* $A \subset V\setminus U$ *exists which is finite and neighbouring.*

PROOF.

(i) $\Rightarrow$ (ii).

Let X be T_2; let U be an s.c. and let W_1, W_2 be distinct m.c.'s such that $U \subset W_1 \cap W_2$. Define $F \subset X$ by $F = \bigcap\{S \mid S \in U\}$, and let x_i be the unique point in $\bigcap\{S \mid S \in W_i\}$ $(i=1,2)$. Then $x_i \in F$ $(i=1,2)$ and $x_1 \neq x_2$. Since X is T_2, it is easily verified that there exist $S_1,\ldots,S_k \in \mathcal{S}$ such that

$$1) \quad X = \bigcup_{j=1}^{k} S_j$$

and

$$2) \quad \text{for } 1 \leq j \leq k \text{ either } x_1 \notin S_j \text{ or } x_2 \notin S_j.$$

Now consider $A = \{S_1,\ldots,S_k\} \subset V$. First note that $A \subset V \backslash U$ if $S_j \in U$, then S_j does not contain, say, x_1. But $x_1 \in F = \bigcap\{S \mid S \in U\}$; therefore, $S_j \notin U$.

Secondly, every m.c. $M \subset V$ determines a point $x \in X$. If j is such that $x \in S_j$, then $S_j \in M$. So A is neighbouring.

(ii) $\Rightarrow$ (i).

Suppose (ii) holds, and let $x_1, x_2 \in X$, $x_1 \neq x_2$. Then $U = \{S \mid S \in \mathcal{S}$ and $x_1, x_2 \in S\}$ is an s.c. (even if it is empty), as it is contained in $W_1 \cap W_2$ where $W_i = \{S \mid x_i \in S \in \mathcal{S}\}$ $(i=1,2)$.

By condition (ii), a finite set $A \subset V \backslash U$ exists which is neighbouring. It is easily verified that A covers X and that no $S \in A$ contains both x_1 and x_2. Thus X is T_2. □

THEOREM 4. *Γ and Δ define a one-to-one correspondence (up to $\approx$-equivalence) between the class of countable space graphs satisfying condition* (ii) *of theorem 3 and the class of pairs* $(X,\mathcal{S})$ *with* X *a supercompact metrizable space and* $\mathcal{S}$ *a countable binary subbase for the closed sets of* X.

PROOF. If X is supercompact metric, and $\mathcal{S}$ is countable, then evidently $\Gamma(X,\mathcal{S})$ is a countable space graph satisfying condition (ii) of theorem 3.

Conversely, if (V,K) is a countable space graph satisfying condition (ii) of theorem 3, then (V,K) is a compact T_2-space with a countable (sub-) base. By the Urysohn Metrization Theorem, X is metrizable. □

REMARK. By O'CONNOR's theorem (page 30), every compact metric space has a (countable) binary subbase. It therefore follows that compact metric spaces can be studied in terms of countable graphs.

We conclude this section by stating

THEOREM 5. *If* $(X,S) \approx (X',S')$, *then* $\Gamma(X,S) \approx \Gamma(X',S')$; *if* $(V,K) \approx (V',K')$, *then* $\Delta(V,K) \approx \Delta(V',K')$.

We omit the trivial proof.

2. EXAMPLES

2.1. Countable space with cofinite topology

A countable discrete graph is the space graph of a countable set with the cofinite topology; the subbase consists of all one-point subsets.

The same space is also obtained from the graph $(\mathbb{N}, \{\{k,k+1\} \mid k \in \mathbb{N}\})$.

o——o——o——o——o——o——. . . .
1 2 3 4 5 6

Each subbase element is generated by a point of the graph; $1 \in \mathbb{N}$ generates $\{\{1,2\}\}$, a one-point set (the m.c. $\{1,2\}$ is a point of the space), and $k+1 \in \mathbb{N}$ generates the subbase element $\{\{k,k+1\},\{k+1,k+2\}\}$.

2.2. The Cantor set

Consider the Cantor set $C = \prod_{i=1}^{\infty} \{0,1\}$, with the closed binary subbase $S = \{\pi_i^{-1}(\varepsilon) \mid i \in \mathbb{N}, \varepsilon \in \{0,1\}\}$. Then $\Gamma(C,S)$ is equivalent to the following graph (V,K):

$$V = \mathbb{N} \times \{0,1\};$$

$$K = \{\{(k,i),(\ell,j)\} \mid k,\ell \in \mathbb{N},\ i,j \in \{0,1\}, \text{ and } (k\neq\ell \text{ or } i=j)\}.$$

This is easily seen by identifying $\pi_k^{-1}(i)$ with (k,i).

The complementary graph (V,K') (i.e. $(v,w) \in K'$ iff $(v,w) \notin K$) does look like

(1,1) (2,1) (3,1) (4,1)

(1,0) (2,0) (3,0) (4,0) .....

2.3. <u>The converging point sequence</u>

Let $X = \{0\} \cup \{\frac{1}{n} \mid n \in \mathbb{N}\}$, considered as a subspace of $\mathbb{R}$. As a subbase we select

$$\mathcal{S} = \{\{\tfrac{1}{n}\} \mid n \in \mathbb{N}\} \cup \{X \backslash \{\tfrac{1}{n}\} \mid n \in \mathbb{N}\}.$$

Then $\Gamma(X,\mathcal{S}) \approx (V,K)$ with $V = \mathbb{N} \times \{0,1\}$ and with $\{(k,i),(\ell,j)\} \in K$ iff ($i+j = 1$ and $k \neq \ell$ or $i = j = 1$) (in fact, $(n,0)$ represents $\{\frac{1}{n}\} \in \mathcal{S}$, and $(n,1)$ represents $X \backslash \{\frac{1}{n}\} \in \mathcal{S}$).

The complementary graph of (V,K) is indicated below:

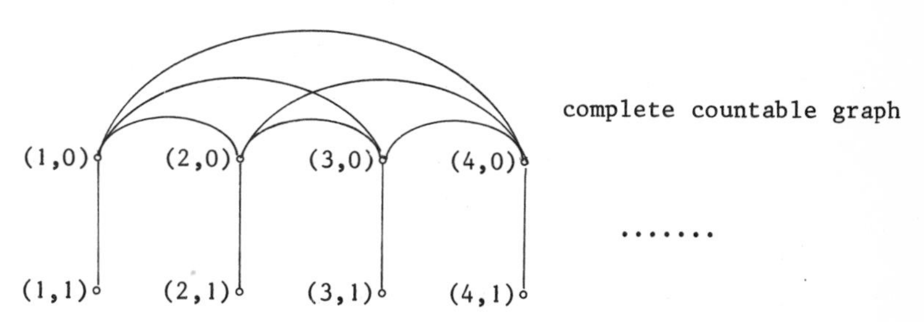

2.4. <u>The unit square</u>

Let X be the unit square I^2, and let $\mathcal{S}$ be the collection of all closed subsquares of I^2 of the form

$$I^2 \cap \{(x,y) \mid \max(|x-p|,|y-q|) \leq \frac{1}{n+1}\}$$

for some $p,q \in \mathbb{Q} \cap I$ and $n \in \mathbb{N}$. (This is a binary subbase for the closed sets in I^2, with the euclidean topology).

Let $V = (I^2 \cap \mathbb{Q}^2) \times \mathbb{N}$. We let $((p,q),n)$ represent the subbase element with centre (p,q) and "radius" $\frac{1}{n+1}$. Then $\Gamma(I^2,\mathcal{S}) \approx (V,K)$, with K defined by

$$K = \{\{((q_1,q_2),n),((r_1,r_2),m)\} \mid \max(|r_1-q_1|,|r_2-q_2| \le \frac{1}{n+1} + \frac{1}{m+1}\}.$$

2.5. Topological products

Suppose we are given a collection $\{(X_\alpha,\mathcal{S}_\alpha) \mid \alpha \in A\}$ of compact T_1-spaces with binary closed subbases. We also suppose (without loss of generality) that $X_\alpha \notin \mathcal{S}_\alpha$, for all $\alpha \in A$. We write (V_α,K_α) for $\Gamma(X_\alpha,\mathcal{S}_\alpha)$.

For each $\alpha \in A$, the following holds true, as a consequence of our assumption that $X_\alpha \notin \mathcal{S}_\alpha$:

$$\forall v \in V_\alpha\ \exists w \in V_\alpha : \{v,w\} \notin K_\alpha.$$

This follows from the following

LEMMA. *If* $x \notin S_1 \in \mathcal{S}$, *then an* $S_2 \in \mathcal{S}$ *exists such that* $x \in S_2 \subset X\backslash S_1$.

PROOF. Let $\mathcal{S}' = \{S \in \mathcal{S} \mid x \in S\}$. Since X is T_1, $\cap\mathcal{S}' = \{x\}$. Define $\mathcal{S}'' = \mathcal{S}' \cup \{S_1\}$; then $\cap\mathcal{S}'' = \emptyset$. Therefore there exist $S',S'' \in \mathcal{S}''$ such that $S' \cap S'' = \emptyset$. Necessarily, $S' = S_1$ or $S'' = S_1$. □

Next, let X be the topological product $\prod_{\alpha\in A} X_\alpha$; a subbase for the closed sets of X is the collection

$$\mathcal{S} = \{\pi_\alpha^{-1}(S_\alpha) \mid \alpha \in A \text{ and } S_\alpha \in \mathcal{S}_\alpha\}.$$

We define the *join* of the graphs (V_α,K_α) to be the graph (V,K) with

$$V = \bigcup_{\alpha\in A} V_\alpha;$$

$$K = \{\{v_1,v_2\} \mid (\exists\alpha,\beta\in A)\ [v_1 \in V_\alpha \text{ and } v_2 \in V_\beta \text{ and } (\alpha \neq \beta \text{ or } (\alpha = \beta \text{ and } \{v_1,v_2\} \in K_\alpha))]\}.$$

(Implicitly we are assuming that $V_\alpha \cap V_\beta = \emptyset$ whenever $\alpha \neq \beta$). It is easily verified that

$$\Gamma(X,\mathcal{S}) \approx (V,K).$$

REMARK. Example 2.2 is a special case of this situation.

REFERENCES

[1] GROOT, J. DE, *Topological characterizations of metrizable cubes*, in: *Theory of sets and topology* (Felix Hausdorff Gedenkband), VEB Deutscher Verlag Wiss., Berlin, 1972, pp. 209-214.

[2] GROOT, J. DE, *Gekleurde en ongekleurde graphen als hulpmiddel bij algebra en meetkunde* in: *Vacantiecursus 1972, Grafentheorie en haar toepassingen*, Mathematical Centre Report VC 26, Amsterdam, 1972, pp. III.1 - III.6, (in Dutch).

[3] O'CONNOR, J.L., *Supercompactness of compact metric spaces*, Nederl. Akad. Wetensch. Proc. Ser. A, 73 (= Indag. Math., 32) (1970) 30-34.

MATHEMATICAL CENTRE TRACTS 52, 1974, 38-47

APPENDIX

CHARACTERIZATION OF I^n AND I^∞ USING THE GRAPH THEORETICAL REPRESENTATION OF J. DE GROOT

J. BRUIJNING *)

In [1] DE GROOT proved a topological characterization of finite-dimensional cubes and of the Hilbert cube in terms of a certain subbase for the closed sets. Using the graph-theoretical representation this characterization can be formulated in terms of graph-theoretical concepts. Moreover, the proof of the characterizations in these terms consists of simple manipulation with diagrams.

It should be stressed that the present proof is, to a great extent, a translation of the proof in [1]. However, it is felt that in some aspects it can be considered to be a simplification; in particular the product structure becomes a triviality, using example 2.5 of the preceding paper. A disadvantage is the need for a graph-theoretical characterization of the real interval, whereas in the original proof a well known topological characterization could be used.

In the sequel all space graphs are assumed to be countable.

In the characterization mentioned above the following concept of *comparability* is used.

DEFINITION 1. A closed subbase S for a space X is called *comparable* provided that each pair $S_1, S_2 \in S$, such that both S_1 and S_2 have an empty intersection with some third member $S_3 \in S$, is inclusion comparable ($S_1 \subseteq S_2$ or $S_2 \subseteq S_1$).

In order to translate this concept of comparability in graph-theoretical terms we need first the translation of inclusion-comparability of subbase

*) University of Amsterdam, The Netherlands.

elements. Consequently we need to define a partial order on the vertices of a graph. This order is defined as follows:

DEFINITION 2. Let (V,K) be a space graph. The relation $<$ is defined by

$$v_1 < v_2 \quad \text{iff} \quad \{v_1,v_2\} \in K \quad \text{and}$$

$$\forall v \in V\ [\{v_2,v\} \in K \Rightarrow (\{v_1,v\} \in K \text{ or } v=v_1)].$$

Hence $v_1 < v_2$ means that v_1 and v_2 are neighbours in K such that all neighbours of v_2 are neighbours of v_1. If v_1 and v_2 are thought of as being the points corresponding to subbase elements S_1 and S_2 then $v_1 < v_2$ means that $S_2 \subseteq S_1$. This can be shown using the following lemma which was formulated in example 2.5 of the preceding paper.

LEMMA 1. *If* $x \notin S_1 \in \mathcal{S}$ *then an* $S_2 \in \mathcal{S}$ *exists such that* $x \in S_2 \subset X \backslash S_1$.

We write $v_1 \leq v_2$ for $v_1 < v_2$ or $v_1 = v_2$. Clearly $v_1 \leq v_2 \leq v_1$ implies that v_1 and v_2 have the same neighbours; since (V,K) is a space graph this means that $v_1 = v_2$. This shows that $\leq$ is a well defined partial order (transitivity and reflexivity being trivial).

In the course of our argument we frequently use diagrams representing (incomplete) information on vertices, edges and the ordering $\leq$ in the graph. In these diagrams an arc: $v_1 \bullet\!\!-\!\!-\!\!-\!\!\bullet v_2$ denotes that $v_1 \neq v_2$ and $\{v_1,v_2\} \in K$. Absence of an edge between distinct points v_1 and v_2 is represented by an interrupted arc: $v_1 \bullet\text{-----}\bullet v_2$. A directed arc from v_1 to v_2 represents a pair $v_1 \neq v_2$ such that $v_2 < v_1$: $v_1 \bullet\!\!\rightarrow\!\!\bullet v_2$. Finally a pair $v_1 \neq v_2$ such that v_1,v_2 are $\leq$-comparable ($v_1 \leq v_2$ or $v_2 \leq v_1$) is denoted by $v_1 \bullet\!\!\leftrightarrow\!\!\bullet v_2$.

We should emphasize that in our diagrams distinct points represent distinct vertices of V. Part of the argumentations is dedicated showing that vertices assumed to be distinct in fact are so.

As an example we present two graphical conclusions from the fact that $\leq$ is a partial order.

LEMMA 2. (a) $v_1 \bullet\!\!\rightarrow\!\!\bullet v_2 \Rightarrow \exists v_3[$ $v_1 \bullet\!\!\rightarrow\!\!\bullet v_2$, $v_1 \bullet\text{-----}\bullet v_3$, $v_3 \bullet\!\!-\!\!-\!\!\bullet v_2$ $]$

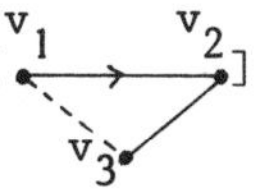

(*If* $v_1 > v_2$ *then* $\exists v_3[\{v_1,v_3\} \notin K, \{v_2,v_3\} \in K]$).

(b) $v_1 \quad v_2 \quad v_3 \Rightarrow v_1 \quad v_2 \quad v_3$

(*If* $v_1 > v_2$ *and* $\{v_1,v_3\} \in K$ *then* $\{v_2,v_3\} \in K$).

Using this partial order we now can formulate the translation of "comparability" in terms of space graphs.

DEFINITION 3. The space graph (V,K) is called *comparable* provided that for each pair of vertices v_1,v_2 such that for some $v_3 \in V$ both $(v_1,v_3) \notin K$ and $(v_2,v_3) \notin K$ either $v_1 < v_2$ or $v_2 < v_1$.

In our graphical representation

Another concept which may be translated is connectivity (combined with binarity). If $S_1 \cap S_2 = \emptyset$ then there exists an $x \notin S_1 \cup S_2$; consequently there exist S_3 and S_4 such that $x \in S_3 \cap S_4$ and $S_1 \cap S_3 = S_2 \cap S_4 = \emptyset$ (use lemma 1). If, moreover, S is comparable it is certain that $S_3 \neq S_4$.

DEFINITION 4. The space graph (V,K) is called *contiguous* provided for each pair (v_1,v_2) such that $(v_1,v_2) \notin K$ a pair of vertices v_3,v_4 can be found such that $(v_3,v_4) \in K$, $(v_1,v_3) \notin K$, $(v_2,v_4) \notin K$.

Clearly a space graph corresponding to a comparable binary subbase of a connected space is contiguous.

The corresponding diagrams are:

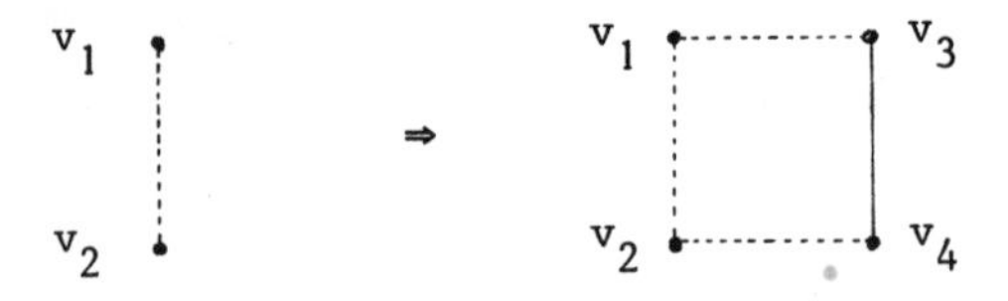

Using the above terminology we now can characterize a collection of space graphs for the real interval.

PROPOSITION 1. *Let* (V,K) *be a countable space graph. Let* $\le$ *be the partial order from definition 2. Suppose that the following conditions are satisfied:*

(i) *The relation of* $\le$*-comparability on* V *is an equivalence relation, partitioning* V *into two equivalence classes* V_1 *and* V_2. *Moreover,* $\le$ *restricted to either of these classes is a total dense order without smallest element.*

(ii) *If* $v_2 > w_2$ *then there exist* v_1 *and* w_1 *such that* $v_1 > w_1$, $\{v_1,w_2\} \in K$ *and* $\{w_1,v_2\} \notin K$, *or in our graphical representation:*

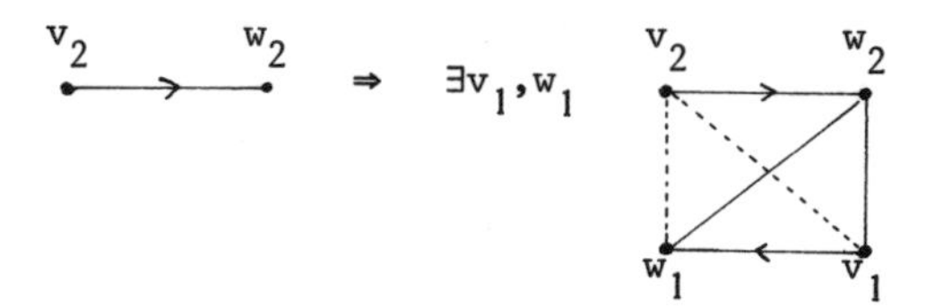

Then $\Delta(V,K)$ *is equivalent to the real interval. equipped with a subbase* S *of the following type:*

$$S = \{[0,d] \mid d \in D_1\} \cup \{[d,1] \mid d \in D_2\} ,$$

where D_1,D_2 *are countable dense subsets of* $[0,1)$ *and* $(0,1]$ *respectively.*

REMARK. For the space graph corresponding to a subbase S of the above type (i) is trivial, whereas (ii) follows from the fact that D_1 and D_2 are dense.

PROOF. Since V is countable and the ordering $\le$ restricted to V_2 is dense and has no smallest element, there exists an order preserving bijection ϕ from V_2 into $(0,1]$, such that $D_2 = \phi(V_2)$ is a dense subset of $(0,1]$.

For a given point $v_1 \in V_1$ we define a cut in V_2 as follows: $C(v_1) = C(v_1) = (L(v_1),R(v_1))$, where $L = L(v_1) = \{v \mid v \in V_2 \text{ and } \{v,v_1\} \in K\}$ and $R = R(v_1) = \{v \mid v \in V_2 \text{ and } \{v,v_1\} \notin K\}$.

Indeed, from the definition of $\le$ it is clear that $v \in L$, $w \in R$ implies that $w \le v$ is impossible; hence, since v and w are comparable, $v < w$. R is not empty; since V_1 contains no smallest element there exists a $w_1 < v_1$. Consequently, by lemma 2, one has:

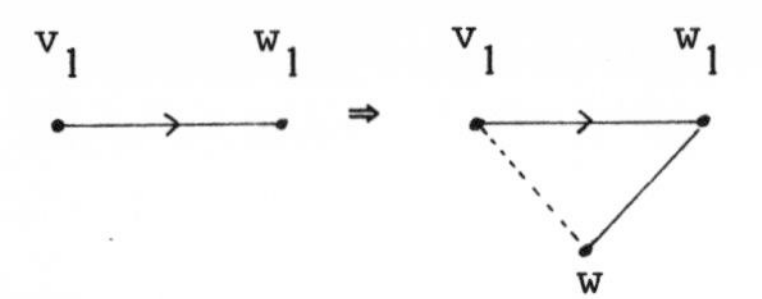

(there exists a w such that $\{v_1,w\} \notin K$, $\{w_1,w\} \in K$); clearly $w \in V_2$ and hence $w \in R$.

If v_1 is not the $\leq$-largest element of V_1 one proves in the same way that $L = L(v_1)$ is not empty.

Using the order-preserving dense embedding ϕ: $V_2 \to D_2$, one finds that v_1 also defines a cut in D_2 and hence a cut in I, represented by a real number < 1 (since R is not empty). This number is denoted by $\psi(v_1)$. We prove that $\psi(V_1) = D_1$ is dense in $[0,1)$ and that ψ is 1-1 order reversing from V_1, $\leq$ onto D_1 equipped with the natural order in I.

D_1 is dense in $[0,1)$: since D_2 is dense in $(0,1]$ it is sufficient to show that in between any two points of D_2 lies a point of D_1. This, however, is clear from the diagrams:

$v_2 \quad w_2 \quad \Rightarrow \quad \exists v_1 \quad v_2 \quad w_2 \quad v_1$

$$(v_2 \leq w_2 \Rightarrow \exists v_1 \; [\{v_2,v_1\} \in K, \{w_2,v_1\} \notin K] \Rightarrow$$

$$\Rightarrow \exists v_1 \; [v_2 \in L(v_1), w_2 \in R(v_1)] \Rightarrow$$

$$\Rightarrow \exists v_1 \; [\phi(v_2) \leq \psi(v_1) \leq \phi(w_2)]) .$$

ψ is one-one. Suppose $v_1 < w_1$. Using (ii) there exist v_2 and w_2 such that $\{v_1,w_2\} \in K$, $\{w_1,v_2\} \notin K$.

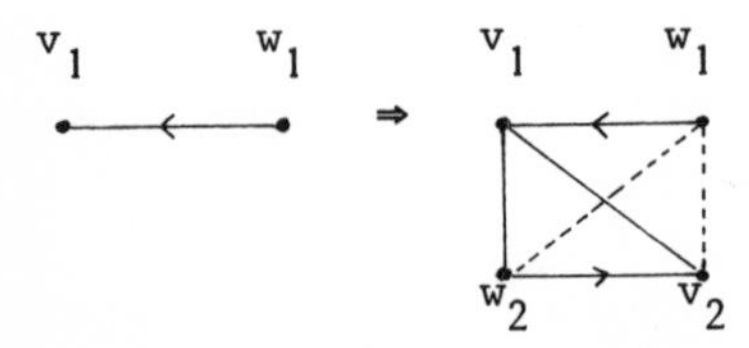

This shows that $v_2,w_2 \in L(v_1) \cap R(w_1)$. Since, moreover, $v_2 < w_2$, this implies

$\psi(w_1) \leq \phi(v_2) < \phi(w_2) \leq \psi(v_1)$; hence $\psi(w_1) \neq \psi(v_1)$. In fact $\psi(w_1) < \psi(v_1)$, which shows that ψ is order reversing.

Now consider the subbase $S = \{[0,d] \mid d\in D_1\} \cup \{[d,1] \mid d\in D_2\}$. Defining $\chi: S\to V$ by $\chi([0,d]) = \psi^{-1}(d)$, $\chi([d,1]) = \phi^{-1}(d)$, it is easily seen that $\Gamma(I,S) \approx (V,K)$ by χ. This proves our characterization. □

The characterization of the cube by DE GROOT [1] read as follows: A cube X (I^n or I^∞) is topologically characterized by the following properties:

(1) X is a T_1 space,

(2) X is a connected space,

(3) X satisfies the second axiom of countability,

(4) X has a closed subbase S which is both binary and comparable (without loss of generality we can assume that S itself is countable and that $X \notin S$).

The translation of this characterization reads as follows.

THEOREM 1. *Let* (V,K) *be a space graph which is both comparable and contiguous. Then* $\Delta(V,K)$ *is equivalent to a cube equipped with a comparable binary subbase.*

PROOF. From the conditions it cannot be excluded that the graph (V,K) contains a vertex corresponding to the whole space as a subbase element, i.e. a vertex which is connected to all other vertices. If present, such a vertex is uniquely determined and may be removed from the graph without changing $\Delta(V,K)$ essentially. Hence we assume in the sequel that (V,K) contains no such vertex. The proof depends on some lemmas.

LEMMA 3. *Under the assumptions of the theorem, the relation of* $\leq$*-comparability is an equivalence relation.*

PROOF. Since $\leq$ is a partial order it is sufficient to prove that

(i) $v_1 \leq v_3$ and $v_2 \leq v_3 \Rightarrow v_1 \leq v_2$ or $v_2 \leq v_1$,

(ii) $v_3 \leq v_1$ and $v_3 \leq v_2 \Rightarrow v_1 \leq v_2$ or $v_2 \leq v_1$.

Both cases become trivial if $v_1 = v_2$, and also if $v_1 = v_3$ or if $v_2 = v_3$. Therefore, we may assume v_1, v_2 and v_3 to be distinct vertices.

(ii) Suppose $v_3 \leq v_1$ and $v_3 \leq v_2$. Let w be a vertex such that $(v_3,w) \notin K$ (such a w exists because of our assumption that (V,K) contains no vertex connected with all vertices). By the definition of $\leq$ we conclude that (v_1,w), $(v_2,w) \notin K$, and using the comparability of (V,K), we see that $v_1 \leq v_2$ or $v_2 \leq v_1$.

In our graphical representation:

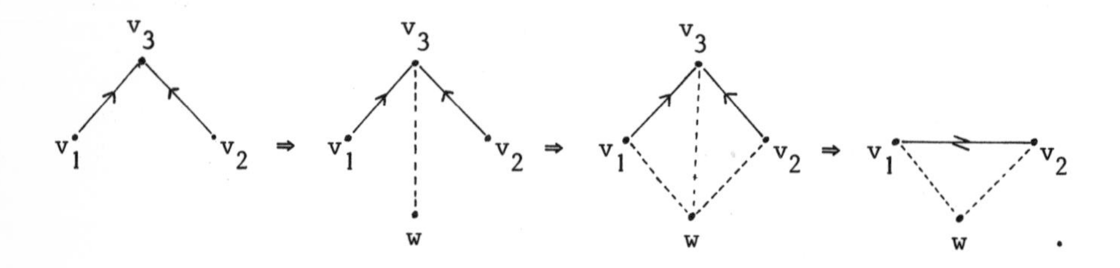

(i) Let $v_3 \geq v_1$ and $v_3 \geq v_2$. By the definition of $\leq$ we conclude that $(v_1,v_2) \in K$. Let v_4 and v_5 be vertices such that $(v_1,v_4),(v_2,v_5) \notin K$. If $v_4 = v_5$ then, by comparability, v_1 and v_2 are $\leq$-comparable. Otherwise we conclude that (v_3,v_4), $(v_3,v_5) \notin K$. Consequently v_4 and v_5 are $\leq$-comparable; say $v_4 \leq v_5$. Then $(v_1,v_5) \notin K$. Again, by comparability, $v_1 \leq v_2$ or $v_2 \leq v_1$.

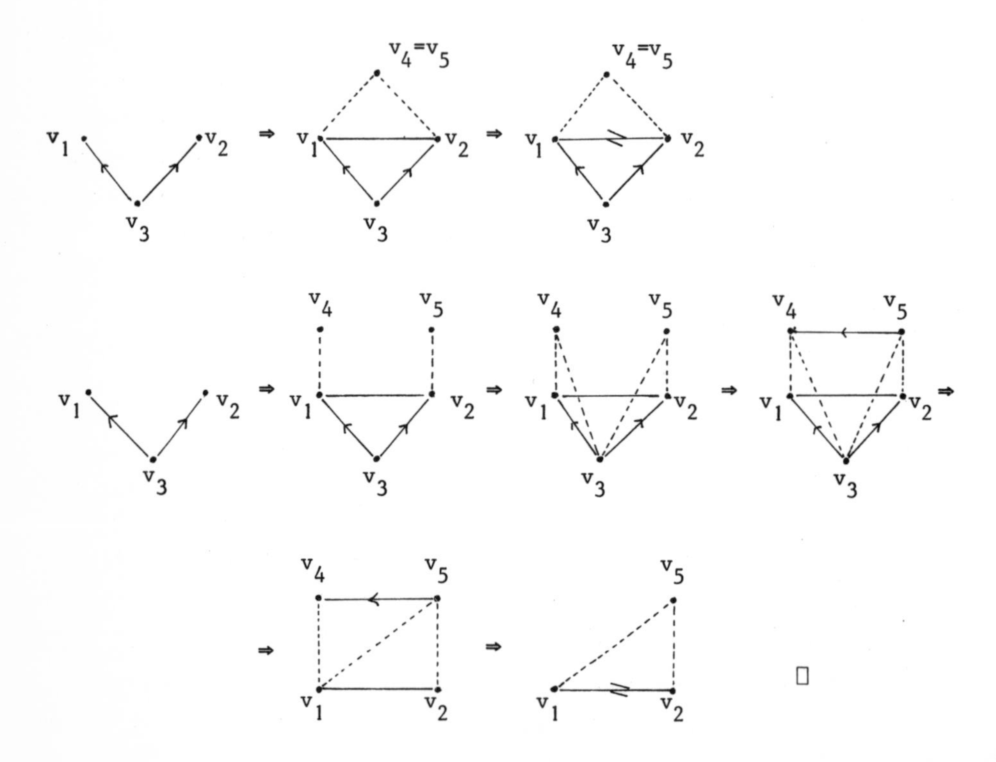

□

The equivalence relation of $\leq$-comparability is denoted $\lesseqgtr$.

LEMMA 4. *For every* $\lesseqgtr$*-equivalence class* w *there exists a unique* $\lesseqgtr$*-equivalence class* w' *such that* $(\forall w \in W)\ (\exists w' \in W')\ ((w,w') \notin K)$.

PROOF. By assumption, for each $w \in V$ there exists a w' such that $(w,w') \notin K$. Moreover, two of such elements w' and w'' are $\lesseqgtr$-equivalent by the comparability condition.

If $v < w$ then $(v,w') \notin K$ implies $(w,w') \notin K$. Hence the "complementary class" is independent from the choice of the representant $w \in W$. □

By lemma 4, the space graph (V,K) may be decomposed as the join of a (countable) sequence of graphs (V_i,K_i), where V_i is the union of a $\lesseqgtr$-equivalence class W_i with its complementary class W_i' and $K_i = K \cap V_i \times V_i$. This is sufficient to show that $\Delta(V,K)$ is the topological product of the spaces $\Delta(V_i,K_i)$. To see this we need the following converse to section 2.5 in the preceding paper.

LEMMA 5. *Let* (V,K) *be a space graph which as a graph is the join of a sequence of graphs* (V_i,K_i). *Then* $\Delta(V,K)$ *is equivalent to the topological product of the spaces* $\Delta(V_i,K_i)$.

PROOF. Since $v \in V_i$ is connected with all vertices in $\bigcup_{j \neq i} V_j$, it is clear that $v,w \in V_i$ have distinct neighbours within V_i if they have so in V. This shows that each (V_i,K_i) is again a countable space graph. Since $\Gamma(\Delta(V_i,K_i)) = (V_i,K_i)$ and $\Gamma(\prod_i \Delta(V_i,K_i))$ is the join of the graphs $\Gamma(\Delta(V_i,K_i))$ we conclude that $\Gamma(\prod_i \Delta(V_i,K_i)) = (V,K)$. This implies $\prod_i \Delta(V_i,K_i) = \Delta(V,K)$. □

To complete the proof of theorem 1 we must show that each (V_i,K_i) is a space graph of the real interval.

LEMMA 6. *Each* (V_i,K_i) *satisfies conditions (i) and (ii) from proposition 1.*

PROOF. The first part of condition (i) is evident from the construction. We must prove, however, that $\leq$ is a dense order without smallest element.

Let W be a fixed $\lesseqgtr$-equivalence class and let W' be its complementary class. Assume $w_2 < w_1$, $w_1,w_2 \in W$. First we find a vertex $w_3 \in W'$ such that $(w_2,w_3) \in K$ and $(w_1,w_3) \notin K$. By contiguity we find w_4 and w_5 such that $(w_4,w_5) \in K$ and (w_1,w_4), $(w_3,w_5) \notin K$. (Note that these vertices all are distinct, and that, moreover, $w_4 \in W'$ and $w_5 \in W$.) Now both $w_1 \lesseqgtr w_5$ and

$w_2 \lessgtr w_5$. The only possible orientations are $w_1 > w_5$ and $w_5 > w_2$, which proves the order > to be dense.

The diagrams are:

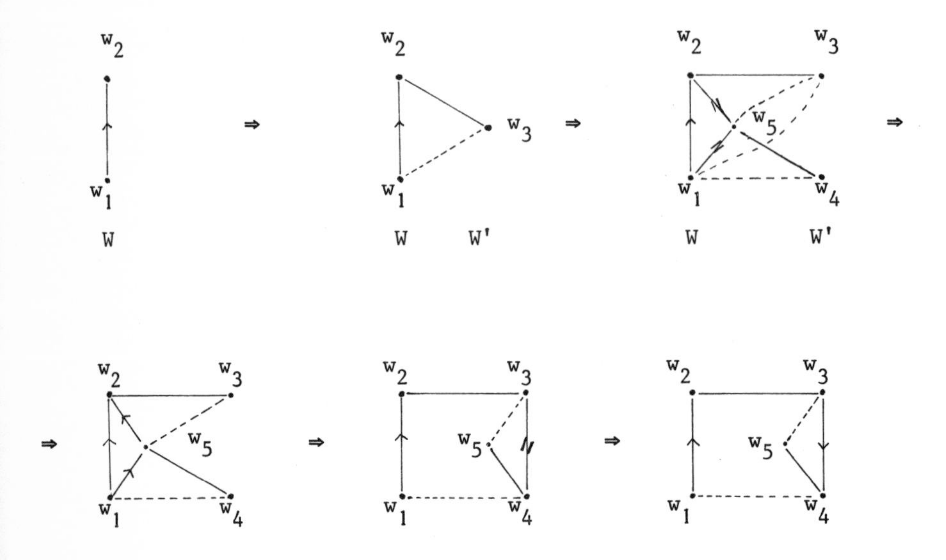

The above diagrams may be used still further. Since w_3, w_4 both are elements of W' we know $w_3 \lessgtr w_4$. Again the only admissible orientation is $w_3 > w_4$; this completes the proof of condition (ii).

Next we have some $w_1 \in W$. Let $w_2 \in W'$ such that $(w_1, w_2) \notin K$. By contiguity there exist w_3, w_4 such that $(w_3, w_4) \in K$, $(w_1, w_3) \notin K$ and $(w_2, w_4) \notin K$. Then $w_3 \in W'$ and $w_4 \in W$. Now w_1 and w_4 are $\leq$-comparable, and again the only possibility is $w_1 > w_4$. This shows that W has no smallest element, completing the proof of condition (i).

In our pictorial representation:

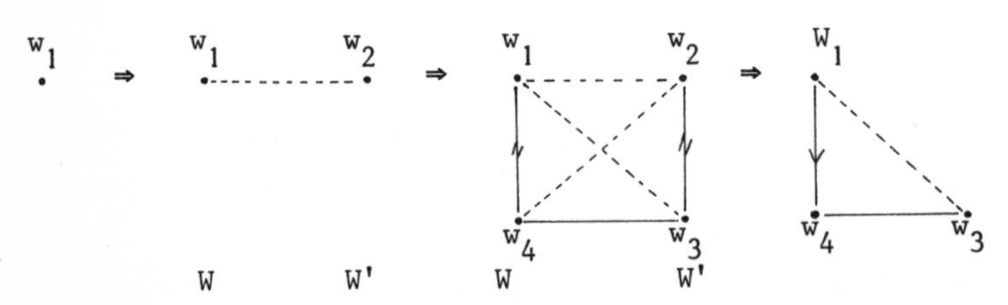

This completes the proof of the lemma. □

Given the lemmas 3, 4, 5 and 6, theorem 1 becomes evident. □

Finally it should be noted that the dimension of the cube may be recognized from the number of pairs of $\leqslant$-equivalence classes.

REFERENCE

[1] GROOT, J. DE, *Topological characterizations of metrizable cubes*, in: *Theory of sets and topology* (Felix Hausdorff Gedenkband), VEB Deutscher Verlag Wiss., Berlin, 1972, pp.209-214.

MATHEMATICAL CENTRE TRACTS 52, 1974, 48-54

THE PRODUCT OF BAIRE SPACES

J.M. AARTS *)

INTRODUCTION

One of the problems concerning Baire spaces, to which much attention has been given, is the unification problem: is there a natural class of topological spaces for which the Baire category theorem holds and which contains the classical examples of Baire spaces, namely the completely metrizable spaces and the locally compact Hausdorff spaces?

In this paper [15], which has greatly influenced his later work (cf. [7]), Professor DE GROOT has introduced the notion of *subcompactness* as a unifying concept. As a matter of fact the unifying concept of a Čech-complete space had already been introduced several years before. Since one of the main differences of these two concepts lies in the invariance under the taking of topological products, I shall discuss in this talk these and other concepts giving special emphasis to the various product theorems.

The presentation will be rather sketchy. A detailed exposition of the concepts and the theorems mentioned here can be found in a joint paper by D.J. LUTZER and myself [6].

All spaces are assumed to be at least T_1.

1. BAIRE SPACES

Here we list several properties of Baire spaces which will be dealt

*) Delft Institute of Technology, Delft, The Netherlands.

with in the sequel.

A topological space X is called a *Baire space*, if every open subset of X is of the second category, or, equivalently, if the intersection of countably many dense, open subsets of X is a dense subset of X.

Every locally compact Hausdorff space and every completely metrizable space is a Baire space. Any open subspace and any dense G_δ-subspace of a Baire space is a Baire space. A closed subset of a Baire space need not be a Baire space.

If a space X is locally a Baire space (i.e. each point of X has an open neighborhood which is a Baire space in its relative topology), then X is a Baire space.

As for mappings the positive results are as follows. Let f: X → Y be a continuous map of X onto Y. If f is open and X is a Baire space, then Y is a Baire space. If f is closed and irreducible *), then X is a Baire space if and only if Y is a Baire space.

A counterexample by OXTOBY [17] shows that the product of Baire spaces need not be a Baire space. For many applications it is useful to know under what extra condition the product of a collection of Baire spaces is a Baire space. The following is an example of such a condition ([8],§5, Excercise 17). Any product of a collection of completely metrizable spaces is a Baire space. From this result it then follows that the collection of all real-valued functions on a set A endowed with the topology of pointwise convergence is a Baire space.

2. PSEUDO-COMPLETENESS

The first systematic discussion of product theorems for Baire spaces is given in OXTOBY's paper [17], where also the above mentioned counter-example of a Baire space, whose square fails to be a Baire space, is presented. For stating the most important results from this paper we need some definitions.

A space X is *quasi-regular*, if each non-empty open subset of X contains the closure of some non-empty open set. A family P of non-empty open sets in a topological space is called a *pseudo-base*, if every non-empty open set contains some member of P.

---

*) A mapping f: X → Y is *irreducible* if no proper, closed subset of X is mapped onto Y by f.

A quasi-regular space is *pseudo-complete*, if there is a sequence $\{P(n)\}$ of pseudo-bases for X such that if $P_n \in P(n)$ and $\overline{P}_{n+1} \subset P_n$, then $\cap\{P_n | n=1,2,\ldots\} \neq \emptyset$. It is easily verified that any pseudo-complete space is a Baire space. As for products there are the following results.

THEOREM (cf. [17]). *If* X *and* Y *are Baire spaces and if at least one of them has a pseudo-base* P *such that each member of* P *contains only countably many members of* P, *then* X × Y *is a Baire space.*

THEOREM (cf. [17]). *The topological product of any family of Baire spaces, each of which has a countable pseudo-base, is a Baire space.*

THEOREM (cf. [17]). *The topological product of any family of pseudo-complete spaces is pseudo-complete. In particular such a product is a Baire space.*

The concept of pseudo-completeness is an elegant solution to the unification problem. Indeed, most of the known unifying concepts -in particular subcompactness and Čech completeness- are encompassed by pseudo-completeness.

Also, pseudo-completeness shares many invariance properties with the property of being a Baire space as may be seen from the following results.

THEOREM (cf. [5]). *Any open subspace of a pseudo-complete space is pseudo-complete. If a space* X *is locally pseudo-complete, then* X *is pseudo-complete.*

THEOREM (cf. [5], [6]). *Let* f: X → Y *be a continuous map of* X *onto* Y. *If* Y *is a metrizable space (or, more generally a Moore space, i.e. a regular space which admits a development) and if* f *is an open map, then* Y *is pseudo-complete, whenever* X *is pseudo-complete. If* f *is closed and irreducible, then* Y *is pseudo-complete if and only if* X *is pseudo-complete.*

The problem whether a dense G_δ-subspace of a pseudo-complete space is pseudo-complete is still unresolved.

3. SUBCOMPACTNESS

Quite another approach to the unification problem has been given by DE GROOT [15].

A collection $\mathcal{F}$ of non-empty subsets of a space X is called a *regular filterbase* if, whenever $F_1, F_2 \in \mathcal{F}$, some $F_3 \in \mathcal{F}$ has $\overline{F_3} \subset F_1 \cap F_2$. A regular space is *subcompact* if there is a base $\mathcal{B}$ of open sets for X such that for every regular filterbase $\mathcal{F} \subset \mathcal{B}$ we have $\cap\mathcal{F} \neq \emptyset$.

By DE GROOT the notion of subcompactness was considered the right generalization of topological completeness in view of the following theorem.

THEOREM (cf. [15]). *A metrizable space is subcompact if and only if it is topologically complete.*

It should be noticed that there is no similar result for pseudo-completeness. Indeed, there exist very "incomplete" spaces, which are pseudo-complete. Since every locally compact Hausdorff space is subcompact relative to the base of open sets with compact closure, subcompactness is a unifying concept.

As for topological products the following theorem holds.

THEOREM (cf. [15]). *Subcompactness is invariant under the forming of topological products.*

Recently the following results have been obtained.

THEOREM (cf. [6]). *If a regular space is locally subcompact, then it is subcompact.*

THEOREM (cf. [6]). *Suppose* f *is a continuous and open map of a space* X *onto a regular space* Y. *Suppose either* X *or* Y *is metrizable. If* X *is subcompact, then so is* Y.

The question whether a dense G_δ-subset of a subcompact space is subcompact will be discussed in the next section.

4. OTHER COMPLETENESS PROPERTIES

The first solution to the unification problem was given by ČECH [9]. A completely regular space X is *Čech-complete* if X is a G_δ-subset of its Čech-Stone compactification βX.

THEOREM (cf. [9]). *A metrizable space is Čech-complete if and only if it is topologically complete.*

A locally compact Hausdorff space is Čech-complete, as it is an open subset of any of its compactifications.

Čech completeness is countably productive, but it fails to be productive in general. The uncountable product of real lines is a specific example of a product of Čech-complete spaces, which is not Čech-complete. These results about products are closely related to the result that closed subsets of Čech-complete spaces are Čech-complete. An elucidating discussion of this phenomenon has been given by VAN DER SLOT [18].

As subcompactness is productive, the uncountable product of real lines provides an example of a subcompact space which is not Čech-complete. The question whether every Čech-complete space is subcompact, and also the more general question whether a dense G_δ-subset of a subcompact space is subcompact, is still unresolved.

Besides the above mentioned solutions to the unification problem, in the same spirit many other concepts have been defined [1], [2], [3], [10], [11], [12], [13], [14], [18], [22], [23]. For a systematic discussion of many of these completeness properties and their interrelations see [6]. This paper also reveals the many consequences of a recent example by TALL [20], which has been designed to show that a Čech-complete space may fail to be cocompact [2] or base-compact [18].

5. RECENT RESULTS

Until recently the following question has not been considered. Under what conditions on the space X is the product X × Y of X and any Baire space Y a Baire space? An answer to this question is given in the following

THEOREM (cf. [5]). *If* Y *is a quasi-regular Baire space and* X *is pseudo-complete, then* X × Y *is a Baire space.*

This result has been generalized by WHITE [21].

Another recent result is a solution to the following problem, which was first posed by SIKORSKI [19]. Is there a metrizable Baire space X such that X × X is not a Baire space? (Of course, if metrizability is not required, the counterexample of OXTOBY is such a space.) This problem is resolved by the following theorem of KROM in connection with OXTOBY's counterexample.

THEOREM (cf. [16]). *For any topological space* X *there is an associated metrizable zero-dimensional space* $\mathcal{U}(X)$ *such that the product* $\mathcal{U}(X) \times Y$ *with any other space* Y *is a Baire space if and only if* $X \times Y$ *is a Baire space.*

REFERENCES

[1] AARTS, J.M. (ed), *Colloquium Cotopologie 1964/65*, Mathematical Centre Report ZC 65, Amsterdam, 1966.

[2] AARTS, J.M., J. DE GROOT & R.H. MCDOWELL, *Cocompactness*, Nieuw Arch. Wisk., 18 (1970) 2-15.

[3] AARTS, J.M., J. DE GROOT & R.H. MCDOWELL, *Cotopology for metrizable spaces*, Duke Math. J., 37 (1970) 291-295.

[4] AARTS, J.M. & D.J. LUTZER, *The product of totally non-meagre spaces*, Proc. Amer. Math. Soc., 38 (1973) 198-200.

[5] AARTS, J.M. & D.J. LUTZER, *Pseudo-completeness and the product of Baire spaces*, Pacific J. Math., 48 (1973) 1-10.

[6] AARTS, J.M. & D.J. LUTZER, *Completeness properties designed for recognizing Baire spaces*, Rozprawy Math. (= Dissertations Math.), 116 (1974) 1-48.

[7] BAAYEN, P.C. & M.A. MAURICE, *Johannes de Groot 1914-1972*, General Topology and Appl., 3 (1973) 3-32.

[8] BOURBAKI, N., *Eléments de mathématique*, Livre III, Chapitre 9, Paris, 1958.

[9] ČECH, E., *On bicompact spaces*, Ann. of Math., 38 (1937) 823-844.

[10] CHOQUET, G., *Une classe régulière d'espaces de Baire*, C.R. Acad. Sci. Paris, Sér. A, 246 (1958) 218-220.

[11] CHOQUET, G., *Lectures on analysis, Vol. 1*, New York, 1969.

[12] CHABER, J., M.M. ČOBAN & K. NAGAMI, *On monotonic generalizations of Moore spaces, Čech-complete spaces and p-spaces*, to appear.

[13] FROLÍK, Z., *Baire spaces and some generalizations of complete metric spaces*, Czechoslovak Math. J., 11 (1961) 237-247.

[14] FROLÍK, Z., *Locally topologically complete spaces*, Soviet Math. Dokl., 2 (1961) 355-357.

[15] GROOT, J. DE, *Subcompactness and the Baire category theorem*, Indag. Math., 25 (1963) 761-767.

[16] KROM, M.R., *Cartesian products of metric Baire spaces*, Notices Amer. Math. Soc., 20 (1973) A-355, # 702-G3.

[17] OXTOBY, J.C., *Cartesian products of Baire spaces*, Fund. Math., 49 (1961) 157-166.

[18] SLOT, J. VAN DER, *Some properties related to compactness*, Mathematical Centre Tracts 19, Amsterdam, 1968.

[19] SIKORSKI, R., *On the cartesian product of metric spaces*, Fund. Math., 34 (1947) 288-292.

[20] TALL, F.D., *A counterexample in the theories of compactness and of metrization*, Indag. Math., 35 (1973) 471-474.

[21] WHITE JR., H.E., *Topological spaces that are α-favorable for a player with perfect information*, Notices Amer. Math. Soc., 20 (1973) A-28, # 73T-G15.

[22] WICKE, H.H., *Base of countable order theory and some generalizations*, Proc. of the Univ. of Houston Point Set Topology Conf. 1971, Houston, Texas.

[23] WICKE, H.H. & J.M. WORRELL, *Completeness of first countable Hausdorff spaces II*, to appear.

MATHEMATICAL CENTRE TRACTS 52, 1974, 55-58

SOME CLASSES OF QUOTIENT MAPS [†)]

E. MICHAEL [*)]

This note is a brief summary of some recent work on various kinds of quotient maps.

Recall that a map [**)] $f: X \to Y$ is *quotient* if a set $V \subset Y$ is open in Y if and only if $f^{-1}(V)$ is open in X. The most important property of these maps (which, in fact, characterizes them) is that, if $f: X \to Y$ is quotient, then a function $g: Y \to Z$ is continuous if and only if $g \circ f$ is continuous.

The classes of quotient maps which interest us here are indicated in the following diagram.

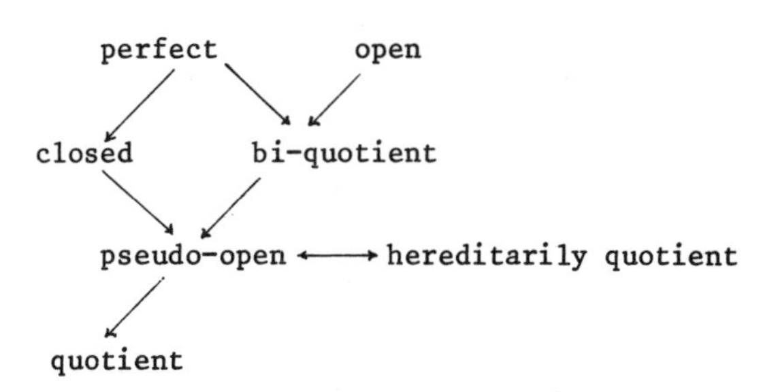

The above classes are defined as follows. A map $f: X \to Y$ is *hereditarily quotient* if, for every $S \subset Y$, the map $f|f^{-1}(S): f^{-1}(S) \to S$ is quotient.

---

†) Partly supported by an N.S.F. contract.

*) University of Washington, Seattle, Wash., USA; temp.Ⓐ.

**) All *maps* in this paper are continuous and onto.

A map $f: X \to Y$ is *pseudo-open* [1] if, whenever $y \in Y$ and $f^{-1}(y) \subset U$ with U open in Y, then $y \in \operatorname{Int} f(U)$. A map $f: X \to Y$ is *bi-quotient* [11] (an equivalent concept was defined in [7]) if, whenever $y \in Y$ and $\mathcal{U}$ is a cover of $f^{-1}(y)$ by open subsets of X, then there are $U_1,\ldots,U_n$ in $\mathcal{U}$ such that $y \in \operatorname{Int} f(U_1 \cup \ldots \cup U_n)$. *Open* maps and *closed* maps are, of course, well known. A map $f: X \to Y$ is *perfect* *) if f is closed and $f^{-1}(y)$ is compact for every $y \in Y$.

The implications in the diagram are easily verified. Moreover, these are the only valid implications; in particular, [6, Example 1.8] shows that a quotient map need not be hereditarily quotient, and [11, Example 8.1] shows that a closed map need not be bi-quotient.

Let us now consider how the classes of maps in the diagram behave with respect to products. (Recall that, if $f_\alpha: X_\alpha \to Y_\alpha$ is a family of maps, then their *product* is the map $f: \Pi_\alpha X_\alpha \to \Pi_\alpha Y_\alpha$ which sends (x_α) to $(f_\alpha(x_\alpha))$.) In this respect, the classes in the diagram are of two distinct types. On the one hand, quotient, pseudo-open and closed maps are not even preserved by binary products; this is shown by an example [11, Example 8.1] of a closed map f and a space Z such that $f \times i_Z$ is not even a quotient map.**) On the other hand, open, perfect and bi-quotient maps are preserved by arbitrary products; for open maps this is trivial, for perfect maps it was proved in [2], and for bi-quotient maps it was proved in [11]. It should be observed that the preservation of perfect maps under arbitrary products immediately implies the Tychonoff product theorem (just consider maps with one-point ranges), while the converse implication takes a bit more work.

The above results imply half of each of the following two characterizations:

(1) [2, p.117, Theorem 1]. *A map* f *is perfect if and only if* $f \times i_Z$ *is closed for every space* Z.

(2) [7, Proposition 2], [11, Theorem 1.3]. *A map* f *with Hausdorff range is bi-quotient if and only if* $f \times i_Z$ *is quotient for every space* Z. (This motivates the term "bi-quotient".)

---

*) In the terminology of BOURBAKI [2], such maps are called *proper*. However, the term "proper" has also been applied to a somewhat larger class of maps (namely maps $f: X \to Y$ such that $f^{-1}(K)$ is compact for every compact $K \subset Y$), and may thus be subject to confusion.

**) i_Z denotes the identity map on Z.

There are many results characterizing images of familiar kinds of spaces (such as metrizable spaces) under the various maps appearing in the diagram. For open, bi-quotient, hereditarily quotient and quotient maps, many such results are summarized in [12, Table 1]. Perfect maps appear to preserve most kinds of spaces; in particular, this was proved for metrizable spaces by A.H. STONE [16] and K. MORITA & S. HANAI [14] and for Hausdorff spaces admitting a perfect map onto a metrizable space by V.V. FILIPPOV [4] and T. ISHII [9]. Closed images of metrizable spaces were characterized by N.S. LAŠNEV [10].

We now conclude this note with an interesting -and somehwat surprising- result. (Recall that a map $f: X \to Y$ is an *s-map* if every $f^{-1}(y)$ is separable, and that a map $f: X \to Y$ is *compact-covering* if every compact $K \subset Y$ is the image of some compact $C \subset X$.)

THEOREM 1. *The following properties of a Hausdorff space* Y *equivalent:*

(a) Y *has a point-countable base.*

(b) Y *is a compact-covering, open s-image of a metrizable space.*

(c) Y *is an open s-image of a metrizable space.*

(d) Y *is a bi-quotient s-image of a metrizable space.*

In the above theorem, the implications (b)→(c)→(d) and (c)→(a) are trivial. That (a)→(c) was proved by V.I. PONOMAREV [15] and S. HANAI [8], and it was shown in [13] that the same construction actually yields (a)→(b). The implication (d)→(a) (which, unlike (c)→(a), is not at all trivial) was obtained by V.V. FILIPPOV [5]; a somewhat shorter proof can be found in [3].

It should finally be observed that, in contrast to Theorem 1, the classes of spaces obtained when the prefix "s-" is omitted from (b),(c) and (d) are all distinct.

REFERENCES

[1] ARHANGEL'SKIĬ, A.V., *Some types of factor mappings and the relations between classes of topological spaces*, Dokl. Akad. Nauk SSSR, 151 (1963) 751-754 (= Soviet Math. Dokl, 4 (1963) 1051-1055).

[2] BOURBAKI, N., *Topologie générale*, Chapters 1 and 2, Hermann, Paris, 1961.

[3] BURKE, D. & E. MICHAEL, *On a theorem of V.V. Filippov*, Israel J. Math., 11 (1972) 394-397.

[4] FILIPPOV, V.V., *The perfect image of paracompact feathery space*, Dokl. Akad. Nauk SSSR, 176 (1967) 533-535 (=Soviet Math. Dokl., 8 (1967) 1151-1153).

[5] FILIPPOV, V.V., *Quotient spaces and multiplicity of a base*, Mat. Sb., 80 (1969) 521-532 (=Math. USSR-Sb., 9 (1969) 487-496).

[6] FRANKLIN, S.P., *Spaces in which sequences suffice*, Fund. Math., 57 (1965) 107-115.

[7] HÁJEK, O., *Notes on quotient maps*, Comm. Math. Univ. Carolinae, 7 (1966) 319-323.

[8] HANAI, S., *On open mappings, II*, Proc. Japan Acad., 37 (1961) 233-238.

[9] ISHII, T., *On closed mappings and M-spaces. I,II*, Proc. Japan Acad., 43 (1967) 752-756; 757-761.

[10] LAŠNEV, N.S., *Closed images of metric spaces*, Dokl. Akad. Nauk SSSR, 170 (1966) 505-507 (=Soviet Math. Dokl., 7 (1966) 1219-1221).

[11] MICHAEL, E., *Bi-quotient maps and cartesian products of quotient maps*, Ann. Inst. Fourier (Grenoble), 18 (2) (1968) 287-302.

[12] MICHAEL, E., *A quintuple quotient quest*, General Topology and Appl., 2 (1972) 91-138.

[13] MICHAEL, E. & K. NAGAMI, *Compact-covering images of metric spaces*, Proc. Amer. Math. Soc., 37 (1973) 260-266.

[14] MORITA, K. & S. HANAI, *Closed mappings and metric spaces*, Proc. Japan Acad., 32 (1956) 10-14.

[15] PONOMAREV, V.I., *Axioms of countability and continuous mappings*, Bull. Acad. Polon. Sci., Sér. Sci. Math. Astronom. Phys., 8 (1960) 127-133.

[16] STONE, A.H., *Metrizability and decomposition spaces*, Proc. Amer. Math. Soc., 7 (1956) 690-700.

MATHEMATICAL CENTRE TRACTS 52, 1974, 59-122

TOPOLOGICAL STRUCTURES

HORST HERRLICH *)

CONTENTS

---

*) Universität Bremen, Bremen, GFR.

INTRODUCTION

To handle problems of a "topological" nature general topologists have created a major host of topological structures of varying importance such as topological spaces, uniform spaces, proximity spaces, contiguity spaces, limit spaces, uniform convergence spaces and a number of generalizations and variations of these concepts. Many mathematicians considered this situation to be unsatisfactory and have tried more or less successfully to create a unified theory of topological structures. The solutions offered fall into two categories:

A. The categorical approach

Each of the various topological concepts mentioned above gives rise to a concrete category. The striking similarities between the so obtained "topological categories" can be described in categorical terms and can be analyzed by means of categorical methods. The resulting theory is fairly young and far from its final form. But the crucial role played by "initial" and "final" structures in the sense of N. BOURBAKI [A5,A4] is now well understood. Appendix A contains an introduction into this theory which is designed for topologists and is accompanied by a fairly complete bibliography.

B. The conceptual approach

The aim of this approach is to find a basic topological concept -if possible intuitively easily accessible- by means of which any topological concept or idea can be expressed.

1. Topological spaces

The general belief that the concept of a topological space serves this purpose is certainly not justified. This concept -defined in a slightly restricted sense by F. HAUSDORFF [33] and in the sense which is nowadays generally accepted by K. KURATOWSKI [50]- can be considered as an axiomatization of any of the following two equivalent concepts:

(1) convergence of a filter (or a Moore-Smith-sequence) to a point,

(2) nearness between a set and a point.

Obviously these concepts are rather "local" and not suitable to express such "global" topological concepts as "uniform covers", "completeness", "total boundedness" and "uniform continuity". Also, the concept of a topological space has another disadvantage, since in passing from a topological space to a subspace in general some topological information gets lost. If, for instance, X is a subset of $\mathbb{R}$ obtained by removing one point and Y is a subset of $\mathbb{R}$ obtained by removing a closed interval of length one then X and Y are essentially different and the difference is of a "topological" nature. But X and Y considered as topological subspaces of $\mathbb{R}$ with the usual topology are homeomorphic and hence intrinsically essentially the same. Considered, for instance, as uniform (or proximal) subspaces of $\mathbb{R}$ with the usual uniformity (proximity) X and Y are essentially different. The reason why uniform (proximity) spaces behave "good" with respect to the formation of subobjects and topological spaces behave so "bad" will become clear in the realm of nearness structures: a subspace of a uniform (proximal) nearness space is again uniform (proximal), a subspace of a topological nearness space is not topological but supplied with a "richer" structure. This also explains why the theorem concerning the extendibility of uniformly continuous maps from dense subspaces into complete uniform spaces has no direct counterpart in the theory of topological spaces.

2. *Uniform spaces*

The concept of a uniform space introduced by A. WEIL [82] and described by J.W. TUKEY [79] as an axiomatization of the concept of

(3) uniform covers

has none of the drawbacks mentioned above. Also, in passing from a pseudometric space to its underlying uniform space no relevant topological information get lost whereas in passing from a pseudometric space to its underlying topological space usually some such information gets lost. This, by the way, seems to be the main reason why uniform spaces in general are wrongly supposed to be "richer" in structure than topological spaces (cf. 4.24). But uniform spaces have another disadvantage not due to the basic concept of uniform covers but due to its axiomatization which is so restrictive that it excludes many topological structures of interest from being uniform spaces. Because of this several authors have offered generalizations by weakening the axioms. Especially worth mentioning are the P-spaces of Z.FROLÍK [21] which are identical with the quasi-uniform spaces of J.R. ISBELL [44] who used them as intermediate constructs in his transfinite construction of the locally fine coreflection of a uniform space. Since these constructs satisfy our axiom (U5) in 3.6 for uniform covers they can be considered as nearness spaces and J.R. ISBELL's construction can be carried out in the category *Near*. K. MORITA [55] generalized uniform structures by blending uniform and topological concepts together in order to study extensions of topological spaces. These structures which have been rediscovered by D. HARRIS [29] will be discussed shortly in Appendix B. The most important generalization of uniform structures, the concepts of semi-uniform structures, has been obtained recently by A.K. STEINER & E.F. STEINER [70] by abstracting the uniform (topology-free) part of K. MORITA's regular T-uniformities.

3. Proximity spaces

Proximity spaces are obtained as an axiomatization of the concept of

(4) nearness of two sets.

This concept, although already known to F. RIESZ [61], was first axiomatized by V.A. EFREMOVIČ [20]. It plays a crucial role in the study of Hausdorff compactifications of completely regular spaces as has been shown by Yu.M. SMIRNOV [67,68]. In order to study arbitrary T_1-compactifications several authors offered weaker axioms than the strong separation axiom of V.A. EFREMOVIČ. An axiom due to M.W. LODATO [52], corresponding to our axiom (N5) in 2.1, paved the way.

4. Contiguity spaces

Using M.W. LODATO's axiom V.M. IVANOVA & A.A. IVANOV [46] introduced contiguity spaces by axiomatizing the concept of

(5) nearness of finite collections of sets.

This concept has also been studied by W.L. TERWILLIGER [76]. It is of central importance for the study of T_1-compactifications of topological spaces. A.K. STEINER & E.F. STEINER [69] defined binding spaces by blending together the concept of a contiguity space and the concept of a separating closed base.

5. *Merotopic spaces*

M. KATĚTOV [47,48,49] created the concept of merotopic spaces by axiomatizing the concept of

(6) collections of sets containing arbitrary small members

and proved that the category of merotopic spaces and merotopic maps is isomorphic to the category of quasi-uniform spaces in the sense of J.R. ISBELL (resp. P-spaces in the sense of Z. FROLIK) and uniformly continuous maps. Somewhat earlier V. SANDBERG [63] had demonstrated that uniform structures can be characterized by their corresponding merotopic structure.
A.G. MORDKOVIČ [54] investigated the merotopic structure of proximity spaces.

6. *Nearness spaces*

Nearness spaces where introduced by the author [35] as an axiomatization of the concept of

(7) nearness of arbitrary collections of sets.

Already earlier H.H. CORSON [13] invented for uniform spaces the concept of a "weakly Cauchy filter" which, in our terminology, is a near-filter, i.e. a filter belonging to ξ. H.H. CORSON's problem to characterize paracompactness among topological spaces by means of suitable uniformities has in the realm of nearness structures an elegant solution: A.H. STONE's theorem can be expressed in the form *the paracompact spaces are precisely those nearness sapces which are simultaneously topological and uniform* (cf. 4.22(2)). Recently, A.K. STEINER & E.F. STEINER [70] defined the concept of a "bound" collection of sets in a semi-uniform space. In our terminology these are precisely the collections which are "near", i.e. belong to ξ. H.L. BENTLEY [6] and M.S. GAGRAT & W.J. THRON [24] have shown that the concept of nearness is of crucial importance for the investigation of T_1-extensions of topological spaces. H.L. BENTLEY [5], S.A. NAIMPALLY [57] and the author [36] have used nearness structures to study extensions of continuous functions. W.N. HUNSAKER & P.L. SHARMA [39] have studied the lattice of all nearness structures compatible with a given topology and the same authors [66] have investigated special reflectors and coreflectors in *Near*.
P. CAMERON, J.G. HOCKING & S.A. NAIMPALLY [8] advocate strongly and convincingly to teach topology using "nearness" as a basic concept.

7. *Topological structures*

In chapter 3 of this treatise it will be shown that the following concepts are equivalent

(1) nearness of collections of sets

(2) farness of collections of sets

(3) uniform covers

(4) collections of sets containing arbitrary small members.

This is a strong indication that the basic problem concerning the conceptual approach has found a satisfactory solution. Especially the categories of topological R_0-spaces, uniform spaces, proximity spaces, and contiguity spaces are nicely embedded in the category of nearness spaces. But not all topological spaces are included. The reason to the author seems to be that the general concept of a topological space as opposed to the purely topological concepts of T_1-spaces, uniform spaces, proximity spaces, contiguity spaces, merotopic spaces, and nearness spaces contains a basically non-topological order-theoretic component ($x \le y$ iff $x \in cl\{y\}$). Appendix B contains a short discussion of theories dealing simultaneously with topological structures and this additional order-structure. They are necessarily more complicated and more technical in nature.

NOTATIONAL CONVENTIONS

$X, Y, \ldots$	usually denote sets
PX	denotes the power set $\{A \mid A \subset X\}$ of X
$x, y, \ldots$	usually denote elements of $X, \ldots$
$A, B, \ldots$	usually denote subsets of $X, \ldots$
$\mathcal{A}, \mathcal{B}, \ldots$	usually denote subsets of $PX, \ldots$
$\alpha, \beta, \ldots$	usually denote subsets of $P^2X, \ldots$
$\Omega, \Lambda, \ldots$	usually denote subsets of $P^3X, \ldots$

For subsets $\mathcal{A}$, $\mathcal{B}$ of PX:

$$\text{sec}\, \mathcal{A} = \{B \subset X \mid \forall A \in \mathcal{A} \quad B \cap A \neq \emptyset\}$$

$$\text{stack}\, \mathcal{A} = \text{sec}^2 \mathcal{A} = \{B \subset X \mid \exists A \in \mathcal{A} \quad A \subset B\}$$

$$\mathcal{A} \vee \mathcal{B} = \{A \cup B \mid A \in \mathcal{A} \text{ and } B \in \mathcal{B}\}$$

$\mathcal{A} \wedge \mathcal{B} = \{A \cap B \mid A \in \mathcal{A} \text{ and } B \in \mathcal{B}\}$

$\mathcal{A} \prec \mathcal{B} \Leftrightarrow \forall A \in \mathcal{A} \ \exists B \in \mathcal{B} \ A \subset B \Leftrightarrow \mathcal{A}$ refines $\mathcal{B}$

$\mathcal{A} < \mathcal{B} \Leftrightarrow \forall A \in \mathcal{A} \ \exists B \in \mathcal{B} \ B \subset A \Leftrightarrow \mathcal{A}$ corefines $\mathcal{B}$

$\mathcal{A} \sim \mathcal{B} \Leftrightarrow (\mathcal{A} < \mathcal{B}$ and $\mathcal{B} < \mathcal{A})$.

For a (pre-, quasi-) nearness-structure ξ on X:

$\bar{\xi} = \{\mathcal{A} \subset PX \mid \mathcal{A} \notin \xi\}$ associated (pre-, quasi-) farness-structure on X

$\mu = \{\mathcal{U} \subset PX \mid \{X-U \mid U \in \mathcal{U}\} \in \bar{\xi}\}$ associated (pre-, quasi-) covering-structure on X

$\gamma = \{\mathcal{C} \subset PX \mid \forall \mathcal{U} \in \mu \ \ \mathcal{U} \cap \text{stack } \mathcal{C} \neq \emptyset\}$ associated (pre-, quasi-) merotopic structure on X

$cl_\xi A = \{x \in X \mid \{A,\{x\}\} \in \xi\}$ associated (pre-, quasi-) closure-operator on X

$int_\mu A = \{x \in X \mid \{A, X-\{x\}\} \in \mu\}$ associated (pre-, quasi-) interior-operator on X

ξ_t denotes the topological coreflection (= underlying topological structure) of ξ

ξ_u denotes the uniform reflection of ξ

ξ_c denotes the contigual reflection of ξ

ξ_r denotes the regular reflection of ξ

ξ_p denotes the proximal reflection of ξ

ξ_1 denotes the N1-reflection of ξ

ξ_q denotes the quasinear coreflection of a prenearness structure

ξ_n denotes the near reflection of a quasinearness structure

(X^*,ξ^*) denotes the completion of (X,ξ)

$A <_\xi B \Leftrightarrow \{A, X-B\} \in \bar{\xi}$

$\mathcal{A}(<_\xi) = \{B \subset X \mid \exists A \in \mathcal{A} \ \ A <_\xi B\}$

$\xi(\mathcal{A}) = \{B \subset X \mid (\{B\} \cup \mathcal{A}) \in \xi\}$

If x is a point and $\mathcal{A}$ is a collection of subsets of a topological space then x is an *adherencepoint* of $\mathcal{A}$ iff $x \in \bigcap\{cl\, A \mid A \in \mathcal{A}\}$;
$\mathcal{A}$ *converges* to x iff the neighbourhoodfilter $\mathcal{U}$ of x corefines $\mathcal{A}$.

CONVENTIONS

(1) All topological spaces (X,cl) in this treatise are assumed to be *symmetric* (= R_0-*spaces* = *weakly regular*), i.e. to satisfy the following axiom:

(R_0) *If* $x \in cl\{y\}$ *then* $y \in cl\{x\}$.

(R_0) *If* $x \in cl\{y\}$ *then* $y \in cl\{x\}$.

(2) $\cap\emptyset \neq \emptyset$.

Top denotes the category of (symmetric) topological spaces and continuous maps

Unif denotes the category of uniform spaces and uniformly continuous maps

Cont denotes the category of contiguity spaces and contiguity-preserving maps

Prox denotes the category of proximity spaces and δ-maps

Near denotes the category of N-spaces and N-maps

T-Near denotes the category of topological N-spaces and N-maps

U-Near denotes the category of uniform N-spaces and N-maps

C-Near denotes the category of contigual N-spaces and N-maps

Pr-Near denotes the category of proximal N-spaces and N-maps

R-Near denotes the category of regular N-spaces and N-maps

Q-Near denotes the category of quasi-N-spaces and N-maps

P-Near denotes the category of pre-N-spaces and N-maps.

If $f\colon X \to Y$ is a map, $\mathcal{A} \subset PX$, $\mathcal{B} \subset PY$, $\xi \subset P^2X$, $\eta \subset P^2Y$ then:

$$f\mathcal{A} = \{f[A] \mid A \in \mathcal{A}\}$$
$$f^{-1}\mathcal{B} = \{f^{-1}[B] \mid B \in \mathcal{B}\}$$
$$f(\xi) = \{\mathcal{B} \subset PY \mid f^{-1}\mathcal{B} \in \xi\}$$
$$f^{-1}(\eta) = \{\mathcal{A} \subset PX \mid f\mathcal{A} \in \eta\}.$$

Chapter I. BASIC CONCEPTS

1. SET-THEORETIC PRELIMINARIES

A topological structure on a set X is -as we will see in section 2- a subset ξ of P^2X, i.e. a collection of collections of subsets of X. To describe and analyze such collections properly we introduce the following simple but useful concepts.

Let $\mathcal{A}$ and $\mathcal{B}$ be subsets of PX.

1.1. DEFINITIONS.

$\sec \mathcal{A} = \{B \subset X \mid \forall A \in \mathcal{A}\ A \cap B \neq \emptyset\}$.

$\text{stack } \mathcal{A} = \{B \subset X \mid \exists A \in \mathcal{A}\ A \subset B\}$.

$\mathcal{A} \vee \mathcal{B} = \{A \cup B \mid A \in \mathcal{A} \text{ and } B \in \mathcal{B}\}$.

$\mathcal{A} \wedge \mathcal{B} = \{A \wedge B \mid A \in \mathcal{A} \text{ and } B \in \mathcal{B}\}$.

$\mathcal{A} \prec \mathcal{B} \iff \forall A \in \mathcal{A}\ \ \exists B \in \mathcal{B}\ \ A \subset B \iff \mathcal{A}$ refines $\mathcal{B}$.

$\mathcal{A} < \mathcal{B} \iff \forall A \in \mathcal{A}\ \ \exists B \in \mathcal{B}\ \ B \subset A \iff \mathcal{A}$ corefines $\mathcal{B}$.

$\mathcal{A} \sim \mathcal{B} \iff (\mathcal{A} < \mathcal{B} \text{ and } \mathcal{B} < \mathcal{A})$.

$\mathcal{A}$ is called a *stack* in X iff $\mathcal{A} = \text{stack } \mathcal{A}$.

$\mathcal{A}$ is called a *grill* in X iff $\emptyset \neq \mathcal{A} \neq PX$ and $A \cup B \in \mathcal{A} \iff (A \in \mathcal{A} \text{ or } B \in \mathcal{A})$.

$\mathcal{A}$ is called a *filter* in X iff $\emptyset \neq \mathcal{A} \neq PX$ and $A \cap B \in \mathcal{A} \iff (A \in \mathcal{A} \text{ and } B \in \mathcal{A})$.

1.2. REMARK. $\mathcal{A} \subset \sec \mathcal{A}$ iff $\mathcal{A}$ is a linked system in the sense of J. DE GROOT, $\mathcal{A} = \sec \mathcal{A}$ iff $\mathcal{A}$ is a maximal linked system.

1.3. EXAMPLE. If x is a point in a topological space (X,cl), $\mathcal{A}$ is the collection of all $A \subset X$ with $x \in \text{cl } A$ and $\mathcal{B}$ is the neighbourhoodfilter of x then $\mathcal{A} = \sec \mathcal{B}$ and $\mathcal{B} = \sec \mathcal{A}$.

1.4. DEFINITIONS. If x is a point and $\mathcal{A}$ is a collection of subsets of a topological space (X,cl) then:

(a) x is an *adherencepoint* of $\mathcal{A}$ iff $x \in \bigcap\{\text{cl } A \mid A \in \mathcal{A}\}$.

(b) $\mathcal{A}$ *converges* to x iff the neighbourhoodfilter of x corefines $\mathcal{A}$.

1.5. COROLLARY. *Under the assumptions of* 1.4:

(1) x *is an adherencepoint of* $\mathcal{A}$ *iff* $\sec \mathcal{A}$ *converges to* x.

(2) $\mathcal{A}$ *converges to* x *iff* x *is an adherencepoint of* $\sec \mathcal{A}$.

1.6. PROPOSITIONS (characterizations of sec, stack, < and ~).

(1) $\sec \mathcal{A} = \{B \subset X \mid X-B \notin \text{stack } \mathcal{A}\}$.

(2) $\text{stack } \mathcal{A} = \sec^2 \mathcal{A}$.

(3) $\mathcal{A} < \mathcal{B} \iff \mathcal{A} \subset \text{stack } \mathcal{B} \iff \{X-A \mid A \in \mathcal{A}\} \quad \{X-B \mid B \in \mathcal{B}\}$.

(4) $\mathcal{A} \sim \mathcal{B} \iff \sec \mathcal{A} = \sec \mathcal{B} \iff \text{stack } \mathcal{A} = \text{stack } \mathcal{B}$.

1.7. PROPOSITIONS

(1) $\mathcal{A} \subset \mathcal{B} \Rightarrow \sec \mathcal{B} \subset \sec \mathcal{A}$.

(2) $\sec^3 \mathcal{A} = \sec \mathcal{A}$ (i.e. $\sec \mathcal{A}$ *is a stack*).

(3) $\sec(\mathcal{A} \vee \mathcal{B}) = \sec \mathcal{A} \cup \sec \mathcal{B}$.

(4) $\sec(\mathcal{A} \cup \mathcal{B}) = \sec \mathcal{A} \cap \sec \mathcal{B}$.

(5) $\mathcal{A} < \mathcal{B} \Leftrightarrow \sec \mathcal{B} < \sec \mathcal{A}$.

1.8. PROPOSITIONS

(1) stack *is a topological closure operator on* PX, *i.e.*

(a) $\text{stack } \emptyset = \emptyset$.

(b) $\mathcal{A} \subset \text{stack } \mathcal{A}$.

(c) $\text{stack}(\mathcal{A} \cup \mathcal{B}) = \text{stack } \mathcal{A} \cup \text{stack } \mathcal{B}$.

(d) $\text{stack}^2 \mathcal{A} = \text{stack } \mathcal{A}$.

(2) $\text{stack}(\mathcal{A} \vee \mathcal{B}) = \text{stack } \mathcal{A} \vee \text{stack } \mathcal{B} = \text{stack } \mathcal{A} \cap \text{stack } \mathcal{B}$.

(3) $\mathcal{A} < \mathcal{B} \Rightarrow \text{stack } \mathcal{A} < \text{stack } \mathcal{B}$.

1.9. PROPOSITIONS

(1) $<$ *and* $\prec$ *are reflexive and transitive relations on* P^2X.

(2) $\emptyset < \mathcal{A} < PX$.

(3) $\mathcal{A} \cup \mathcal{B} = \sup_{<}\{\mathcal{A},\mathcal{B}\}$.

(4) $\mathcal{A} \vee \mathcal{B} = \inf_{<}\{\mathcal{A},\mathcal{B}\}$.

(5) $\sim$ *is an equivalence relation on* P^2X.

1.10. REMARK. It will turn out that many topologically interesting properties of a collection $\mathcal{A}$ (e.g. that $\mathcal{A}$ belongs to ξ, $\bar{\xi}$, γ resp.) depends only on the equivalence class of $\mathcal{A}$ with respect to $\sim$. Especially $\mathcal{A}$ has such a property iff stack $\mathcal{A}$ has it. This suggests to focus attention on the set of all stacks.

1.11. PROPOSITIONS. *Let* SX *be the set of all stacks in* X, *and let* $\mathcal{A}$ *and* $\mathcal{B}$ *be elements of* SX. *Then*

(1) $\mathcal{A} < \mathcal{B} \Leftrightarrow \mathcal{A} \subset \mathcal{B} \Leftrightarrow \sec \mathcal{B} \subset \sec \mathcal{A}$.

(2) $\mathcal{A} \sim \mathcal{B} \Leftrightarrow \mathcal{A} = \mathcal{B}$.

(3) $\mathcal{A} \vee \mathcal{B} = \mathcal{A} \cap \mathcal{B}$.

(4) $\mathcal{A} = \sec \mathcal{B} \Leftrightarrow \mathcal{B} = \sec \mathcal{A}$.

(5) $\mathcal{A}$ *is a filter* $\Leftrightarrow \sec \mathcal{A}$ *is a grill.*

1.12. HISTORICAL REMARK. Filters were introduced by H. CARTAN [9], grills by G. CHOQUET [11], stacks by G. GRIMEISEN [26]. The papers of J. SCHMIDT [64] and W.J. THRON [77] contain detailed discussions of these concepts. Refinements seem to go back to J.W. TUKEY [79]. Corefinements were introduced by H.L. BENTLEY & P. SLEPIAN [7a], implicitly they appear already in M. KATĚTOV's paper [48].

2. NEARNESS AXIOMS

2.1. DEFINITIONS. Let X be a set and let ξ be a subset of P^2X. Consider the following axioms:

(N1) *if* $\mathcal{A} < \mathcal{B}$ *and* $\mathcal{B} \in \xi$ *then* $\mathcal{A} \in \xi$.

(N2) *if* $\cap\mathcal{A} \neq \emptyset$ *then* $\mathcal{A} \in \xi$.

(N3) $\emptyset \neq \xi \neq P^2X$.

(N4) *if* $(\mathcal{A} \vee \mathcal{B}) \in \xi$ *then* $\mathcal{A} \in \xi$ *or* $\mathcal{B} \in \xi$.

(N5) *if* $\{cl_\xi A \mid A \in \mathcal{A}\} \in \xi$ *then* $\mathcal{A} \in \xi$, *where* $cl_\xi A = \{x \in X \mid \{A,\{x\}\} \in \xi\}$.

ξ is called a *prenearness structure* on X iff ξ satisfies (N1), (N2) and (N3).

ξ is called a *quasinearness structure* on X iff ξ satisfies (N1), (N2), (N3), and (N4).

ξ is called a *nearness structure* on X iff ξ satisfies (N1), (N2), (N3), (N4) and (N5).

The pair (X,ξ) is called a *(pre-, quasi-) nearness space* -shortly: a *(pre-, quasi-)* N*-space*- iff ξ is a (pre-, quasi-) nearness structure on X.

2.2. REMARKS

(1) (N1) holds iff the following two axioms hold simultaneously:

(N1.1) *if* $\mathcal{A} \subset \mathcal{B}$ *and* $\mathcal{B} \in \xi$ *then* $\mathcal{A} \in \xi$.

(N1.2) *if* $\mathcal{A} \in \xi$ *then* stack $\mathcal{A} \in \xi$.

(2) If (N1) holds then (N2) holds if the following two axioms hold simultaneously:

(N2.1) $\emptyset \in \xi$ (because of our convention $\cap\emptyset \neq \emptyset$).

(N2.2) *if* $x \in X$ *then* $\{\{x\}\} \in \xi$.

The condition (N2.1) is implied by (N1) and (N3).

(3) (N3) holds iff the following two axioms hold simultaneously:

(N3.1) $\xi \neq \emptyset$.

(N3.2) $\xi \neq P^2X$.

The condition (N3.1) is implied by (N2) and hence superfluous. It has been included because of symmetry.

If (N1) holds then (n.3.2) is equivalent to each of the following axioms:

(N3.2') $PX \notin \xi$.

(N3.2") $\{\emptyset\} \notin \xi$.

(N3.2"') *if* $\emptyset \in A$ *then* $A \notin \xi$.

2.3. DEFINITIONS. If (X,ξ) and (Y,η) are pre-N-spaces then a function $f: X \to Y$ is called a *nearness preserving map* -shortly: an N-*map*- $f: (X,\xi) \to (Y,\eta)$ from (X,ξ) to (Y,η) iff $A \in \xi$ implies $fA \in \eta$. The category of pre-N-spaces and N-maps is denoted by *P-Near*. Its full subcategory whose objects are the quasi-N-spaces is denoted by *Q-Near*. Its full subcategory whose objects are the N-spaces is denoted by *Near*.

2.4. REMARKS

(1) The categories *P-Near*, *Q-Near* and *Near* will be shown to be extremely nice -in fact: topological- categories. Our main interest lies in the category *Near*.

(2) If (X,ξ) is a pre-N-space then cl_ξ can be regarded as an operator on PX satisfying the following axioms:

(T0) $cl_\xi\{x\} \cap cl_\xi A \neq \emptyset$ *implies* $x \in cl_\xi A$ (Symmetry-Axiom).

(T1) $cl_\xi\emptyset = \emptyset$.

(T2) $A \subset cl_\xi A$.

(T3) $A \subset B$ *implies* $cl_\xi A \subset cl_\xi B$.

Vice versa any operator on PX satisfying these axioms can be obtained in this way.

If (X,ξ) is a quasi-N-space then cl_ξ satisfies in addition the axiom:

(T4) $cl_\xi(A \cup B) = cl_\xi A \cup cl_\xi B$ (Infinity-Axiom).

If (X,ξ) is an N-space then cl_ξ satisfies in addition the axiom:

(T5) $cl_\xi(cl_\xi A) = cl_\xi A$.

Thus any nearness structure ξ on X induces on X a symmetric, topological closure operator. The topological space (X,cl_ξ) will be called *the underlaying topological space* of (X,ξ). The relations between (X,ξ) and (X,cl_ξ) will be studied in greater detail in section 4.

(3) If (X,ξ) is a nearness space then the relation δ on PX defined by

$$A \, \delta \, B \Longleftrightarrow \{A,B\} \in \xi$$

is a Lodato-proximity [52] on X, i.e. it satisfies

(P0) $A \, \delta \, B$ *implies* $B \, \delta \, A$.

(P1) $A \subset B$ *and* $A \, \delta \, C$ *imply* $B \, \delta \, C$.

(P2) $A \cap B = \emptyset$ *implies* $A \, \delta \, B$.

(P3) $A \, \delta \, B$ *implies* $A \neq \emptyset$.

(P4) $A \, \delta \, (B \cup C)$ *implies* $A \, \delta \, B$ *or* $A \, \delta \, C$.

(P5) $A \, \delta \, B$ *and* $B \subset cl_\delta C$ *imply* $A \, \delta \, C$, *where* $cl_\delta C = \{x \in X \mid \{x\} \, \delta \, C\}$.

One might call δ *the underlying Lodato proximity structure* on X. This will not be studied in this treatise. Instead, the collection ξ_f consisting of all finite elements $\mathcal{A} = \{A_1,\ldots,A_n\}$ of ξ, will play an important role in our study. If we modify the axioms (Ni) by requiring all collections $\mathcal{A}$, $\mathcal{B}$ in question to be finite then ξ_f obviously satisfies the modified axioms, thus forming what has been called by IVANOVA & IVANOV [46] a contiguity structure on X. Hence (X,ξ_f) will be called *the underlying contiguity space* of (X,ξ). The relations between (X,ξ) and (X,ξ_f) will be studied in greater detail in section 4.

3. FARNESS, UNIFORM COVERS, MEROTOPIES

In this section we will associate with any prenearness structure ξ on a set X the following three structures on X:

(1) $\bar{\xi} \subset P^2X$, containing all "collections which are far".

(2) $\mu \subset P^2X$, containing all "uniform covers" of X.

(3) $\gamma \subset P^2X$, containing all "collections which have arbitrary small members".

The crucial point is that any of these structures inherit all the information contained in ξ. In other words: ξ can be recovered from each of the structures $\bar{\xi}$, μ and γ. So, instead of axiomatizing the concept of "collections which are near" we could have axiomatized any of the three other concepts mentioned above. All four concepts are logically equivalent, and through suitable axiomatization give rise to isomorphic categories. We will formulate the corresponding axiomatizations below and in this way connect our work with the work of Z. FROLÍK [21] and J.R. ISBELL [44] on quasi-uniform spaces and of M. KATĚTOV [48] on merotopic spaces.

We have chosen the nearness concept as our starting point, first because when we started our work we were not aware of the equivalences mentioned above, second because we feel that the nearness concept has a greater intuitive appeal than any of the others and that one can handle it in a simpler and more direct way in most cases (an exception being e.g. the embedding of $\mathcal{Unif}$ in $\mathcal{Near}$). Even though many readers will be more familiar thinking in terms of covers they will soon find that thinking in terms of nearness is more convenient in many cases. It may also be worth mentioning that P. CAMERON, J.G. HOCKING & S.A. NAIMPALLY [8] advocate very convincingly to teach topology using "nearness" as basic concept (topology = = nearness between points and sets, proximity = nearness between paired sets, contiguity = nearness of finite collections of sets, nearness = = nearness of arbitrary collections of sets).

3.1. DEFINITIONS. Let ξ be a (pre-, quasi-) nearness structure on X. Then

(1) $\bar{\xi} = P^2X - \xi$ is called the (pre-, quasi-) *farness structure* induced on X by ξ;

(2) $\mu = \mu_\xi = \{\mathcal{A} \subset PX \mid \{X-A \mid A \in \mathcal{A}\} \in \bar{\xi}\}$ is called the (pre-, quasi-) *covering structure* induced on X by ξ;

(3) $\gamma = \gamma_\xi = \{\mathcal{A} \subset PX \mid \forall \mathcal{B} \in \mu \;\; \mathcal{B} \cap \text{stack}\, \mathcal{A} \neq \emptyset\}$ is called the (pre-, quasi-) *merotopic structure* induced on X by ξ.

3.2. PROPOSITIONS. *Let* ξ *be a prenearness structure on* X *and let* $\bar{\xi}$, μ *and* γ *be the associated structures. Then*

(1) ξ, $\bar{\xi}$, μ *and* γ *are subsets of* P^2X.

(2) *If* $\mathcal{A} \sim \mathcal{B}$ *then* $\mathcal{A} \in \xi(\bar{\xi},\gamma$ *resp.*) *iff* $\mathcal{B} \in \xi(\bar{\xi},\gamma$ *resp.*).

(3) $\mathcal{A} \in \xi$ *iff* $\text{sec}\, \mathcal{A} \in \gamma$.

(4) $\mathcal{A} \in \gamma$ *iff* $\text{sec}\, \mathcal{A} \in \xi$.

(5) $\mathcal{A} \in \bar{\xi}$ *iff* $\{X-A \mid A \in \mathcal{A}\} \in \mu$.

(6) $\mathcal{A} \in \mu$ *iff* $\forall \mathcal{B} \in \xi \;\; \mathcal{A} \cap \text{sec}\, \mathcal{B} \neq \emptyset$.

(7) $\mathcal{A} \in \xi$ *iff* $\forall \mathcal{B} \in \mu \;\; \mathcal{B} \cap \text{sec}\, \mathcal{A} \neq \emptyset$.

(8) $\mathcal{A} \in \mu$ *iff* $\forall \mathcal{B} \in \gamma \;\; \mathcal{A} \cap \text{stack}\, \mathcal{B} \neq \emptyset$.

(9) $\mathcal{A} \in \gamma$ *iff* $\forall \mathcal{B} \in \bar{\xi} \;\; \exists A \in \mathcal{A} \;\; \exists B \in \mathcal{B} \;\; A \cap B = \emptyset$.

(10) $\mathcal{A} \in \xi$ *iff* $\forall \mathcal{B} \in \gamma \;\; \exists A \in \mathcal{A} \;\; \exists B \in \mathcal{B} \;\; A \cap B = \emptyset$.

(11) *Equivalent are:*

(a) $x \in \text{cl}_\xi A$.

(b) $\sec\{\mathcal{A},\{x\}\} \in \gamma$.

(c) $\{X-A, X-\{x\}\} \notin \mu$.

(12) *Equivalent are:*

(a) $x \in \mathrm{int}_\xi A$, *i.e.* $x \notin \mathrm{cl}_\xi(X-A)$.

(b) $\sec\{X-A,\{x\}\} \notin \gamma$.

(c) $\{A, X-\{x\}\} \in \mu$.

(13) *If* $f\colon (X,\xi) \to (Y,\eta)$ *is a map between pre-N-spaces then the following conditions are equivalent:*

(a) $\mathcal{A} \in \xi \Rightarrow f\mathcal{A} \in \eta$.

(b) $\mathcal{B} \in \bar{\eta} \Rightarrow f^{-1}\mathcal{B} \in \bar{\xi}$.

(c) $\mathcal{A} \in \gamma_\xi \Rightarrow f\mathcal{A} \in \gamma_\eta$.

(d) $\mathcal{B} \in \mu_\xi \Rightarrow f^{-1}\mathcal{B} \in \mu_\xi$.

3.3. <u>DIAGRAM</u>.

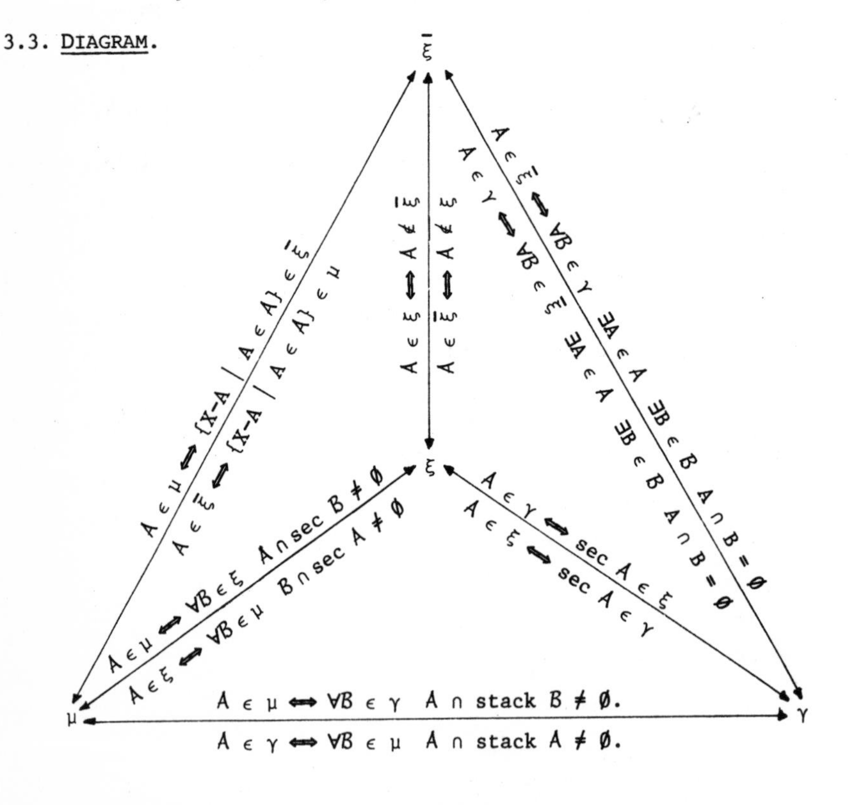

(1) ξ consists of all "collections which are near".

$\bar{\xi}$ consists of all "collections which are far".

γ consists of all "collections which contain arbitrary small members".

μ consists of all "uniform covers".

(2) For a function f the following conditions are equivalent:

(a) f preserves nearness.

(b) f preserves smallness.

(c) f^{-1} preserves farness.

(d) f^{-1} preserves uniform covers.

Having established the equivalence of the concepts of nearness, farness, smallness and uniform covers it poses no difficulty to formulate axiomatizations for the latter three concepts which correspond to the one given for the nearness concept. We arrange the axioms in such a way that the first three always correspond to prenearness structures, the first four to quasi-nearness structures, and all five to nearness structures.

3.4. AXIOMS FOR "FARNESS". *Let* $\bar{\xi}$ *be a subset of* P^2X:

(F1) *if* $\mathcal{A} < \mathcal{B}$ *and* $\mathcal{A} \in \bar{\xi}$ *then* $\mathcal{B} \in \bar{\xi}$.

(F2) *if* $\mathcal{A} \in \bar{\xi}$ *then* $\bigcap\mathcal{A} = \emptyset$.

(F3) $\emptyset \neq \bar{\xi} \neq P^2X$.

(F4) *if* $\mathcal{A} \in \bar{\xi}$ *and* $\mathcal{B} \in \bar{\xi}$ *then* $(\mathcal{A} \vee \mathcal{B}) \in \bar{\xi}$.

(F5) *if* $\mathcal{A} \in \bar{\xi}$ *then* $\{\mathrm{cl}\, A \mid A \in \mathcal{A}\} \in \bar{\xi}$, *where* $\mathrm{cl}\, A = \{x \in X \mid \{A,\{x\}\} \notin \bar{\xi}\}$.

3.5. AXIOMS FOR "SMALLNESS". *Let* γ *be a subset of* P^2X:

(S1) *if* $\mathcal{A} < \mathcal{B}$ *and* $\mathcal{A} \in \gamma$ *then* $\mathcal{B} \in \gamma$.

(S2) $\forall x \in X \quad \{\{x\}\} \in \gamma$.

(S3) $\emptyset \neq \gamma \neq P^2X$.

(S4) *if* $(\mathcal{A} \cup \mathcal{B}) \in \gamma$ *then* $\mathcal{A} \in \gamma$ *or* $\mathcal{B} \in \gamma$.

(S5) $\sec\{\mathrm{cl}\, A \mid A \in \mathcal{A}\} \in \gamma \Rightarrow \sec \mathcal{A} \in \gamma$, *where* $\mathrm{cl}\, A = \{x \in X \mid \sec\{A,\{x\}\} \in \gamma\}$.

3.6. AXIOMS FOR "UNIFORM COVERS". *Let* μ *be a subset of* P^2X:

(U1) *if* $\mathcal{A} \prec \mathcal{B}$ *and* $\mathcal{A} \in \mu$ *then* $\mathcal{B} \in \mu$.

(U2) *if* $\mathcal{A} \in \mu$ *then* $\bigcup\mathcal{A} = X$.

(U3) $\emptyset \neq \mu \neq P^2X$.

(U4) *if* $\mathcal{A} \in \mu$ *and* $\mathcal{B} \in \mu$ *then* $(\mathcal{A} \wedge \mathcal{B}) \in \mu$.

(U5) *if* $\mathcal{A} \in \mu$ *then* $\{\mathrm{int}_\mu A \mid A \in \mathcal{A}\} \in \mu$ *with* $\mathrm{int}_\mu A = \{x \in X \mid \{A, X - \{x\}\} \in \mu\}$.

As an immediate consequence we obtain the following result:

3.7. THEOREM. *The following categories are pairwise isomorphic (as concrete categories):*

(a) *the category* $\mathcal{Q}$-*Near of quasi-*N*-spaces and* N*-maps*;

(b) *the category of quasiuniform spaces and uniformly continuous maps for the sense of* J.R. ISBELL [44];

(c) *the category of merotopic spaces and merotopic maps in the sense of* M. KATĚTOV [48].

4. EXAMPLES: TOPOLOGICAL, CONTIGUAL, UNIFORM AND PROXIMAL N-SPACES

4.1. PROPOSITION. *If* (X,ξ) *is an* N*-space then*:

(1) *if* $\cap\{cl_\xi A \mid A \in \mathcal{A}\} \neq \emptyset$ *then* $\mathcal{A} \in \xi$.

(2) *if* $\mathcal{A}$ *converges then* $\mathcal{A} \in \gamma$.

(3) *if* $\mathcal{A} \in \mu$ *then* $X = \cup\{int_\mu A \mid A \in \mathcal{A}\}$.

4.2. PROPOSITION. *If* (X,ξ) *is an* N*-space then the following conditions are equivalent*:

(T) *if* $\mathcal{A} \in \xi$ *then* $\cap\{cl_\xi A \mid A \in \mathcal{A}\} \neq \emptyset$.

(T') *if* $\mathcal{A} \in \gamma$ *then* $\mathcal{A}$ *converges*.

(T") *if* $X = \cup\{int_\mu A \mid A \in \mathcal{A}\}$ *then* $\mathcal{A} \in \mu$.

4.3. DEFINITION. An N-space is called a *topological* N*-space* iff it satisfies the condition (T) above. The full subcategory of *Near* whose objects are the topological N-spaces is denoted by *T-Near*.

4.4. THEOREM. *If* (X,cl) *is a topological space* *) *then*

$$\xi = \{\mathcal{A} \subset PX \mid \cap\{cl\ A \mid A \in \mathcal{A}\} \neq \emptyset\}$$

is a topological N*-structure on* X *with* $cl_\xi = cl$. *The map* $cl \rightsquigarrow \xi$ *induces an isomorphism from the category Top of all topological spaces and continuous maps onto the category* T-*Near of all topological* N*-spaces and* N*-maps*.

4.5. REMARK. By means of the above isomorphism $cl \longleftrightarrow \xi$ we can identify *Top* and *T-Near* and can consider *Top* as a full subcategory of *Near*.

---

*) In this treatise all topological spaces are assumed to be symmetric, i.e. to satisfy the condition $x \in cl\{y\} \Rightarrow y \in cl\{x\}$.

4.6. THEOREM. *T-Near is a bicoreflective subcategory of Near. For any nearness structure* ξ *on* X *the set*

$$\xi_t = \{\mathcal{A} \subset PX \mid \cap\{cl_\xi A \mid A \in \mathcal{A}\} \neq \emptyset\}$$

is a topological nearness structure on X *with* $cl_{\xi_t} = cl_\xi$, *and the map*

$$1_X: (X,\xi_t) \to (X,\xi)$$

is the T-Near-coreflection of (X,ξ).

4.7. REMARK. The coreflector T: *Near* → *T-Near* can be considered as a "forgetful" functor associating with any N-space (X,ξ) its "underlying" topological space $(X,\xi_t) \approx (X,cl_\xi)$.

4.8. PROPOSITION. *If* (X,ξ) *is an* N-*space then the following conditions are equivalent:*

(C) *if every finite subset of* $\mathcal{A}$ *belongs to* ξ *then* $\mathcal{A}$ *belongs to* ξ.

(C') *if* $\mathcal{A} \in \bar{\xi}$ *then there exists a finite subset* $\mathcal{B}$ *of* $\mathcal{A}$ *with* $\mathcal{B} \in \bar{\xi}$.

(C") *if* $\mathcal{A} \in \mu$ *then there exists a finite subset* $\mathcal{B}$ *of* $\mathcal{A}$ *with* $\mathcal{B} \in \mu$.

4.9. DEFINITION. An N-space is called a *contigual N-space* iff it satisfies the condition (C) above. The full subcategory of *Near* whose objects are the contigual N-spaces is denoted by *C-Near*.

4.10. THEOREM. *If* (X,η) *is a contiguity space then*

$$\xi = \{\mathcal{A} \subset PX \mid \forall\mathcal{B} \subset \mathcal{A}\ (\mathcal{B} \text{ finite} \Rightarrow \mathcal{B} \in \eta)\}$$

is a contigual N-*structure on* X *with* $\xi_f = \{\mathcal{A} \in \xi \mid \mathcal{A} \text{ finite}\} = \eta$. *The map* $\eta \rightsquigarrow \xi$ *induces an isomorphism from the category Cont of all contiguity spaces and contiguity preserving maps* (V.M. IVANOVA & A.A. IVANOV [46]) *onto the category C-Near of all contigual* N-*spaces and* N-*maps*.

4.11. REMARK. By means of the above isomorphism $\eta \leftrightsquigarrow \xi$ we can identify *Cont* and *C-Near* and can consider *Cont* as a full subcategory of *Near*.

4.12. THEOREM. *C-Near is a bireflective subcategory of Near. For any nearness structure* ξ *on* X *the set*

$$\xi_c = \{\mathcal{A} \subset PX \mid \forall\mathcal{B} \subset \mathcal{A}\ (\mathcal{B} \text{ finite} \Rightarrow \mathcal{B} \in \xi)\}$$

is a contigual nearness structure on X *with* $(\xi_c)_f = \xi_f$, *and the map*

$$1_X\colon (X,\xi) \to (X,\xi_c)$$

is the C-Near-reflection of (X,ξ).

4.13. REMARK. The reflector C: *Near* → *C-Near* can be considered as a "forgetful" functor associating with any N-space (X,ξ) its "underlying" contiguity space $(X,\xi_c) \approx (X,\xi_f)$.

4.14. PROPOSITION. *If* (X,ξ) *is an* N-*space then the following conditions are equivalent:*

(U) *if* $\mathcal{A} \in \bar{\xi}$ *then there exists* $\mathcal{B} \in \bar{\xi}$ *such that for each* $B \in \mathcal{B}$ *there exists* $A \in \mathcal{A}$ *with* $A \subset \cap\{C \in \mathcal{B} \mid C \cup B \neq X\}$.

(U') *if* $\mathcal{A} \in \bar{\xi}$ *then there exists* $\mathcal{B} \in \bar{\xi}$ *such that for each* $x \in X$ *there exists* $A \in \mathcal{A}$ *with* $A \subset \cap\{B \notin \mathcal{B} \mid x \in B\}$.

(U") *if* $\mathcal{A} \in \mu$ *then there exists* $\mathcal{B} \in \mu$ *such that for each* $B \in \mathcal{B}$ *there exists* $A \in \mathcal{A}$ *with* $\cup\{C \in \mathcal{B} \mid B \cap C \neq \emptyset\} \subset A$, *i.e. every uniform cover has a uniform star-refinement.*

4.15. DEFINITION. An N-space is called a *uniform* N-*space* iff it satisfies the condition (U) above. The full subcategory of *Near* whose objects are the uniform N-spaces is denoted by *U-Near*.

4.16. THEOREM. *If* (X,μ) *is a uniform space then*

$$\xi = \{\mathcal{A} \subset PX \mid \forall \mathcal{B} \in \mu \quad \mathcal{B} \cap \sec \mathcal{A} \neq \emptyset\}$$

is a uniform N-*structure on* X *with* $\mu_\xi = \mu$. *The map* $\mu \rightsquigarrow \xi$ *induces an isomorphism from the category Unif of uniform spaces and uniformly continuous maps onto the category U-Near of all uniform* N-*spaces and* N-*maps.*

4.17. REMARK. By means of the above isomorphism $\mu \leftrightsquigarrow \xi$ we can identify *Unif* and *U-Near* and can consider *Unif* as a full subcategory of *Near*.

4.18. THEOREM. *U-Near is a bireflective subcategory of Near. For any nearness structure* ξ *on* X *with the corresponding cover structure* μ, *the set* μ_u *consisting of all* $\mathcal{A} \in \mu$ *for which there exists a sequence* $\ldots \mathcal{B}_3 \prec^* \mathcal{B}_2 \prec^* \mathcal{B}_1 \prec^* \mathcal{B}$ *of star-refinements in* μ *is a uniform structure on* X. *The corresponding nearness structure* ξ_u *is a uniform nearness structure on* X, *and the map*

$$1_X : (X,\xi) \to (X,\xi_u)$$

is the U-*Near*-*reflection of* (X,ξ).

4.19. REMARK. The reflector U: *Near* → U-*Near* can be considered as a "forgetful" functor associating with any N-space (X,ξ) its "underlying" uniform space $(X,\xi_u) \approx (X,\mu_u)$.

4.20. NOTATIONAL CONVENTIONS. From now on we will make the following identifications which are justified by the above remarks:

T-*Near* = *Top*
C-*Near* = *Cont*
U-*Near* = *Unif*
T: *Near* → *Top* topological coreflector
C: *Near* → *Cont* contigual reflector
U: *Near* → *Unif* uniform reflector.

4.21. THEOREM. *A nearness space is*

(1) *topological and contigual iff it is a compact topological space.*
(2) *topological and uniform iff it is a paracompact topological space.*
(3) *uniform and contigual iff it is a totally bounded (= precompact) uniform space.*

Since the category of all totally bounded uniform spaces and uniformly continuous maps is isomorphic to the category *Prox* of all proximity spaces and δ-maps the following definitions are justified:

4.22. DEFINITIONS. An N-space is called

(1) *compact* iff it is topological and contigual;
(2) *paracompact* iff it is topological and uniform;
(3) *proximal* iff it is contigual and uniform.

The full subcategory of *Near* whose objects are the proximal N-spaces will be denoted by *Pr*-*Near*.

4.23. THEOREM.

(1) *The categories Pr-Near and Prox are isomorphic (and will from now on be identified).*

(2) *Prox is a bireflective subcategory of Near. If* (X,ξ) *is an N-space,* (X,ξ_u) *is the uniform reflection of* (X,ξ) *and* (X,ξ_{uc}) *is the contigual reflection of* (X,ξ_u) *then* $\xi_p = \xi_{uc}$ *is a proximal nearness structure on* X*, and the map*

$$1_X: (X,\xi) \to (X,\xi_p)$$

is the Prox-reflection of (X,ξ).

4.24. <u>REMARK</u>. Whereas usually uniform spaces and topological spaces are treated in a non-symmetric way and it is commonly believed that uniform spaces are richer in structure than topological spaces, in the realm of nearness structures it becomes quite apparent that the relation between uniform and topological structures is completely symmetric.

The "forgetful" functor *Unif* → *Top* is the domain-restriction of the topological coreflector T: *Near* → *Top*. Its counterpart, the domain-restriction of the uniform reflector U: *Near* → *Unif*, is precisely the "fine" functor *Top* → *Unif*. It can equally well be considered as a "forgetful" functor from *Top* to *Unif*.

A topological space (X,ξ) is "uniformizable" (= completely regular) iff there exists a uniform structure η on X with $\xi = \eta_t$, equivalently iff $\xi = \xi_{ut}$. Likewise a uniform space (X,ξ) could be called "topologizable" (= fine) iff there exists a topological structure η on X with $\xi = \eta_u$, equivalently iff $\xi = \xi_{tu}$.

The "uniformizable" reflection of a topological space (X,ξ) is just

$$1_X: (X,\xi) \to (X,\xi_{ut}).$$

The "topologizable" coreflection of a uniform space (X,ξ) is just

$$1_X: (X,\xi_{tu}) \to (X,\xi).$$

Suitable restrictions of T: *Near* → *Top* and U: *Near* → *Unif* provide isomorphisms between

(a) the category of "uniformizable" (= completely regular) topological spaces and continuous maps;
(b) the category of "topologizable" (= fine) uniform spaces and uniformly continuous maps.

Similar relations hold for any pair of full subcategories of *Near*, one being bireflective the other being bicoreflective in *Near*. Cf. A.11 and the paper [66] by P.L. SHARMA and W.N. HUNSAKER.

5. CLUSTERS, CLANS AND FILTERS

This section, being of a more technical nature, provides some useful terminology, especially for the study of completions.

5.1. DEFINITIONS. Let (X,ξ) be an N-space. A non-empty subset $\mathcal{A}$ of PX is called:

(1) a *ξ-cluster* -shortly: a *cluster*- iff $\mathcal{A}$ is a maximal element of the set ξ, ordered by inclusion.
(2) a *γ-cocluster* -shortly: a *cocluster*- iff $\mathcal{A}$ is a minimal element of the set $\{\mathcal{B} \in \gamma \mid \mathcal{B} = \text{stack } \mathcal{B}\}$, ordered by inclusion.
(3) a *ξ-clan* iff $\mathcal{A}$ is a grill and $\mathcal{A} \in \xi$.
(4) a *γ-filter* -or *Cauchy filter*- if $\mathcal{A}$ is a filter and $\mathcal{A} \in \gamma$.

The proof of the next proposition follows immediately from the observation that the sec-operator induces an order-reversing bijection on the set SX of all stacks in X and from the next lemma.

5.2. LEMMA

(1) *If* $\mathcal{A}$ *is a filter in* X *then* $\mathcal{A} \subset \text{sec } \mathcal{A}$.
(2) *If* $\mathcal{A}$ *is a clan in* X *then* $\text{sec } \mathcal{A} \subset \mathcal{A}$.

5.3. PROPOSITION. *Let* (X,ξ) *be an* N-*space. For non-empty stacks* $\mathcal{A}$ *in* X *the following implications hold:*

$$\begin{array}{lcl}
\mathcal{A} \textit{ is a } \xi\textit{-cluster} & \Longleftrightarrow & \text{sec } \mathcal{A} \textit{ is a } \gamma\textit{-cocluster} \\
\Downarrow & & \Downarrow \\
\mathcal{A} \textit{ is a maximal } \xi\textit{-clan} & \Longleftrightarrow & \text{sec } \mathcal{A} \textit{ is a minimal } \gamma\textit{-filter} \\
\Downarrow & & \Downarrow \\
\mathcal{A} \textit{ is a } \xi\textit{-clan} & \Longleftrightarrow & \text{sec } \mathcal{A} \textit{ is a } \gamma\textit{-filter} \\
\Downarrow & & \Downarrow \\
\mathcal{A} \in \xi \cap \gamma & \Longleftrightarrow & \text{sec } \mathcal{A} \in \gamma \cap \xi \\
\Downarrow & & \Downarrow \\
\mathcal{A} \in \xi & \Longleftrightarrow & \text{sec } \mathcal{A} \in \gamma
\end{array}$$

5.4. REMARKS

(1) (D. HARRIS [29]) The γ-coclusters are precisely the "round" Cauchy filters, i.e. the γ-filters $\mathcal{F}$ satisfying the condition:
$\forall F \in \mathcal{F} \ \exists \mathcal{B} \in \mu \ \ \cup(\mathcal{F} \cap \mathcal{B}) \subset F$.

(2) In general none of the above arrows $\Downarrow$ can be reversed. But under very mild conditions the maximal ξ-clans are precisely the ξ-clusters and the minimal γ-filters are precisely the γ-coclusters. Cf. 5.5(2) and 10.4.

5.5. EXAMPLES

(1) If (X,ξ) is an N-space and $x \in X$ then

(a) $\xi(x) = \{A \in X \mid x \in cl_\xi A\}$ is a ξ-cluster.

(b) the neighbourhoodfilter $\mathcal{U}(x)$ of x is a γ-cocluster.

(2) If (X,ξ) is uniform or contigual or topological then $\mathcal{A}$ is a maximal ξ-clan iff it is a ξ-cluster and $\mathcal{B}$ is a minimal γ-filter iff it is a γ-cocluster.

(3) If (X,ξ) is topological then the ξ-clusters are precisely the collections $\xi(x)$ and the ξ-coclusters are precisely the neighbourhoodfilters $\mathcal{U}(x)$.

(4) If (X,ξ) is topological then $\mathcal{A} \in \xi \cap \gamma$ iff $\mathcal{A}$ has an adherencepoint and a convergencepoint. It may happen that there is no point which is simultaneously an adherencepoint and a convergencepoint.

(5) If (X,ξ) is contigual then every $\mathcal{A} \in \xi$ is contained in some ξ-cluster, every $\mathcal{B} \in \gamma$ is corefined by some γ-cocluster and every γ-filter contains some γ-cocluster.

Chapter II. THE CATEGORIES *P-Near*, *Q-Near* AND *Near*

Before we turn our attention to the "topological" properties of *Near* we investigate the basic categorical properties of *Near* and the larger categories *P-Near* and *Q-Near*. Most of the results follow immediately from the theory developed in Appendix A.

6. *P-Near*

6.1. DEFINITION. For any set X, the nearness structure defined by

(1) $\xi = \{\mathcal{A} \subset PX \mid \cap\mathcal{A} \neq \emptyset\}$ is called the *discrete* nearness structure on X and (X,ξ) is called the discrete nearness space with underlying set X.

(2) $\xi = \{\mathcal{A} \subset PX \mid \emptyset \notin \mathcal{A}\}$ is called the *indiscrete* nearness structure on X and (X,ξ) is called the indiscrete nearness space with underlying set X.

6.2. PROPOSITION. *For any set* X, *the set of all prenearness structures on* X, *ordered by inclusion, is a complete lattice. Especially:*

(1) *the discrete nearness structure on* X *is the smallest element;*

(2) *the indiscrete nearness structure on* X *is the largest element;*

(3) *if* Ω *is a non-empty set of prenearness structures on* X *then:*

$\inf \Omega = \cap\Omega$

$\sup \Omega = \cup\Omega$.

6.3. PROPOSITION. *If* X *is a set,* $(Y_i,\eta_i)_{i\in I}$ *is a family of pre-N-spaces and* $(f_i\colon X \to Y_i)_{i\in I}$ *is a family of maps then* $\xi = \cap\{f_i^{-1}(\eta_i) \mid i \in I\}$ *is a prenearness structure on* X, *initial with respect to* $(X,(f_i)_{i\in I},(Y_i,\eta_i)_{i\in I})$.

6.4. THEOREM. *P-Near is a property fibred topological category.*

6.5. REMARK. Because of 6.4 all results of Appendix A are applicable. Final structures can be described in the following way: if Y is a set, (X_i,ξ_i) is a family of pre-N-spaces, and $(f_i\colon X_i \to Y)_{i\in I}$ is a family of maps then $\eta = \{\mathcal{B} \subset PY \mid \cap\mathcal{B} \neq \emptyset\} \cup \cup\{f_i(\xi_i) \mid i \in I\}$ is a prenearness structure on Y, final with respect to $((X_i,\xi_i)_{i\in I},(f_i)_{i\in I},Y)$.

7. *Q-Near*

7.1. DEFINITION. If ξ is a prenearness structure on X then ξ_q denotes the collection of all $\mathcal{A} \subset PX$ such that there do not exist finitely many elements $\mathcal{A}_1,\mathcal{A}_2,\ldots,\mathcal{A}_n$ of $\bar{\xi}$ with $\mathcal{A}_1 \vee \mathcal{A}_2 \vee \ldots \vee \mathcal{A}_n < \mathcal{A}$.

7.2. PROPOSITION. *Q-Near is bicoreflective in P-Near. For any pre-N-space* (X,ξ) *the map* $1_X\colon (X,\xi_q) \to (X,\xi)$ *is the Q-Near-coreflection of* (X,ξ).

7.3. THEOREM. *Q-Near is a properly fibred topological category.*

7.4. REMARK. Because of 7.3 all results of Appendix A are applicable. Initial and final structures in *Q-Near* can be described as follows:

(1) if X is a set, $(Y_i,\eta_i)_{i\in I}$ is a family of quasi-N-spaces, and $(f_i\colon X \to Y_i)_{i\in I}$ is a family of maps then $\xi = (\cap\{f_i^{-1}(\eta_i) \mid i \in I\})_q$ is a quasinearness structure on X, initial with respect to $(X,(f_i)_{i\in I},(Y_i,\eta_i)_{i\in I})$.

(2) especially, if $f\colon X \to Y$ is a map and η is a quasinearness structure on Y then $\xi = f^{-1}(\eta)$ is a quasinearness structure on X, initial with respect to $(X,f,(Y,\eta))$.

(3) if Y is a set, $(X_i,\xi_i)_{i\in I}$ is a family of quasi-N-spaces and $(f_i\colon X_i \to Y)_{i\in I}$ is a family of maps then $\eta = \{\mathcal{B} \subset PY \mid \cap\mathcal{B} \neq \emptyset\} \cup \cup\{f_i(\xi_i) \mid i \in I\}$ is a quasinearness structure on Y, final with respect to $((X_i,\xi_i)_{i\in I},(f_i)_{i\in I},Y)$.

(4) especially, if $f\colon X \to Y$ is a surjective map and ξ is a quasinearness structure on X then $\eta = f(\xi)$ is a quasinearness structure on Y, final with respect to $((X,\xi),f,Y)$.

7.5. <u>PROPOSITION</u>. *Q-Near is a subcategory of P-Near containing all discrete spaces and all indiscrete spaces and being closed under the formation of subobjects, quotientobjects and coproducts in P-Near.*

8. *Near*

8.1. <u>THEOREM</u>. *Near is bireflective in Q-Near.*

<u>PROOF</u>. Let (X,ξ) be a quasi-N-space. By transfinite induction define operators cl^α on PX:

(1) $\mathrm{cl}^0 A = A$

(2) $\mathrm{cl}^{\alpha+1} A = \{x \in X \mid \{\mathrm{cl}^\alpha A, \mathrm{cl}^\alpha\{x\}\} \in \xi\}$

(3) $\mathrm{cl}\, A = \cup\{\mathrm{cl}^\alpha A \mid \alpha < \beta\}$ if β is a limit ordinal.

If $\mathrm{cl}\, A = \cup\{\mathrm{cl}^\alpha A \mid \alpha \text{ ordinal}\}$ then cl is the smallest operator on PX satisfying the following conditions:

(T1) $\mathrm{cl}\, \emptyset = \emptyset$,

(T2) $A \subset \mathrm{cl}\, A$,

(T3) $\mathrm{cl}(A\cup B) = \mathrm{cl}\, A \cup \mathrm{cl}\, B$,

(T4) $\mathrm{cl}^2 A = \mathrm{cl}\, A$,

(T5) if $\{\mathrm{cl}\, A, \mathrm{cl}\{x\}\} \in \xi$ then $x \in \mathrm{cl}\, A$.

This implies that $\xi_n = \{\mathcal{A} \subset PX \mid \{\mathrm{cl}\,A \mid A \in \mathcal{A}\} \in \xi\}$ is a nearness structure on X with $\mathrm{cl} = \mathrm{cl}_{\xi_n}$.

To show that $1_X\colon (X,\xi) \to (X,\xi_n)$ is the *Near*-reflection of (X,ξ), consider an N-space (Y,η) and an N-map $f\colon (X,\xi) \to (Y,\eta)$. The operator cl_f, defined on PX by $\mathrm{cl}_f A = f^{-1}[\mathrm{cl}_\eta(fA)]$, satisfies (T1)-(T5). Hence $\mathrm{cl}\,A \subset \mathrm{cl}_f A$ for each $A \subset X$. Therefore the following implications hold:

$$\mathcal{A} \in \xi_n \Rightarrow \{\mathrm{cl}\,A \mid A \in \mathcal{A}\} \in \xi \Rightarrow \{\mathrm{cl}_f A \mid A \in \mathcal{A}\} \in \xi \Rightarrow$$
$$\Rightarrow \{f^{-1}[\mathrm{cl}_\eta(fA)] \mid A \in \mathcal{A}\} \in \xi \Rightarrow \{\mathrm{cl}_\eta(fA) \mid A \in \mathcal{A}\} \in \eta \Rightarrow f\mathcal{A} \in \eta.$$

Hence $f\colon (X,\xi_n) \to (Y,\eta)$ is an N-map. □

8.2. DEFINITION. The *Near-reflection* of a quasi-N-space (X,ξ) will be denoted by $1_X\colon (X,\xi) \to (X,\xi_n)$.

8.3. THEOREM. *Near is a properly fibred topological category.*

8.4. REMARK. Because of 8.3 all results of Appendix A are applicable. Initial and final structures in *Near* can be described as follows:

(1) if X is a set, $(Y_i,\eta_i)_{i\in I}$ is a family of N-spaces, and $(f_i\colon X \to Y_i)_{i\in I}$ is a family of maps then $\xi = (\bigcap\{f_i^{-1}(\eta_i) \mid i \in I\})_q$ is a nearness structure on X, initial with respect to $(X,(f_i)_{i\in I},(Y_i,\eta_i)_{i\in I})$.

(2) especially, if $f\colon X \to Y$ is a map and η is a nearness structure on Y then $\xi = f^{-1}(\eta)$ is a nearness structure on X, initial with respect to $(X,f,(Y,\eta))$.

(3) if Y is a set, $(X_i,\xi_i)_{i\in I}$ is a family of N-spaces, and $(f_i\colon X_i \to Y)_{i\in I}$ is a family of maps then $\eta = (\{\mathcal{B} \subset PY \mid \bigcap\mathcal{B} \neq \emptyset\} \cup \bigcup\{f_i(\xi_i) \mid i \in I\})_n$ is a nearness structure on Y, final with respect to $((X_i,\xi_i)_{i\in I},(f_i)_{i\in I},Y)$.

(4) especially, if $f\colon X \to Y$ is a surjective map and ξ is a nearness structure on X then $\eta = (f(\xi))_n$ is a nearness structure on Y, final with respect to $((X,\xi),f,Y)$.

8.5. PROPOSITION. *Near is a subcategory of Q-Near containing all discrete spaces and all indiscrete spaces and being closed under the formation of subobjects, products and coproducts in Q-Near.*

8.6. PROPOSITION. *An isomorphism-closed full subcategory $\underline{A}$ of Near is bireflective in Near iff it satisfies the following conditions:*

(1) *any indiscrete space belongs to* $\underline{A}$,

(2) *if* $f: X \to Y$ *is a map and* (Y,η) *belongs to* $\underline{A}$ *then* $(X,f^{-1}(\eta))$ *belongs to* $\underline{A}$,

(3) *if* $\{\xi_i \mid i \in I\}$ *is a non-empty family of* $\underline{A}$*-structures on a set* X *then* $\inf\{\xi_i \mid i \in I\} = (\cap\{\xi_i \mid i \in I\})_q$ *is an* $\underline{A}$*-structure on* X.

CHAPTER III. SEPARATION AXIOMS

9. N1-SPACES

9.1. PROPOSITION. *If* (X,ξ) *is a pre-N-space and if* γ *and* μ *are the associated structures then the following conditions are equivalent:*

(1) *if* $\{\{x\},\{y\}\} \in \xi$ *then* $x = y$.

(2) *if* $\{\{x,y\}\} \in \gamma$ *then* $x = y$.

(3) *if* $x \neq y$ *then* $\{X-\{x\},X-\{y\}\} \in \mu$.

9.2. DEFINITION. A (pre-,quasi-) N-space is called a *(pre-,quasi-)* N1*-space* iff it satisfies the above conditions.

9.3. PROPOSITION. *An* N*-space* (X,ξ) *is an* N1*-space iff the underlying topological space* (X,ξ_t) *is a* T1*-space.*

9.4. PROPOSITION. *The full subcategory Near-1 of Near whose objects are the* N1*-spaces is epireflective in Near. It is closed under the formation of subobjects, products and coproducts in Near and contains all discrete spaces.*

9.5. REMARKS

(1) *Near-1* is properly fibred but not topological. If X is a set, $(Y_i,\eta_i)_{i\in I}$ is a family of N1-spaces and $(f_i: X \to Y_i)_{i\in I}$ is a family of maps then the following conditions are equivalent:

(a) there exists an N1-structure on X, initial with respect to $(X,(f_i)_{i\in I},(Y_i,\eta_i)_{i\in I})$ in *Near-1*.

(b) if ξ is the N-structure on X, initial with respect to $(X,(f_i)_{i\in I},(Y_i,\eta_i)_{i\in I})$ in *Near* then (X,ξ) is an N1-space.

(c) the family $(f_i)_{i\in I}$ separates points.

But *Near-1* is relatively topological in the sense of [Al 3]

(2) A nearness space is topological (contigual, uniform, proximal) iff its N1-reflection has the corresponding property.

10. SEPARATED N-SPACES AND N2-SPACES

10.1. DEFINITION. If $\mathcal{A} \subset PX$ and $\xi \subset P^2X$ then $\xi(\mathcal{A}) = \{A \subset X \mid (\{A\} \cup \mathcal{A}) \in \xi\}$.

10.2. DEFINITION. A pre-N-space (X,ξ) is called *separated* iff $\mathcal{A} \in \xi \cap \gamma$ implies $\xi(\mathcal{A}) \in \xi$. A (pre-,quasi-) N-space is called a *(pre-,quasi)* N2-*space* iff it is a separated (pre-,quasi-) N1-space.

10.3. PROPOSITION.

(1) *A topological* N-*space is separated iff it satisfies the axiom* H0 *of* K. CSÁSZÁR [16].
(2) *A topological* N-*space is an* N2-*space iff it is a Hausdorff space.*
(3) *For any* N2-*space (resp. separated* N-*space)* (X,ξ) *the underlying topological space* (X,ξ_t) *is a Hausdorff space (resp. an* H0-*space).*
(4) *Every uniform* N-*space is separated.*

10.4. PROPOSITION. *If* (X,ξ) *is a separated* N-*space and* $\mathcal{A}$ *is a stack in* X, *then the following conditions are equivalent:*

(1) $\mathcal{A}$ *is a* ξ-*cluster.*
(2) $\mathcal{A}$ *is a maximal* ξ-*clan.*
(3) sec $\mathcal{A}$ *is a minimal* γ-*filter.*
(4) sec $\mathcal{A}$ *is a* γ-*cocluster.*

10.5. PROPOSITION. *If* (X,ξ) *is a separated* N-*space then the following hold:*

(1) *if* $\mathcal{A} \in \xi \cap \gamma$ *(especially if* $\mathcal{A}$ *is a* ξ-*clan) then there exists a unique* ξ-*cluster containing* $\mathcal{A}$, *namely* $\xi(\mathcal{A})$.
(2) *if* $\mathcal{A} \in \xi \cap \gamma$ *(especially if* $\mathcal{A}$ *is a* γ-*filter) then there exists a unique minimal* γ-*filter contained in* stack $\mathcal{A}$, *namely*
$\{A \subset X \mid (\{X-A\} \cup \text{sec}\,\mathcal{A}) \notin \xi\} = \text{sec}\,\xi(\text{sec}\,\mathcal{A})$.

10.6. REMARK. The full subcategory *Near-2* of *Near* whose objects are the N2-spaces contains all discrete N-spaces and is closed under the formation of subobjects and coproducts in *Near* but not under the formation of quotients or products.

11. REGULAR N-SPACES AND N3-SPACES

In this section one of the most important concepts of the theory of nearness structures will be introduced, the concept of regular N-structures and N3-structures. These structures are equivalent (in the sense of section 3) to the semi-uniform structures (resp. the regular T-uniformities) of A.K. STEINER & E.F. STEINER [70] (resp. K. MORITA [55]). Especially the category *Near-3*, defined below, and the category of semi-uniform spaces and uniformly continuous maps are isomorphic. Several of the results in [35,36] concerning regular N1-spaces have been obtained independently in the realm of semi-uniform spaces (resp. regular T-uniform spaces) by the above mentioned authors (cf. espec. 14.5, 15.6(2), 15.10(1), 16.9(2), 16.10(d)).

11.1. <u>DEFINITION</u>. If (X,ξ) is a pre-N-space, $\mathcal{A} \subset PX$, $A \subset X$ and $B \subset X$ then:

(1) $A <_\xi B$ iff the following equivalent conditions hold:
   (a) $\{A,X-B\} \in \bar{\xi}$.
   (b) $\{X-A,B\} \in \mu$.
   (c) there exists $\mathcal{B} \in \mu$ with $\mathrm{star}(A,\mathcal{B}) \subset B$.

(2) $\mathcal{A}(<_\xi) = \{B \subset X \mid \exists A \in \mathcal{A} \;\; A <_\xi B\}$.

11.2. <u>LEMMA</u>. *If* (X,ξ) *is a pre-N-space and* $\mathcal{A} \subset PX$ *then* $\mathrm{sec}(\mathcal{A}(<_\xi)) = \{B \subset X \mid \forall A \in \mathcal{A} \;\; \{A,B\} \in \xi\}$.

11.3. <u>PROPOSITION</u>. *If* (X,ξ) *is a pre-N-space then the following conditions are equivalent:*

(1) *if* $\mathcal{A}(<_\xi) \in \xi$ *then* $\mathcal{A} \in \xi$.
(2) *if* $\mathcal{A} \in \gamma$ *then* $\mathcal{A}(<_\xi) \in \gamma$.
(3) *if* $\mathcal{A} \in \mu$ *then* $\{B \subset X \mid \exists A \in \mathcal{A} \;\; B <_\xi A\} \in \mu$.
(4) $\mathcal{A} \in \mu$ *iff* $\forall \mathcal{B} \in \gamma \;\; \exists A \in \mathcal{A} \;\; \exists B \in \mathcal{B} \;\; B <_\xi A$.
(5) $\mathcal{B} \in \gamma$ *iff* $\forall \mathcal{A} \in \mu \;\; \exists A \in \mathcal{A} \;\; \exists B \in \mathcal{B} \;\; B <_\xi A$.
(6) $\mathcal{A} \in \gamma$ *iff* $\{B \subset X \mid \forall A \in \mathcal{A} \;\; \{A,B\} \in \xi\} \in \xi$.
(7) $\mathcal{A} \in \xi$ *iff* $\{B \subset X \mid \forall A \in \mathcal{A} \;\; \{A,B\} \in \xi\} \in \gamma$.

11.4. <u>DEFINITION</u>. A pre-N-space is called *regular* iff it satisfies the above conditions. A (pre-,quasi-) N-space is called a *(pre-,quasi-) N3-space* iff it is a regular (pre-,quasi-) N1-space.

11.5. PROPOSITION

(1) *A topological* N-*space is regular as* N-*space iff it is regular as topological space.*
(2) *A topological* N-*space is an* N3-*space iff it is a* T3-*space.*
(3) *For any* N3-*space (respectively regular* N-*space)* (X,ξ) *the underlying topological space* (X,ξ_t) *is a* T3-*space (resp. regular space).*
(4) *Every uniform* N-*space is regular.*
(5) *Every regular* N-*space is separated.*
(6) *Every regular quasi*-N-*space is an* N-*space.*

11.6. PROPOSITION. *If* (X,ξ) *is a regular* N-*space and* $\mathcal{A} \in \xi \cap \gamma$ *then*

(1) $\sec(\xi(\mathcal{A})) = \mathcal{A}(<_\xi)$,
(2) $\sec(\mathcal{A}(<_\xi)) = \xi(\mathcal{A})$,
(3) $\xi(\mathcal{A}) = \{B \subset X \mid \forall A \in \mathcal{A} \ \ \{A,B\} \in \xi\}$ *is the unique* ξ-*cluster containing* $\mathcal{A}$,
(4) $(\sec \mathcal{A})(<_\xi)$ *is the unique minimal* γ-*filter contained in* $\mathcal{A}$,
(5) *if* $\mathcal{A}$ *is a* γ-*filter then* $\mathcal{A}(<_\xi)$ *is the unique minimal* γ-*filter contained in* $\mathcal{A}$.

11.7. REMARK. 11.6(5) is not true for separated spaces. E.g. if (X,ξ) is a non-regular Hausdorff topological space and if $\mathcal{A}$ is a non-regular neighbourhoodfilter of a point x, then $\mathcal{A}$ is a minimal γ-filter but $\mathcal{A} \neq \mathcal{A}(<_\xi)$.

11.8. PROPOSITION. *If* (X,ξ) *is a regular* N-*space*, $x \in X$, *and* $A \subset X$ *then*

(1) *equivalent are:*
    (a) $\{x\} <_\xi A$,
    (b) $\exists B \ \ \{x\} <_\xi B <_\xi A$.
(2) *equivalent are:*
    (a) $x \notin \mathrm{cl}_\xi A$,
    (b) $\exists U \subset X \ \ \exists V \subset X \ \ (\{x\} <_\xi U$ *and* $A <_\xi V$ *and* $U \cap V = \emptyset)$,
    (c) $\exists U \subset X \ \ \exists V \subset X \ \ (\{x\} <_\xi U$ *and* $A <_\xi V$ *and* $\{U,V\} \in \bar{\xi})$.

11.9. THEOREM. *The full subcategory* R-*Near of Near whose objects are the regular* N-*spaces is bireflective in Near.*

PROOF. The theorem follows from 8.6 as demonstrated in [35]. A constructive proof is the following. Let (X,ξ) be an N-space. Define by transfinite induction quasinear structures ξ^α on X as follows:

(1) $\xi^0 = \xi$,
(2) $\xi^{\alpha+1} = \{\mathcal{A} \subset PX \mid \{B \subset X \mid \exists A \in \mathcal{A} \ \mathrm{cl}_{\xi\alpha} A <_{\xi\alpha} B\} \in \xi_\alpha\}$,

(3) $\xi^\beta = \cup\{\xi^\alpha \mid \alpha < \beta\}$ for any limit ordinal β.

Then $\xi_r = \cup\{\xi^\alpha \mid \alpha \text{ ordinal}\}$ is a regular N-structure on X and $1_X: (X,\xi) \to (X,\xi_r)$ is the regular reflection of (X,ξ). □

11.10. DEFINITION. The *regular reflection* of an N-space (X,ξ) will be denoted by $1_X: (X,\xi) \to (X,\xi_r)$.

11.11. COROLLARY. *R-Near is a properly fibred topological category.*

11.12. COROLLARY. *The full subcategory Near-3 of Near whose objects are the N3-spaces is epireflective in Near. The reflection is the composition of the regular reflection with the N1-reflection.*

11.13. PROPOSITION. *R-Near contains all discrete and all indiscrete N-spaces and is closed under the formation of subobjects, products and coproducts in Near.*

12. UNIFORM AND NORMAL N-SPACES

Uniform N-spaces have already been defined and studied in section 4. In this section we will show that uniformity implies some strong normality conditions.

12.1. PROPOSITION. *For any pre-N-space the following conditions are equivalent:*

(1) *if* $\mathcal{A} \in \bar{\xi}$ *then there exists a function* $f: \mathcal{A} \to PX$ *such that*

 (a) $A <_\xi fA$ *for each* $A \in \mathcal{A}$, *and*

 (b) $\{fA \mid A \in \mathcal{A}\} \in \bar{\xi}$.

(2) *if* $\mathcal{A} \in \gamma$ *then there exists a function* $f: \mathcal{A} \to PX$ *such that*

 (a) $A <_\xi fA$ *for each* $A \in \mathcal{A}$, *and*

 (b) $\{fA \mid A \in \mathcal{A}\} \in \gamma$.

(3) *if* $\mathcal{A} \in \mu$ *then there exists a function* $f: \mathcal{A} \to PX$ *such that*

 (a) $fA <_\xi A$, *and*

 (b) $\{fA \mid A \in \mathcal{A}\} \in \mu$.

12.2. DEFINITION. A (pre-, quasi-) N-space is called *weakly normal* iff it satisfies the above conditions.

12.3. PROPOSITION. *For any pre-N-space* (X,ξ) *the following conditions are equivalent:*

(1) *if* $\mathcal{A} \in \bar{\xi}$ *then there exists a function* $f\colon \mathcal{A} \to PX$ *satisfying the following conditions:*

(a) $A <_{\xi} fA$ *for each* $A \in \mathcal{A}$,

(b) $\{fA \mid A \in \mathcal{A}\} \in \bar{\xi}$,

(c) $\mathcal{B} \cup \{X - \cap\{fB \mid B \in \mathcal{B}\}\} \in \bar{\xi}$ *for any* $\mathcal{B} \subset \mathcal{A}$.

(2) *if* $\mathcal{A} \in \mu$ *then there exists a function* $f\colon \mathcal{A} \to PX$ *satisfying the following conditions:*

(a) $fA <_{\xi} A$ *for each* $A \in \mathcal{A}$,

(b) $\{fA \mid A \subset \mathcal{A}\} \in \mu$,

(c) $\mathcal{B} \cup \{X - \cup\{fB \mid B \in \mathcal{B}\}\} \in \mu$ *for any* $\mathcal{B} \subset \mathcal{A}$.

12.4. DEFINITION. A (pre-, quasi-) N-space is called *normal* iff it satisfies the above conditions.

12.5. PROPOSITION. *For any pre-N-space* (X,ξ) *each of the following conditions implies all subsequent ones:*

(1) (X,ξ) *is uniform,*

(2) (X,ξ) *is normal,*

(3) (X,ξ) *is weakly normal,*

(4) (X,ξ) *is regular,*

(5) (X,ξ) *is separated.*

12.6. PROPOSITION. *For any topological N-space* (X,ξ) *the following conditions are equivalent:*

(1) (X,ξ) *is uniform,*

(2) (X,ξ) *is normal as N-space,*

(3) (X,ξ) *is paracompact.*

PROOF. The equivalence of (1) and (3) has been proved by A.H. STONE [74], the equivalence of (2) and (3) by E. MICHAEL [53]. □

12.7. THEOREM. *Unif is a properly fibred topological category.*

12.8. PROPOSITION. *U-Near is a full subcategory of Near, containing all discrete and all indiscrete N-spaces and being closed under the formation of subobjects, products and coproducts in Near.*

Chapter IV. COMPLETENESS, COMPLETIONS AND EXTENSIONS

The diagram in 5.3 suggests five possibilities to define completeness by requiring that every ξ-cluster (maximal ξ-clan, ξ-clan, $\mathcal{A} \in \xi \cap \gamma$, $\mathcal{A} \in \xi$ respectively) has an adherencepoint, or equivalently that every γ-cocluster (minimal γ-filter, γ-filter, $\mathcal{A} \in \gamma \cap \xi$, $\mathcal{A} \in \gamma$ respectively) converges. It turns out that for any separated space all of these concepts, except the strongest one, coincide. The strongest form of completeness is just topology.

13. TOPOLOGICAL AND SUBTOPOLOGICAL N-SPACES

Topological N-spaces have already been defined in section 4 and it has been shown that

(1) the categories *Top* and *T-Near* are isomorphic.

(2) *T-Near* is a bicoreflective subcategory of *Near*; the topological coreflection (X,ξ_t) of an N-space (X,ξ) is usually called the underlying topological space (or topological N-space) of (X,ξ).

13.1. THEOREM. *Top is a properly fibred topological category.*

13.2. DEFINITIONS

(1) A morphism $f\colon (X,\xi) \to (Y,\eta)$ is called a *closed embedding* iff it is an embedding and $\mathrm{cl}_\eta(fX) = fX$.

(2) An N-space (X,ξ) is called a *(closed) subspace* of an N-space (Y,η) iff there exists a (closed) embedding $f\colon (X,\xi) \to (Y,\eta)$.

13.3. PROPOSITION. *T-Near contains all discrete N-spaces and all indiscrete N-spaces, is closed under the formation of closed subspaces, quotientobjects and coproducts in Near, but not closed under the formation of arbitrary subspaces or products in Near.*

13.4. PROPOSITION. *A subspace (Y,η) of a topological N-space (X,ξ) is topological iff it satisfies any of the following equivalent conditions:*

(1) *if* $\mathcal{A} \subset PY$ *and* $\cap\{\mathrm{cl}_\xi A \mid A \in \mathcal{A}\} \neq \emptyset$ *then* $\cap\{\mathrm{cl}_\eta A \mid A \in \mathcal{A}\} \neq \emptyset$,

(2) *if* $\mathcal{A} \subset PY$ *and* $\mathcal{A}$ *converges in* (X,ξ) *then* $\mathcal{A}$ *converges in* (Y,η),

(3) *if* $\mathcal{A}$ *is an open cover of* (Y,η) *then* $\{X - \mathrm{cl}_\xi(Y-A) \mid A \in \mathcal{A}\}$ *is an open cover of* (X,ξ).

13.5. REMARK. D. HARRIS [31] has defined a subspace of a topological space to be *extension-closed* iff it satisfies the above conditions and he has proved the following interesting theorem [30]: a topological space is compact iff it can be embedded as an extension-closed subspace into a product of finite spaces.

13.6. DEFINITION. An N-space is called *subtopological* iff it can be embedded in some topological N-space.

13.7. THEOREM (H.L. BENTLEY [6]). *For any* N-*space the following conditions are equivalent:*

(1) (X,ξ) *is subtopological,*

(2) *each* $\mathcal{A} \in \xi$ *can be embedded in some* ξ*-clan,*

(3) *each* $\mathcal{A} \in \gamma$ *can be corefined by some* γ*-filter.*

PROOF.

(1) ⇒ (2). If $f\colon (X,\xi) \to (Y,\eta)$ is an embedding of (X,ξ) in some topological N-space (Y,η) and if $\mathcal{A} \in \xi$ then there exists some $y \in \bigcap\{cl_\eta(fA) \mid A \in \mathcal{A}\}$. Consequently $\mathcal{B} = \{B \subset X \mid y \in cl_\eta(fA)\}$ is a ξ-clan containing $\mathcal{A}$.

(2) ⇒ (3). If $\mathcal{A} \in \gamma$ then there exists some ξ-clan $\mathcal{B}$ with $\sec \mathcal{A} \subset \mathcal{B}$. Hence $\sec \mathcal{B}$ is a γ-filter which corefines $\mathcal{A}$.

(3) ⇒ (1). Embed (X,ξ_t) in a topological N-space (Y,η) by adjoining for every non-convergent γ-filter $\mathcal{A}$ of (X,ξ) a point $y_{\mathcal{A}}$ to (X,ξ_t) whose trace-filter is the neighbourhoodfilter of $\mathcal{A}$. The topological embedding $(X,\xi_t) \to (Y,\eta)$ induces an embedding $(X,\xi) \to (Y,\eta)$ in *Near*. □

13.8. PROPOSITION (H.L. BENTLEY [6]). *For any* N-*space* (X,ξ) *the following properties are equivalent:*

(1) (X,ξ) *is topological,*

(2) (X,ξ) *is subtopological and each* γ*-filter converges.*

13.9. REMARKS

(1) 13.8 implies e.g. that the reals, supplied with the usual metric-induced uniformity, are not subtopological.

(2) If (X,ξ) is subtopological then there can exist $\mathcal{A} \in \xi$ which cannot be embedded into any ξ-cluster.

13.10. PROPOSITION. *Let* $(X_i,\xi_i)_{i\in I}$ *be a family of topological* N*-spaces indexed by a set* I, *and let* $(p_i: (X,\xi) \to (X_i,\xi_i))_{i\in I}$ *be the product of this family in* Near. *Then:*

(1) $(p_i: (X,\xi_t) \to (X_i,\xi_i))_{i\in I}$ *is the product of this family in* T-Near.

(2) $\xi = \xi_t$ *holds iff for any open cover* $\mathcal{U}$ *of* (X,ξ) *there exist finitely many indices* $i_1,\ldots,i_n$ *in* I *and open covers* $\mathcal{U}_\nu$ *of* (X_{i_ν},ξ_{i_ν}) *such that the cover* $\{p_{i_1}^{-1}[U] \mid U \in \mathcal{U}_1\} \wedge \ldots \wedge \{p_{i_n}^{-1}[U] \mid U \in \mathcal{U}_n\}$ *refines* $\mathcal{U}$.

13.11. PROPOSITION. *If* $(X_i,\xi_i)_{i\in I}$ *is a set-indexed family of compact* N*-spaces and* $(p_i: (X,\xi) \to (X_i,\xi_i))$ *is the product of this family in* Near *then* $\xi = \xi_t$, *i.e.* (X,ξ) *is a compact* N*-space.*

PROOF. Let $\mathcal{U}$ be an open cover of (X,ξ). Then $\mathcal{U}$ can be refined by a finite cover consisting of canonical base-elements. Since each of these depends only on a finite number of coordinates we may assume that I is finite, hence that $I = \{1,2\}$ and that $\mathcal{U} \subset \{U_j \times V_j \mid j = 1,\ldots,n\}$ for some open covers $\{U_1,\ldots,U_n\}$ of (X_1,ξ_1) and $\{V_1,\ldots,V_n\}$ of (X_2,ξ_2). For any $x \in X_1$ define $U_x = \bigcap\{U_j \mid x \in U_j\}$ and for any $y \in X_2$ define $V_y = \bigcap\{V_j \mid y \in V_j\}$. Then $\mathcal{U}_1 = \{U_x \mid x \in X_1\}$ is an open cover of (X_1,ξ_1) and $\mathcal{U}_2 = \{V_y \mid y \in X_2\}$ is an open cover of (X_2,ξ_2) such that $\{p_1^{-1}[U] \mid U \in \mathcal{U}_1\} \wedge \{p_2^{-1}[V] \mid V \in \mathcal{U}_2\}$ refines $\mathcal{U}$.

13.12. PROPOSITION. *If* (X,ξ) *is a topological* N*-space such that* $(X,\xi)^{\aleph_0}$, *taken in* Near, *is topological then* (X,ξ) *is countably compact.*

PROOF. Assume, (X,ξ) is not countably compact. Then there exists a countable open cover $\{U_n \mid n \in \mathbb{N}\}$ of (X,ξ) containing no finite cover. Let I be the set of all finite sequences $(n_1,\ldots,n_\ell)$ of natural numbers with $\ell = n_1$ and define an open cover $\mathcal{U} = \{\bigcap\{p_i^{-1}[U_{n_i}] \mid i=1,\ldots,\ell\} \mid (n_1,\ldots,n_\ell) \in I\}$ of $(X,\xi)^{\aleph_0}$. Then $\mathcal{U}$ cannot be refined by some cover of the form required in 13.10. □

13.13. PROPOSITION. *If the product in* Near *of a family of paracompact* N*-spaces is topological then it is paracompact.*

PROOF. If each space of the family is paracompact then it is uniform and hence the product is uniform. □

13.14. REMARK. Since *T-Near* is a bicoreflective subcategory of the properly fibred topological category *Near*, all results of Appendix A, especially A.10-A.14, are applicable.

14. COMPLETE N-SPACES

14.1. DEFINITION. An N-space (X,ξ) is called *complete* iff every ξ-cluster has an adherencepoint.

14.2. PROPOSITION

(1) *Every topological* N-*space is complete.*

(2) *A uniform* N-*space is complete iff it is complete as a uniform space.*

(3) *A contigual* N-*space is complete iff it is compact.*

14.3. PROPOSITION. *For any separated* N-*space* (X,ξ) *the following conditions are equivalent:*

(1) (X,ξ) *is complete,*

(2) *every maximal* ξ-*clan has an adherencepoint,*

(3) *every* ξ-*clan has an adherencepoint,*

(4) *every* $A \in \xi \cap \gamma$ *has an adherencepoint,*

(5) *every* $A \in \xi \cap \gamma$ *converges,*

(6) *every* γ-*filter converges,*

(7) *every minimal* γ-*filter converges,*

(8) *every* γ-*cocluster converges.*

14.4. DEFINITION. An embedding $f: (X,\xi) \to (Y,\eta)$ in *Near* is called *dense* iff $cl_\eta(fX) = Y$.

14.5. THEOREM. *If* $f: (X,\xi) \to (Y,\eta)$ *is a dense embedding in Near then any* N-*map from* (X,ξ) *into a complete, regular* N-*space* (Z,ζ) *can be extended to an* N-*map* (Y,η) *into* (Z,ζ). *The extension is unique if* (Z,ζ) *is an* N1-*space.*

PROOF. See [36]. □

14.6. COROLLARY 1. (A. WEIL [82]). *If* X *is a dense subspace of a uniform space* Y *then any uniformly continuous map from* X *into a complete uniform space* Z *can be extended to a uniformly continuous map from* Y *into* Z. *The extension is unique if* Z *is a* T1-*space.*

14.7. COROLLARY 2 (H. HERRLICH [34]; S.A. NAIMPALLY [57]). *If* (Y,η) *is a topological* N-*space and* f: $(X,\xi) \to (Y,\eta)$ *is a dense embedding in* $\mathcal{N}ear$ *then* f: $(X,\xi_t) \to (Y,\eta)$ *is a dense embedding in* $\mathcal{T}op$*, and for any continuous map* g *from* (X,ξ_t) *into a regular topological* N-*space* (Z,ζ) *the following conditions are equivalent:*

(1) g *can be extended to a continuous map from* (Y,η) *into* (Z,ζ),

(2) g: $(X,\xi) \to (Z,\zeta)$ *is an* N-*map*,

(3) $\forall \mathcal{A} \subset PX\ [\mathcal{A} \in \xi \Rightarrow g\mathcal{A} \in \eta]$,

(4) $\forall \mathcal{B} \subset PZ\ [\mathcal{B} \notin \zeta \Rightarrow g^{-1}\mathcal{B} \notin \xi]$.

14.8. REMARK. If one drops the assumption that (Z,ζ) is regular then 1.5 and 1.7 are no longer true as has been shown in [34].

14.9. REMARK. Without any separation axioms the class of complete N-spaces is not well behaved with respect to the usual constructions in $\mathcal{N}ear$. But the following facts -to be proved in the next section- are worth mentioning:

(1) every N-space has a "natural" completion,

(2) the full subcategory of Near whose objects are the complete N3-spaces is dense-reflective in $\mathcal{N}ear$ and epireflective in $\mathcal{N}ear$-3.

14.10. PROPOSITION. *Let* (X,ξ) *be a regular* N-*space and let* k *be an infinite cardinal number. Then the following conditions are equivalent:*

(1) *each* γ-*filter which is closed under* k-*intersections converges,*

(2) *each* γ-*filter with* k-*intersection property converges,*

(3) *each minimal* γ-*filter with* k-*intersection-property is fixed.*

14.11. DEFINITION. An N-space is called *regular* k-*complete* iff it is regular and satisfies the above conditions.

14.12. THEOREM. *For any infinite cardinal number* k*, the full subcategory of* $\mathcal{N}ear$ *whose objects are the regular* k-*complete* N1-*spaces is closed under the formation of products and closed subspaces in* $\mathcal{N}ear$ *and hence dense-reflective in* $\mathcal{N}ear$ *and epireflective in* $\mathcal{N}ear$-3.

15. THE COMPLETION (X^*,ξ^*) OF AN N-SPACE (X,ξ)

15.1. DEFINITION. Let (X,ξ) be a pre-N-space. Denote by

(1) X^* the set of all ξ-clusters,

(2) $\xi^* = \{\Omega \subset PX^* \mid \cup\{\cap\omega \mid \omega \in \Omega\} \in \xi\}$

(3) $j\colon X \to X^*$ the map defined by $j(x) = \xi(\{x\})$.

15.2. PROPOSITION. *If* (X,ξ) *is a (pre-, quasi-)* N*-space then* (X^*,ξ^*) *is a (pre-, quasi-)* N*-space.*

15.3. PROPOSITION. $j\colon (X,\xi) \to (X^*,\xi^*)$ *is an* N*-map iff the pre-N-space* (X,ξ) *satisfies the axiom* (N5) *of* 2.1.

15.4. THEOREM. *If* (X,ξ) *is an* N*-space,* $A \subset X$, $\mathcal{A} \subset PX$, *and* $\Omega \subset PX^*$ *then*

(1) (X^*,ξ^*) *is a complete* N1*-space,*

(2) $\mathcal{A} \in \xi$ *iff* $f\mathcal{A} \in \xi^*$,

(3) $j\colon (X,\xi) \to (X^*,\xi^*)$ *is an* N*-map, it is*

  (a) *injective (and hence an embedding) iff* (X,ξ) *is an* N1*-space,*

  (b) *surjective (and hence a quotient-map) iff* (X,ξ) *is complete,*

(4) $cl_{\xi^*}j[X] = X^*$,

(5) $cl_{\xi^*}j[A] = \{\mathcal{A} \in X^* \mid A \in \mathcal{A}\}$,

(6) $op\ A = X^* - cl_{\xi^*}j[X-A]$ *is the largest open subset* ω *of* X^* *with* $j^{-1}\omega = int_\xi A$,

(7) $\Omega \in \xi^*$ *iff* $\{A \subset X \mid cl_{\xi^*}j[A] \in \text{stack } \Omega\} \in \xi$,

(8) $\Omega \in \gamma^*$ *iff* $\{A \subset X \mid op\ A \in \text{stack } \Omega\} \in \gamma$,

(9) $\Omega \in \mu^*$ *iff* $\{A \subset X \mid \exists\omega \in \Omega \;\; op\ A \subset \omega\} \in \mu$.

PROOF. See [35]. □

15.5. DEFINITION. If (X,ξ) is an N-space then $j\colon (X,\xi) \to (X^*,\xi^*)$ is called the *completion* of (X,ξ).

15.6. THEOREM. *An* N*-space* (X,ξ) *is*

(1) *separated iff* (X^*,ξ^*) *is separated,*

(2) *regular iff* (X^*,ξ^*) *is regular,*

(3) *normal iff* (X^*,ξ^*) *is normal,*

(4) *uniform iff* (X^*,ξ^*) *is uniform,*

(5) *contigual iff* (X^*,ξ^*) *is contigual,*

(6) *proximal iff* (X^*,ξ^*) *is proximal.*

PROOF. See [35]. □

15.7. REMARK. If (X,ξ) is not an N1-space then one can replace the subspace of (X^*,ξ^*), determined by $j[X]$, by (X,ξ) - obtaining thus a dense embedding of (X,ξ) into a complete N-space. Obviously (X,ξ) is separated (regular, normal, uniform, contigual, proximal) iff the modified complete space is separated (regular, normal, uniform, contigual, proximal).

15.8. DEFINITION. If (X,ξ) is an N-space then $j\colon (X,\xi) \to (X^*,(\xi_r)^*)$ is called the *regular completion* of (X,ξ).

15.9. THEOREM

(1) *The full subcategory of* Near-3 *whose objects are the complete* N3-*spaces is bireflective in* Near-3; *the completion is the reflection,*
(2) *the full subcategory of* Near *whose objects are the complete* N3-*spaces is dense-reflective in* Near; *the regular completion is the reflection.*

15.10. THEOREM. *Let* (X,ξ) *be an* N-*space. Then*

(1) *if* (X,ξ) *is regular then* $j\colon (X,\xi) \to (X^*,\xi^*)$ *is the Morita-simple-extension of* (X,ξ),
(2) *if* (X,ξ) *is uniform then* $j\colon (X,\xi) \to (X^*,\xi^*)$ *is the Weil-completion of* (X,ξ),
(3) *if* (X,ξ) *is proximal then* $j\colon (X,\xi) \to (X^*,\xi^*)$ *is the Smirnov-compactification of* (X,ξ),
(4) *if* (X,ξ) *is uniform then* $j\colon (X,\xi) \to (X^*,(\xi_c)^*)$ *is the Samuel-compactification of* (X,ξ),
(5) *if* (X,ξ) *is topological then* $j\colon (X,\xi) \to (X^*,(\xi_c)^*)$ *is the Wallman-compactification of* (X,ξ),
(6) *if* (X,ξ) *is topological then* $j\colon (X,\xi) \to (X^*,(\xi_p)^*)$ *is the Čech-Stone-compactification of* (X,ξ),
(7) *if* (X,ξ) *is topological then* $j\colon (X,\xi) \to (X^*,((\xi_u)^*)_t)$ *is the topological completion of* (X,ξ), *i.e. (under the assumption that no measurable cardinals exist) the Hewitt-realcompactifiaction of* (X,ξ).

16. EXTENSIONS AND COMPACTIFICATIONS OF TOPOLOGICAL SPACES

The completion of an N-space, constructed in section 15, provides a general method to obtain as many T1-extensions of a topological T1-space as might be reasonably expected, namely all strict extensions in the sense of B. BANASCHEWSKI [3]. Thus the results below generalize results of

(1) YU.M. SMIRNOV [67,68] concerning Hausdorff compactifications by means of proximity structures,

(2) V.M. IVANOVA & A.A. IVANOV [46], and W.L. TERWILLIGER [76] concerning strict T1-compactifications by means of contiguity structures,

(3) H.L. BENTLEY & S.A. NAIMPALLY [7] concerning Wallman-compactifications,

(4) K. MORITA [55], D. HARRIS [27-29], S. LEADER [51], J.R. PORTER & C. VOTAW [59], A.K. STEINER & E.F. STEINER [70] concerning regular extensions,

(5) F. RIESZ [61], M.W. LODATO [52], and A.A. IVANOV [45] concerning strict T1-extensions in general.

All N-spaces in this section are supposed to be N1-spaces. Especially all topological spaces are assumed to be T1-spaces.

16.1. DEFINITIONS. A continuous map $f: (X,\xi) \to (Y,\eta)$ between the topological T1-spaces (X,ξ) and (Y,η) is called

(1) an *extension* of (X,ξ) iff f is a dense topological embedding,

(2) a *strict extensio* of (X,ξ) iff it is an extension of (X,ξ) and $\{cl_\eta f[A] \mid A \in X\}$ is a base for the closed sets in (Y,η),

(3) a *strict compactification* of (X,ξ) iff it is a strict extension and (Y,η) is compact,

(4) a *Hausdorff compactification* of (X,ξ) iff it is an extension of (X,ξ) and (Y,η) is a compact Hausdorff space.

16.2. REMARK. Any dense topological embedding of (X,ξ) into a regular T1-space (Y,η) is a strict extension of (X,ξ).

16.3. DEFINITION. Extensions $f: (X,\xi) \to (Y,\eta)$ and $f': (X,\xi) \to (Y',\eta')$ of (X,ξ) are called *equivalent* iff there exists a homeomorphism $h: (Y,\eta) \to (Y',\eta')$ with $f' = h\circ f$.

16.4. THEOREM (H.L. BENTLEY & S.A. NAIMPALLY [7]). *If* (X,ζ) *is a topological* T1-*space and* $\mathcal{B}$ *is a separating base on* (X,ζ) *in the sense of*

E.F. STEINER [73] *then:*

(1) *if* $\bar{\xi}$ *is the collection of all* $\mathcal{A} \subset$ PX *which are corefined by some finite subset* $\mathcal{C}$ *of* $\mathcal{B}$ *with* $\cap\mathcal{C} = \emptyset$ *then* $\xi = P^2X - \bar{\xi}$ *is a contigual* N-*structure on* X *with* $\zeta = \xi_t$,

(2) j: $(X,\zeta) \to (X^*,\xi^*)$ *and the Wallman compactification of* (X,ζ) *with respect to* $\mathcal{B}$ *are equivalent extensions of* (X,ζ).

16.5. THEOREM (H.L. BENTLEY [5]). *For any* N1-*space* (X,ξ) *the following conditions are equivalent:*

(1) *for each* $\mathcal{A} \in \xi$ *there exists a* ξ-*cluster* $\mathcal{B}$ *with* $\mathcal{A} \subset \mathcal{B}$,

(2) (X^*,ξ^*) *is topological.*

16.6. DEFINITION. An N1-space is called *concrete* iff it satisfies the above conditions.

16.7. COROLLARIES. *Let* (X,ξ) *be an* N1-*space. Then:*

(1) *if* (X,ξ) *is contigual then* (X,ξ) *is concrete,*

(2) *if* (X,ξ) *is topological then* (X,ξ) *is concrete,*

(3) *if* (X,ξ) *is concrete then* (X,ξ) *is subtopological,*

(4) *if* (X,ξ) *is separated then* (X,ξ) *is concrete iff it is subtopological.*

16.8. PROPOSITION. *If* (X,ξ) *is an* N1-*space then* j: $(X,\xi_t) \to (X^*,(\xi^*)_t)$ *is a strict extension of* (X,ξ_t).

16.9. THEOREM [35]. *If* (X,ξ) *is a concrete* N1-*space then* j: $(X,\xi_t) \to (X^*,\xi^*)$ *is a strict extension of* (X,ξ_t).
Vice versa, for any strict extension f: $(X,\zeta) \to (Y,\eta)$ *of a topological* N1-*space* (X,ζ) *there exists precisely one concrete* N1-*structure* ξ *on* X, *namely*

$$\xi = \{\mathcal{A} \subset PX \mid \cap\{cl_\eta fA \mid A \in \mathcal{A}\} \neq \emptyset\}$$

such that j: $(X,\xi_t) \to (X^*,\xi^*)$ *and* f: $(X,\zeta) \to (Y,\eta)$ *are equivalent extensions of* $(X,\xi_t) = (X,\zeta)$.
Moreover:

(1) (Y,η) *is a Hausdorff space iff* (X,ξ) *is separable,*

(2) (Y,η) *is a regular space iff* (X,ξ) *is regular,*

(3) (Y,η) *is a paracompact space iff* (X,ξ) *is uniform,*

(4) (Y,η) *is a compact space iff* (X,ξ) *is contigual,*

(5) (Y,η) *is a compact Hausdorff space iff* (X,ξ) *is proximal.*

16.10. REMARKS

(1) The above results show that

(a) concrete N1-structures are a proper tool to investigate strict extensions,

(b) concrete N2-structures are a proper tool to investigate strict Hausdorff extensions,

(c) contigual N1-structures are a proper tool to investigate strict compactifications,

(d) N3-structures are a proper tool to investigate regular extensions,

(e) proximal N1-structures are a proper tool to investigate Hausdorff compactifications.

(2) The "complexity degree" of N-structures is just sufficient to obtain all strict extensions by a single method as the following results show:

(a) if X is an infinite set then there exist precisely card(P^3X) N-structures on X,

(b) if X is an infinite set then there exist precisely card(P^3X) equivalence classes of strict extensions of the discrete space with underlying set X.

Neither generalized proximity spaces nor generalizations of A. WEIL's description of uniform spaces will do, since -no matter how we choose the axioms- there are at most card(P^2X) such structures on an infinite set X. Even if we restrict our attention to H-closed extensions these other concepts are not sufficiently complex, since any discrete space with underlying infinite set X has card(P^3X) essentially different H-closed extensions as has been shown by J.R. PORTER & C. VOTAW [60].

Chapter V. CARDINAL CONDITIONS

17. TOTALLY BOUNDED N-SPACES

17.1. PROPOSITION. *For any pre-N-space* (X,ξ) *the following conditions are equivalent:*

(1) *if* $\mathcal{A}$ *is a filter on* X *then* $\mathcal{A} \in \xi$,

(2) *if* $\mathcal{A}$ *is a grill on* X *then* $\mathcal{A} \in \gamma$,

(3) *if* $A \in \overline{\xi}$ *then there exists a finite subset* B *of* A *with* $\bigcap B = \emptyset$,

(4) *if* $A \in \mu$ *then there exists a finite subset* B *of* A *with* $\bigcup B = X$.

17.2. DEFINITION. A pre-N-space is called *totally bounded* iff it satisfies the above conditions.

17.3. PROPOSITION. *The full subcategory of P-Near whose objects are the totally bounded pre-N-spaces is*

(1) *closed under the formation of products, finite coproducts, subobjects and N-images in P-Near,*

(2) *bireflective in P-Near; if* (X,ξ) *is a pre-N-space and* η *is the set of all* $A \subset PX$ *which belong to* ξ *or have the finite-intersection-property then* $1_X\colon (X,\xi) \to (Y,\eta)$ *is the reflection.*

17.4. PROPOSITION. *The full subcategory of Q-Near whose objects are the totally bounded quasi-N-spaces is bireflective in Q-Near. The reflection is constructed as in P-Near.*

17.5. PROPOSITION. *The full subcategory of Near whose objects are the totally bounded N-spaces is bireflective in Near. If* (X,ξ) *is an N-space and* η *is the collection of all* $A \subset PX$ *which belong to* ξ *or for which* $\{cl_\xi A \mid A \in A\}$ *has the finite-intersection-property then* $1_X\colon (X,\xi) \to (X,\xi)$ *is the reflection.*

17.6. PROPOSITION. *Let* (X,ξ) *be an N-space. Then:*

(1) *if* (X,ξ) *is contigual then* (X,ξ) *is totally bounded,*

(2) *if* (X,ξ) *is topological (or regular) then* (X,ξ) *is totally bounded iff it is contigual.*

17.7. REMARK. [35] contains an example of a totally bounded complete N-space which is neither contigual nor topological.

17.8. REMARK. For any infinite cardinal number k one might call a pre-N-space (X,ξ) *k-bounded* iff any $A \subset PX$ with k-intersection-property belongs to ξ. Obviously many properties of totally bounded pre-N-spaces carry over to k-bounded pre-N-spaces.

18. CONTIGUAL AND PROXIMAL N-SPACES

Contigual N-structures have been defined and their relations to topological and uniform N-structures have been studied in section 4. In this section the relations between contigual N-structures and various separation axioms are being investigated.

18.1. PROPOSITION. *For any* N-*space* (X,ξ) *the following conditions are equivalent:*

(1) (X,ξ) *is contigual,*

(2) (X^*,ξ^*) *is compact,*

(3) (X,ξ) *can be embedded in a compact* N-*space.*

18.2. THEOREM. *For any* N1-*space* (X,ξ) *the following conditions are equivalent:*

(1) (X,ξ) *is proximal,*

(2) (X,ξ) *is contigual and normal,*

(3) (X,ξ) *is contigual and weakly normal,*

(4) (X,ξ) *is contigual and regular,*

(5) (X,ξ) *is contigual and separated,*

(6) (X^*,ξ^*) *is a separated compact* N-*space,*

(7) (X,ξ) *can be embedded in a separated compact* N-*space,*

(8) (X,ξ) *is totally bounded and uniform,*

(9) (X,ξ) *is totally bounded and normal,*

(10) (X,ξ) *is totally bounded and weakly normal,*

(11) (X,ξ) *is totally bounded and regular.*

PROOF. 14.2, 15.6 and 17.6. □

18.3. REMARKS

(1) The conditions (1)-(11) are equivalent for arbitrary N-spaces.

(2) If (X,ξ) is a proximal N-space then the relation δ on PX, defined by $A\ \delta\ B \Leftrightarrow \{A,B\} \in \xi$ is an Efremovič-proximity, i.e. it satisfies the following axioms:

(P0) $A\ \delta\ B \Rightarrow B\ \delta\ A$,

(P1) $A\ \delta\ (B \cup C)$ *iff* $A\ \delta\ B$ *or* $A\ \delta\ C$,

(P2) $A \cap B \neq \emptyset$ *implies* $A\ \delta\ B$,

(P3) $A \delta B$ *implies* $A \neq \emptyset$,

(P4) *if* $A \bar{\delta} B$ *stands for* "not $A \delta B$" *and* $A <_\delta B$ *stands for* "$A \bar{\delta} (X-B)$" *then* $A \bar{\delta} B$ *implies that there exist sets* U *and* V *with* $A <_\delta U$, $B <_\delta V$, *and* $U \bar{\delta} V$.

It is well-known that every Efremovič-proximity δ on X can be obtained in this way from precisely one proximal N-structure ξ on X. This ξ is characterized (defined) by any of the following equivalent properties:

(a) $\mathcal{A} \in \mu$ iff there exists a finite cover $\mathcal{B}$ of X such that for any $B \in \mathcal{B}$ there exists $A \in \mathcal{A}$ with $B <_\delta A$,

(b) $\mathcal{A} \in \gamma$ iff for any finite family $(A_i, B_i)_{i \in I}$ of pairs of subsets of X with $A_i <_\delta B_i$ for each $i \in I$ and $X = \cup\{A_i \mid i \in I\}$ there exists $i \in I$ and $A \in \mathcal{A}$ with $A \subset B_i$,

(c) $\mathcal{A} \in \xi$ iff for any finite family $(A_i, B_i)_{i \in I}$ as above $\sec \mathcal{A} \cap \{B_i \mid i \in I\} \neq \emptyset$,

(d) $\mathcal{A} \in \bar{\xi}$ iff there exists a finite set $\mathcal{B} \subset PX$ with $\cap\mathcal{B} = \emptyset$ and such that for each $B \in \mathcal{B}$ there exists $A \in \mathcal{A}$ with $A <_\delta B$.

18.4. THEOREM. *If* (X,ξ) *is an* N-*space then:*

(1) *equivalent are:*

(a) (X,ξ) *is contigual,*

(b) (X,ξ) *is a subspace of a compact* N-*space,*

(c) (X^*,ξ^*) *is compact,*

(2) *equivalent are:*

(a) (X,ξ) *is proximal,*

(b) (X,ξ) *is a subspace of a separated compact* N-*space,*

(c) (X^*,ξ^*) *is separated and compact,*

(3) *equivalent are:*

(a) (X,ξ) *is a proximal* N1-*space,*

(b) (X,ξ) *is a subspace of a compact Hausdorff space,*

(c) (X^*,ξ^*) *is a compact Hausdorff space and* (X,ξ) *is an* N1-*space.*

18.5. COROLLARY

(1) *C-Near is the epireflective hull in Near of the full subcategory of Near whose objects are the compact* N-*spaces,*

(2) *Pr-Near is the epireflective hull in Near of the full subcategory of Near whose objects are the separated compact (= regular compact, paracompact, compact)* N-*spaces,*

(3) *Pr-Near-1 is the epireflective hull in Near of the full subcategory of Near whose objects are the compact Hausdorff spaces.*

18.6. PROPOSITION. *If* (X,ξ) *is contigual then* (X,ξ_r) *is proximal.*

PROOF. If (X,ξ) is contigual then it is totally bounded. Consequently (X,ξ_r) is totally bounded and regular, i.e. proximal. □

18.7. THEOREM. *For any N-space the following hold:*

(1) $(X,\xi) \xrightarrow{1_X} (X,\xi_p) = (X,\xi) \xrightarrow{1_X} (X,\xi_c) \xrightarrow{1_X} (X,\xi_{cr})$,

(2) $(X,\xi) \xrightarrow{1_X} (X,\xi_p) = (X,\xi) \xrightarrow{1_X} (X,\xi_c) \xrightarrow{1_X} (X,\xi_{cu})$,

(3) $(X,\xi) \xrightarrow{1_X} (X,\xi_p) = (X,\xi) \xrightarrow{1_X} (X,\xi_u) \xrightarrow{1_X} (X,\xi_{uc})$.

18.8. REMARK. If (X,ξ) is regular then (X,ξ_c) need not be regular; e.g. if (X,ξ) is a regular topological T1-space which is not normal.

18.9. DEFINITION. An N-space is called *proximally* k-*complete* iff it is contigual and regular k-complete.

18.10. THEOREM. *For any infinite cardinal number* k, *the full subcategory of Near whose objects are the proximally* k-*complete* N1-*spaces is closed under the formation of products and closed subspaces in Near and hence dense-reflective in Near and epireflective in Near-3.*

18.11. REMARKS

(1) The proximally k-complete N-spaces are in case $k = \aleph_1$ precisely the realcompact proximity spaces of O. NJÅSTAD [59] and in general precisely the k-complete proximity spaces of M. HUŠEK [43].

(2) M. HUŠEK [43] has proved that a topological N-space (X,ξ) is k-compact in the sense of [34] iff there exists a proximally k-complete N1-structure η on X with $\eta_t = \xi$. Moreover, he has shown that for any infinite cardinal number k there exists an N-space P_k such that the proximally k-complete N1-spaces are (up to isomorphism) precisely the closed subspaces of powers P_k^I of P_k.

(3) It might be interesting to investigate the category of all N-spaces which are regular k-complete for some k and ℓ-contigual for some ℓ. [Here (X,ξ) is called *l-contigual* iff for any $A \in \bar{\xi}$ there exists a subset B of A with less than k elements such that $B \in \bar{\xi}$.] A.K. STEINER &

E.F. STEINER [71] have shown that a regular, $\aleph_1$-contigual N-space need not be uniform.

19. METRIZABLE N-SPACES AND NAGATA-SPACES

19.1. DEFINITIONS. Let (X,ξ) be an N-space. Then

(1) (X,ξ) is called *(pseudo-) metrizable* iff there exists a (pseudo-) metric d on X such that $A \in \xi$ iff for any positive real number ε there exists $x \in X$ with $\{y \in X \mid d(x,y) < \varepsilon\} \in \sec A$.

(2) (X,ξ) is called a *Nagata-space* iff it is metrizable and topological.

(3) $\beta \subset P^2X$ is called

  (a) a *base for* ξ iff the members of ξ are precisely those $A \subset PX$ which corefine some member of β,

  (b) a *base for* $\bar{\xi}$ iff the members of $\bar{\xi}$ are precisely those $A \subset PX$ which are corefined by some member of β,

  (c) a *base for* μ iff the members of μ are precisely those $A \subset PX$ which are refined by some member of β,

  (d) a *base for* γ iff the members of γ are precisely those $A \subset PX$ which are corefined by some members of β.

19.2. REMARKS

(1) The spaces we call Nagata-spaces here are known under the name N-spaces. They were introduced and characterized by J. NAGATA [56] and have been studied also by N. ATSUJI [2], A.H. STONE [75], M. KATĚTOV [48] and others.

(2) The following results are well-known:

19.3. PROPOSITION. *For any* N-*space* (X,ξ) *the following conditions are equivalent:*

(1) (X,ξ) *is pseudo-metrizable,*

(2) (X,ξ) *is uniform and has a countable base for* $\bar{\xi}$,

(3) (X,ξ) *is uniform and has a countable base for* μ.

19.4. PROPOSITION. *U-Near is the epireflective hull in Near of the full subcategory of Near whose objects are the pseudo-metrizable* N-*spaces.*

19.5. PROPOSITION. *For any topological* N-*space* (X,ξ) *the following conditions are equivalent:*

(1) (X,ξ) *is a Nagata-space,*

(2) (X,ξ) *is metrizable as a topological space and the subspace of* (X,ξ) *consisting of all non-isolated points is compact.*

Diagram: The hierarchy of (pre-) N-structures

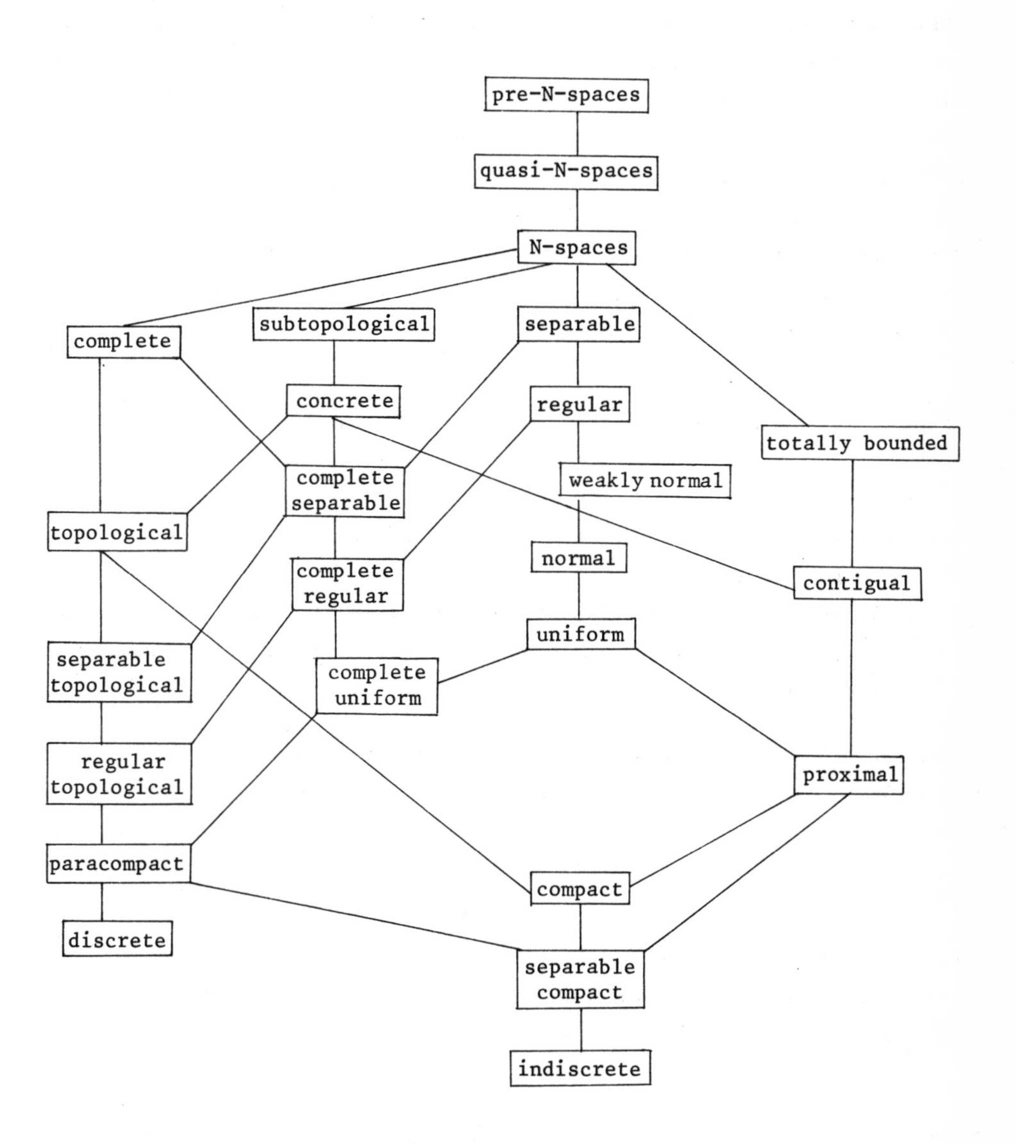

Appendix A. TOPOLOGICAL CATEGORIES

Such categories as *Top*, *Unif*, *Prox*, *Cont*, *Near*, *P-Near*, *Q-Near* have a large number of properties in common. The most crucial one, in the sense that it implies most others, is the existence of "initial" (or dually: of "final") structures in the sense of N. BOURBAKI [A4,A5]. Those readers who are interested in the study of initial structures in the most general setting are referred to the bibliography of Appendix A, especially to the fundamental papers of O. WYLER [A38,A39], the important thesises of G.C.L. BRUMMER [A6] and R.E. HOFFMANN [A16] and to the recent papers [A13,A14] of the author. In this treatise we restrict ourselves to the study of concrete categories. This enables us to present the theory in such way that a reader with just some basic knowledge of categorical terminology will be able to follow. For categorical background material see [A15].

Let A be a *concrete category*, i.e.

(1) objects of A are pairs (X,ξ) where X is a set, called the *underlying set* of (X,ξ), and ξ is some A-structure on X, called the *underlying A-structure* of (X,ξ),

(2) morphisms $f\colon (X,\xi) \to (Y,\eta)$ are certain maps $f\colon X \to Y$, subject to the following conditions:

(M1) for each object (X,ξ) of A the map $1_X\colon (X,\xi) \to (X,\xi)$ is a morphism,

(M2) if $f\colon (X,\xi) \to (Y,\eta)$ and $g\colon (Y,\eta) \to (Z,\zeta)$ are morphisms, then so is $g\circ f\colon (X,\xi) \to (Z,\zeta)$.

A.1. DEFINITION. Let A be a concrete category, let X be a set, let $(Y_i,\eta_i)_{i\in I}$ be a family of objects in A indexed by some class I, and let $(f_i\colon X \to Y_i)_{i\in I}$ be a family of maps indexed by I. An A-structure ξ on X is called *initial* with respect to $(X,(f_i)_{i\in I},(Y_i,\eta_i)_{i\in I})$ iff the following two conditions are satisfied:

(1) $f_i\colon (X,\xi) \to (Y_i,\eta_i)$ is a morphism for each $i \in I$,

(2) if (Z,ζ) is an object in A and $g\colon Z \to X$ is a map such that for each $i \in I$ the map $f_i\circ g\colon (Z,\zeta) \to (Y_i,\eta_i)$ is a morphism, then $g\colon (Z,\zeta) \to (X,\xi)$ is a morphism.

A.2. DEFINITION. A concrete category A is called *topological* iff for any set X, for any family $(Y_i,\eta_i)_{i\in I}$ of objects in A, and for any family $(f_i\colon X \to Y_i)_{i\in I}$ of maps there exists an A-structure on X which is initial with respect to $(X,(f_i)_{i\in I},(Y_i,\eta_i)_{i\in I})$.

A.3. DEFINITION. A morphism $f: (X,\xi) \to (Y,\eta)$ in a concrete category is called

(1) an *embedding* iff $f: X \to Y$ is injective and ξ is initial with respect to $(X,f,(Y,\eta))$,

(2) a *quotient-map* iff $f: X \to Y$ is surjective and η is final (see below) with respect to $((X,\xi),f,Y)$.

A.4. THEOREM. *Any topological category A has the following properties*

(1) *A is cotopological, i.e. for any set* Y, *for any family* $(X_i,\xi_i)_{i\in I}$ *of objects in A, and for any family* $(f_i: X_i \to Y)_{i\in I}$ *of maps there exists an A-structure* η *on* X *final with respect to* $((X_i,\xi_i)_{i\in I},(f_i)_{i\in I},Y)$, *i.e. satisfying the following two conditions:*

(a) $f_i: (X,\xi_i) \to (Y,\eta)$ *is a morphism for each* $i \in I$,

(b) *if* (Z,ζ) *is an object in A and* $g: Y \to Z$ *is a map such that for each* $i \in I$ *the map* $g \circ f_i: (X,\xi_i) \to (Z,\zeta)$ *is a morphism then* $g: (Y,\eta) \to (Z,\zeta)$ *is a morphism.*

(2) *A is complete, and limits are formed by supplying the corresponding limits in Set with the initial structure, e.g.*

(a) *if* $(X_i,\xi_i)_{i\in I}$ *is a family of objects in A indexed by a set* I, *if* ΠX_i *is the Cartesian product of the family* $(X_i)_{i\in I}$ *of sets, if for each* $k \in I$ *the* k*-th projection is denoted by* $p_k: \Pi X_i \to X_k$, *and if* ξ *is an A-structure on* ΠX_i *initial with respect to* $(\Pi X_i,(p_i)_{i\in I},(X_i,\xi_i)_{i\in I})$ *then* $(\Pi X_i,\xi)$ *together with the projection morphisms* $p_k: (\Pi X_i,\xi) \to (X_k,\xi_k)$ *is the product of the family* $(X_i,\xi_i)_{i\in I}$ *in A.*

(3) *A is cocomplete, and colimits are formed by supplying the corresponding colimits in Set with the final structure.*

(4) *For each set* X *there exists a discrete A-structure* ξ *on* X, *characterized (up to isomorphism) by the fact that* $f: (X,\xi) \to (Y,\eta)$ *is a morphism for any object* (Y,η) *in A and any map* $f: X \to Y$.

(5) *For each set* X *there exists an indiscrete A-structure* ξ *on* X *characterized (up to isomorphism) by the fact that* $f: (Y,\eta) \to (X,\xi)$ *is a morphism for any object* (Y,η) *in A and any map* $f: Y \to X$.

(6) *A morphism* $f: (X,\xi) \to (Y,\eta)$ *is*

(a) *a monomorphism iff* $f: X \to Y$ *is injective,*

(b) *an epimorphism iff* f: $X \to Y$ *is surjective,*

(c) *a bimorphism iff* f: $X \to Y$ *is bijective,*

(d) *an isomorphism iff it is an embedding and a quotient-map,*

(e) *an extremal monomorphism iff it is an embedding,*

(f) *an extremal epimorphism iff it is a quotient-map,*

(g) *a regular monomorphism iff it is an embedding,*

(h) *a regular epimorphism iff it is a quotient-map.*

(7) *A is an (epi, extremal mono)-category and an (extremal epi, mono)-category.*

(8) *An object* (X,ξ) *in A is projective iff* ξ *is a discrete structure on* X.

(9) *An object* (X,ξ) *in A is injective iff* $X \neq \emptyset$ *and* ξ *is an indiscrete structure on* X.

(10) *Every discrete object with non-empty underlying set is a separator*

(11) *Every indiscrete object with underlying set containing at least two elements is a coseparator.*

A.5. DEFINITIONS. Let *A* be a concrete category.

(1) The *A-fibre* of a set X is the class of all *A*-structures on X.

(2) *A* is called *properly fibred* iff it satisfies the following conditions:

(a) for each set X the *A*-fibre of X is a set,

(b) for each one-element-set X the *A*-fibre of X has precisely one element,

(c) if ξ and η are *A*-structures on X such that $1_X: (X,\xi) \to (X,\eta)$ and $1_X: (X,\eta) \to (X,\xi)$ are morphisms then $\xi = \eta$.

A.6. THEOREM. *Any properly fibred topological category A has the following properties:*

(1) *initial, final, discrete, and indiscrete structures are uniquely determined by their defining properties,*

(2) *A-structures are transportable, i.e. if* (X,ξ) *is an A-object and* $f: X \to Y$ *is a bijective map then there exists a unique A-structure* η *on* Y *such that* $f: (X,\xi) \to (Y,\eta)$ *is an isomorphism,*

(3) *for any set* X *the fibre of* X *is a complete lattice with respect to the order relation* $\leq$, *defined by*

$$\xi \leq \eta \iff 1_X: (X,\xi) \to (X,\eta) \text{ is a morphism,}$$

(4) *A is wellpowered and cowellpowered,*

(5) *if* $f: X \to Y$ *is a constant map and* (X,ξ), *and* $X \neq \emptyset$ (Y,η) *are objects in A then* $f: (X,\xi) \to (Y,\eta)$ *is a morphism,*

(6) *any object* (X,ξ) *in A with non-empty underlying set* X *is a separator in A.*

A.7. DEFINITION. Let *A* be a concrete category. If (X,ξ) and (Y,η) are objects in *A* then (X,ξ) is called

(1) a *subobject* of (Y,η) iff there exists an embedding $f: (X,\xi) \to (Y,\eta)$,

(2) a *quotientobject* of (Y,η) iff there exists a quotient-map $f: (Y,\eta) \to (X,\xi)$.

A.8. REMARK. The above definitions coincide for concrete categories with the concrete concepts of subobjects and quotientobjects. They do not coincide with the commonly used categorical definitions for arbitrary categories. For topological categories our concepts coincide with the categorical concepts of extremal subobjects and extremal quotientobjects instead.

A.9. THEOREM. *Let A be a full, isomorphism-closed subcategory of a properly fibred topological category B. Then the following hold:*

(1) *equivalent are:*
   (a) *A is epireflective in B,*
   (b) *A is closed under the formation of products and subobjects in B;*

(2) *equivalent are:*
   (a) *A is bireflective in B,*
   (b) *A is epireflective in B and contains all indiscrete objects of B;*

(3) *if A contains at least one object with non-empty underlying set then the following conditions are equivalent:*
   (a) *A is coreflective in B,*
   (b) *A is bicoreflective in B,*
   (c) *A is closed under the formation of coproducts and quotientobjects in B,*
   (d) *A is coreflective in B and contains all discrete objects of B.*

A.10. THEOREM. *Any bireflective (and any bicoreflective) isomorphism-closed full subcategory of a (properly fibred) topological category is a (properly fibred) topological category.*

A.11. THEOREM. *Let A be a properly fibred topological category, let B be a bireflective, and C be a bicoreflective isomorphism-closed full subcategory of A, denote the B-reflector by* $R: A \to B$ *and its domain-restriction to C by* $R_C: C \to B$*, denote the C-coreflector by* $C: A \to C$ *and its domain-restriction to B by* $C_B: B \to C$*, denote the B-reflection of* (X,ξ) *by* $1_X: (X,\xi) \to (X,\xi_B)$ *and denote the C-coreflection* (X,ξ) *by* $1_X: (X,\xi_C) \to (X,\xi)$. *Then:*

(1) R_C *and* C_B *can be considered as "forgetful" functors, i.e. they are faithful,*

(2) R_C *is a left-adjoint to* C_B,

(3) *for any object* (X,ξ) *in C the following conditions are equivalent*

 (a) (X,ξ) *is* B-structurable, *i.e. there exists* (X,η) *in B with* $\eta_C = \xi$,

 (b) $\xi = (\xi_B)_C$,

(4) *for any object* (X,ξ) *in B the following conditions are equivalent:*

 (a) (X,ξ) *is* C-structurable, *i.e. there exists* (X,η) *in C with* $\eta_B = \xi$,

 (b) $\xi = (\xi_C)_B$,

(5) *the full subcategory* C_B *of C whose objects are the B-structurable objects in C is bireflective in C with reflector the suitable codomain-restriction of* $C_B \circ R_B: C \to C$ *and with reflection morphisms* $1_X: (X,\xi) \to (X,\xi_{BC})$,

(6) *the full subcategory* B_C *of B whose objects are the C-structurable objects in B is bicoreflective in B with coreflector the suitable codomain-restriction of* $R_C \circ C_B: B \to B$ *and with coreflection-morphisms* $1_X: (X,\xi_{CB}) \to (X,\xi)$,

(7) *the functor* $R_C: C \to B$ *induces an isomorphism* $C_B \to B_C$*, its inverse* $B_C \to C_B$ *is the suitable restriction of* $C_B: B \to C$.

A.12. APPLICATIONS

(1) A = *Near*, B = *U-Near*, C = *T-Near*. The "uniformizable" topological N-spaces are precisely the completely regular spaces. The "topologizable" uniform spaces are precisely the fine uniform spaces for whom a decent purely uniform characterization doesn't seem to be known. Cf. 4.24 and P.L. SHARMA & W.N. HUNSAKER [66].

(2) A = *Near*, B = *R-Near*, C = *T-Near*. The "regularizable" topological N-spaces are precisely the regular spaces.

(3) A = *Near*, B = *C-Near*, C = *T-Near*. Every topological N-space is "contiguizable". A contigual N-space (X,ξ) is "topologizable" iff every

finite $A \in \xi$ contains an adherencepoint (P.L. SHARMA & W.N. HUNSAKER [66]).

(4) A = *Near*, B = *Pr-Near*, C = *T-Near*. The "proximizable" topological N-spaces are precisely the completely regular spaces.

A.13. THEOREM. *Let A be a properly fibred topological category, let C be a bicoreflective full isomorphism-closed subcategory of A, and let B be an epireflective (resp. bireflective) full isomorphism-closed subcategory of C. Then the full subcategory of A consisting of all objects whose C-coreflection belongs to B is epireflective (resp. bireflective) in A.*

A.14. APPLICATIONS

(1) A = *Near*, C = *T-Near*, B any epireflective (resp. bireflective) full, isomorphism-closed subcategory of *T-Near* = *Top*.

(2) A = *P-Near*, C = *Q-Near*, B = *Near*.

Appendix B. NON-SYMMETRIC TOPOLOGICAL STRUCTURES

All nearness spaces (X,ξ) are symmetric in the sense that $x \in cl_{\xi}\{y\}$ always implies $y \in cl_{\xi}\{x\}$. Because of this in-built symmetry not all topological spaces but only the symmetric (= weakly regular, = R_0-) spaces can be considered as nearness spaces. As has been pointed out in the introduction this restriction is no serious disadvantage. In fact, it has to be expected since the concept of "nearness" is purely topological whereas the nowadays adopted concept of a topological space contains a minor order-theoretic component which is being removed precisely by the R_0-axiom. Nevertheless it is of interest to define a concept which contains all (pre-, quasi-) nearness spaces and all topological spaces as special cases. Naturally, such a concept has to be more complicated and more technical than the intuitivily very appealing concept of nearness.

The probably best known solution to the above problem has been offered by A. CSÁSZÁR [14,15]. Another solution which is much closer related to our investigations has been found independently by K. MORITA [55] and D. HARRIS [29]. The idea is to blend a nearness structure and a topology together. If, for the moment, by a topology on X we understand a set $A \subset PX$ which is closed under the formation of arbitrary intersections and finite unions and contains $\emptyset$ and X -i.e. A is the collection of all closed sets- then a generalized nearness space may be defined to be a triple (X,A,ξ) such that $A \subset PX$, $\xi \subset PA$ and the following axioms are satisfied:

(GN0) *A is a topology on* X.

(GN1) *If $B \subset A$, $B < C$, and $C \in \xi$ then $B \in \xi$.*

(GN2) *If $B \subset A$ and $\cap B \neq \emptyset$ then $B \in \xi$.*

(GN3) $\emptyset \neq \xi \neq PA$.

(GN4) *If $B \subset A$, $C \subset A$, and $(B \vee C) \in \xi$ then $B \in \xi$ or $C \in \xi$.*

Two facts are worth mentioning:

(1) A is determined by ξ since $A = \cup\xi \cup \{\emptyset\}$. Hence a generalized nearness space may be defined equivalently to be a pair (X,ξ) such that $\xi \subset P^2X$, $A = \cup\xi \cup \{\emptyset\}$ is a topology on X, and the axioms (GN1)-(GN4) are satisfied.

(2) The structure ξ may be replaced by any one of the structures $\bar{\xi}$, γ resp. μ to get different descriptions of the same concept of a generalized nearness space. In fact, generalized nearness structures have been defined by K. MORITA [55] and by D. HARRIS [29] by means of μ, i.e. by generalized open uniform covers.

If morphisms are defined in the obvious way a category *Gen-Near* is obtained into which the categories

(1) *Q-Near*,

(2) *Top* of <u>all</u> topological spaces (including the non-R_0-spaces) and continuous maps, and

(3) *POS* of partially ordered sets and order-preserving maps

can be embedded as full bicoreflective subcategories.
Further investigations shedding more light on the relations between all these concepts are desirable.

BIBLIOGRAPHY FOR APPENDIX A

[A1] ANTOINE, P., *Extension minimale de la catégorie des espaces topologiques*, C.R. Acad. Sci. Paris Sér. A, <u>262</u> (1966) 1389-1392.

[A2] ANTOINE, P., *Etude élémentaire des catégories d'ensembles structurés*, Bull. Soc. Math. Belg., <u>18</u> (1966) 142-164 and 387-414.

[A3] BENTLEY, H.L., *T-categories and some representation theorems*, Portugal. Math., <u>32</u> (1973) 201-222.

[A4] BOURBAKI, N., *Théorie des ensembles, ch. IV: Structures*, Hermann, Paris, 1957.

[A5] BOURBAKI, N., *Topologie générale*, Hermann, Paris, 1948.

[A6] BRÜMMER, G.C.L., *A categorical study of initiality in uniform topology*, thesis, Univ. of Capetown, 1971.

[A7] BRÜMMER, G.C.L., *Initial quasi-uniformitiès*, Indag. Math., 31 (1969) 403-409.

[A8] CĂSĂNESCU, V.E., *Familles initiales et finales*, Rev. Roumaine Math. Pures Appl., 17 (1972) 829-836.

[A9] ČECH, E., *Topological spaces*, Z. FROLÍK & M. KATĚTOV (eds.), Prague, 1966.

[A10] ERTEL, H.G., *Algebrenkategorien mit Stetigkeit in gewissen Variablenfamilien*, thesis, Univ. Düsseldorf, 1972.

[A11] FÄHLING P., *Kategorien mit ausgezeichneten Morphismenklassen*, thesis, Free Univ. Berlin, 1973.

[A12] GRAY, J.W., *Fibred and cofibred categories*, Proc. Conf. Categorical Algebra, La Jolla 1965, pp. 21-83, 1966.

[A13] HERRLICH, H., *Topological functors*, General Topology and Appl., 4 (1974).

[A14] HERRLICH, H., *Cartesian closed topological categories*, Math. Coll. Univ. Capetown, 9 (1974).

[A15] HERRLICH, H. & G.E. STRECKER, *Category theory*, Allyn and Bacon, Boston, 1973.

[A16] HOFFMANN, R.E., *Die kategorielle Auffassung der Initial- und Finaltopologie*, thesis, Univ. Bochum, 1972.

[A17] HOFFMANN, R.E., *(E,M)-universally topological functors*, preprint.

[A18] HOFFMANN, R.E., *Semi-identifying lifts and a generalization of the duality theorem for topological functors*, preprint.

[A19] HOFFMANN, R.E., *Topological functors and factorizations*, preprint.

[A20] HOFFMANN, R.E., *Factorization of cones*, preprint.

[A21] HUNSAKER, W.N. & P.L. SHARMA, *Proximity spaces and topological functors*, Proc. Amer. Math. Soc.

[A22] HUŠEK, M., *S-categories*, Comm. Math. Univ. Carolinae, 5 (1964) 37-46.

[A23] HUŠEK, M., *Construction of special functors and its applications*, Comm. Math. Univ. Carolinae, 8 (1967) 555-566.

[A24] HUŠEK, M., *Categorical methods in topology*, Proc. Symp. General Topology Appl., Prague 1966, pp. 190-194, 1966.

[A25] ISBELL, J.R., *Top and its adjoint relatives*, Proc. Topol. Conference, Kanpur 1968, pp. 143-154, 1971.

[A26] KAMNITZER, S.H., *Protoreflections, relational algebras and topology*, thesis, Univ. of Capetown, 1974.

[A27] MARNY, TH., *Rechts-Bikategoriestrukturen in topologischen Kategorien*, thesis, Free Univ. Berlin, 1973.

[A28] MARNY, TH., *TOP-Kategorien*, skript, Free Univ. Berlin, 1973.

[A29] OSIUS, G., *Eine axiomatische Strukturtheorie*, thesis, Free Univ. Berlin, 1969.

[A30] ROBERTS, J.E., *A characterization of initial functors*, J. Algebra, 8 (1968) 181-193.

[A31] SHUKLA, W., *On Top categories*, thesis, Indian Instit. Technology, Kanpur, 1971.

[A32] SRIVASTAVA, A.K., *Non-genuine adjunctions*, thesis, Indian Instit. Technology, New Delhi, 1974.

[A33] TAYLOR, J.C., *Weak families of maps*, Canad. Math. Bull., 8 (1965) 771-781.

[A34] THOLEN, W., *Relative Bildzerlegung und algebraische Kategorien*, thesis, Univ. Münster, 1974.

[A35] WISCHNEWSKY, M., *Initialkategorien*, thesis, Univ. München, 1972.

[A36] WISCHNEWSKY, M., *On the boundedness of initialstructure categories*, manuscripta math. 12 (1974) 205-215.

[A37] WISCHNEWSKY, M., *Partielle Algebren in Initialkategorien*, Math. Z., 127 (1972) 83-91.

[A38] WYLER, O., *Top categories and categorical topology*, General Topology and Appl., 1 (1971) 17-28.

[A39] WYLER, O., *On the categories of general topology and topological algebra*, Archiv Math. (Basel), 22 (1971) 7-17.

REFERENCES

[1] ALFSEN, E.M. & J.E. FENSTAD, *On the equivalence between proximity structures and totally bounded uniform structures*, Math. Scand., 7 (1959) 353-360; *correction*, Math. Scand., 9 (1961) 258.

ALFSEN, E.M. & J.E. FENSTAD, *A note on completion and compactification*, Math. Scand., 8 (1960) 97-104.

[2] ATSUJI, M., *Uniform continuity of continuous functions of metric spaces*, Pacific J. Math., 8 (1958) 11-16.

[3] BANASCHEWSKI, B., *Extensions of topological spaces*, Canad. Math. Bull., 7 (1964) 1-22.

[4] BANASCHEWSKI, B. & J. MARANDA, *Proximity functions*, Math. Nachr., 23 (1961) 1-37.

[5] BENTLEY, H.L., *Extensions of maps on nearness spaces*, preprint.

[6] BENTLEY, H.L., *Nearness spaces and extensions of topological spaces*, preprint.

[7] BENTLEY, H.L. & S.A. NAIMPALLY, *Wallman T_1-compactifications as epireflections*, General Topology and Appl. 4 (1974) 29-41.

[7a] BENTLEY, H.L. & P. SLOPIAN, *Colanders*, Rev. Romaine Math. Pures Appl. 12 (1967) 177-189.

[8] CAMERON, P., J.G. HOCKING & S.A. NAIMPALLY, *Nearness: A better approach to continuity and limits*, Lakehead Univ., Ontario, 1973.

[9] CARTAN, H., *Theorie des filtres*, C.R. Acad. Sci. Paris, 205 (1937) 595-598.

[10] ČECH, E., *Topological spaces*, Z. FROLÍK & M. KATĚTOV (eds.), Prague, 1966.

[11] CHOQUET, G., *Sur les notions de filtre et de grille*, C.R. Acad. Sci. Paris, 224 (1947) 171-173.

[12] COHEN, L.W., *On imbedding a space in a complete space*, Duke Math. J., 5 (1939) 174-183.

[13] CORSON, H.H., *The determination of paracompactness by uniformities*, Amer. J. Math., 80 (1958) 185-190.

[14] CSÁSZÁR, A., *Sur une classe de structures topologiques générales*, Rev. Roumaine Math. Pures Appl., 2 (1957) 399-407.

[15] CSÁSZÁR, A., *Foundations of general topology*, Macmillan, New York, 1963.

[16] CSÁSZÁR, K., *New results on separation axioms*, Topol. Appl. Symp. Herçeg Novi 1968, pp. 118-120, 1969.

[17] DIEUDONNÉ, J., *Une généralisation des espaces compacts*, J. Math. Pures Appl., 23 (1944) 65-76.

[18] DOIČINOV, D., *On a general theory of topological spaces, proximity and uniform spaces*, Dokl. Akad. Nauk. SSSR, 156 (1964) 21-24.

[19] DOIČINOV, D., *A generalization of topological spaces*, Contr. Extension Theory, Symp. Berlin 1967, pp. 59-60, 1969.

[20] EFREMOVIČ, V.A., *Geometry of proximity*, Mat. Sbornik, 31 (73) (1952) 189-200.

[21] FROLÍK, Z., *On the descriptive theory of sets*, Czechoslovak Math. J., 13 (88) (1963) 335-359.

[22] GÁL, I.S., *Proximity relations and precompact structures*, Indag. Math., 21 (1959) 304-326.

[23] GAGRAT, M.S. & S.A. NAIMPALLY, *Proximity approach to extension problems*, Fund. Math., 71 (1971) 63-76.

[24] GAGRAT, M.S. & W.J. THRON, *Nearness and proximity extensions*, preprint.

[25] GINSBURG, S. & J.R. ISBELL, *Some operators on uniform spaces*, Trans. Amer. Math. Soc., 93 (1959) 145-168.

[26] GRIMEISEN, G., *Gefilterte Summation von Filtern und iterierte Grenzprozesse I, II*, Math. Ann., 141 (1960) 318-342 and Math. Ann. 144 (1961) 386-417.

[27] HARRIS, D., *Regular-closed spaces and proximities*, Pacific J. Math., 34 (1970) 675-685.

[28] HARRIS, D., *Regular-closed spaces and structures*, Pacific J. Math., preprint.

[29] HARRIS, D., *Structures in topology*, Memoirs Amer. Math. Soc., 115 (1971)

[30] HARRIS, D., *Compact spaces and products of finite spaces*, Proc. Amer. Math. Soc., 35 (1972) 275-280.

[31] HARRIS, D., *Extension closed and cluster closed subspaces*, Canad. J. Math. 24 (1972) 1132-1136.

[32] HARRIS, D., *Universal compact T_1-spaces*, General Topology and Appl., 3 (1973), 291-318.

[33] HAUSDORFF, F., *Grundzüge der Mengenlehre*, Leipzig, 1914.

[34] HERRLICH, H., *Fortsetzbarkeit stetiger Abbildungen und Kompaktheitsgrad topologischer Räume*, Math. Z., 96 (1967) 64-72.

[35] HERRLICH, H., *A concept of nearness*, General Topology and Appl., 5 (1974).

[36] HERRLICH, H., *On the extendibility of continuous functions*, General Topology and Appl., to appear.

[37] HUNSAKER, W.N. & S.A. NAIMPALLY, *Extensions of continuous functions; reflective functors*, preprint.

[38] HUNSAKER, W.N. & P.L. SHARMA, *Quotients in categories of proximity spaces*, preprint.

[39] HUNSAKER W.N. & P.L. SHARMA, *Nearness structures compatible with a topological space*, preprint.

[40] HUŠEK, M., *Generalized proximity and uniform spaces I, II*, Comment. Math. Univ. Carolinae, 5 (1964) 247-266 and 6 (1965) 119-139.

[41] HUŠEK, M., *Categorical connections between generalized proximity spaces and compactifications*, Contr. Extension Theory, Symp. Berlin 1967, pp. 127-132, 1969.

[43] HUŠEK, M., *The class of k-compact spaces is simple*, Math. Z., 110 (1969) 123-126.

[44] ISBELL, J.R., *Uniform spaces*, Amer. Math. Soc. Math. Surveys 12 (1964).

[45] IVANOV, A.A., *Regular extensions of topological spaces*, Contr. Extension Theory, Symp. Berlin 1967, pp. 133-138, 1969.

[46] IVANOVA, V.M. & A.A. IVANOV, *Contiguity spaces and bicompact extensions*, Izv. Akad. Nauk SSSR, 23 (1959) 613-634.

[47] KATĚTOV, M., *Allgemeine Stetigkeitsstrukturen*, Proc. Intern. Congr. Math. Stockholm 1962, pp. 473-479, 1963.

[48] KATĚTOV, M., *On continuity structures and spaces of mappings*, Comment. Math. Univ. Carolinae, 6 (1965) 257-278.

[49] KATĚTOV, M., *Convergence structures*, Conf. General Topology II, Prague 1966, pp. 207-216, 1967.

[50] KURATOWSKI, K., *Sur l'opération $\overline{A}$ de l'Analysis Situs*, Fund. Math., 3 (1922) 182-199.

[51] LEADER, S., *Regulated bases and completions of regular spaces*, Fund. Math., 68 (1970) 279-287.

[52] LODATO, M.W., *On topologically induced generalized proximity relations I, II*, Proc. Amer. Math. Soc., 15 (1964) 417-422, resp. Pacific J. Math., 17 (1966) 131-135.

[53] MICHAEL, E., *Yet another note on paracompact spaces*, Proc. Amer. Math. Soc., 10 (1959) 309-314.

[54] MORDKOVIČ, A.G., *Systems with small sets and proximity spaces*, Math. Sbornik (N.S.), 67 (109) (1965) 474-480.

[55] MORITA, K., *On the simple extension of a space with respect to a uniformity I-IV*, Proc. Japan Acad., 27 (1951) 65-72, 130-137, 166-171, resp. 632-636.

[56] NAGATA, J., *On the uniform topology of bicompactifications*, J. Inst. Pol. Osaka City Univ., 1 (1950) 28-38.

[57] NAIMPALLY, S.A., *Reflective functors via nearness*, Fund. Math., to appear.

[58] NJÅSTAD, O., *On real-valued proximity mappings*, Math. Ann., 154 (1964) 413-419.

[58a] NJÅSTAD, O., *A proximity without a smallest compatible nearness*, preprint.

[59] PORTER, J.R. & C. VOTAW, *S(α)-spaces and regular Hausdorff extensions*, Pacific J. Math., 45 (1973) 327-345.

[60] PORTER, J.R. & C. VOTAW, *H-closed extensions I*, General Topology and Appl., 3 (1973) 211-224.

[61] RIESZ, F., *Stetigkeitsbegriff und abstrakte Mengenlehre*, Atti IV Congr. Internat. Mat. Roma, II (1908) 18-24.

[61a] ROBERTSON, W.A., *Convergence structures*, preprint.

[62] SAMUEL, P., *Ultrafilters and compactifications of uniform spaces*, Trans. Amer. Math. Soc., 64 (1948) 100-132.

[63] SANDBERG, V., *A new definition of uniform spaces*, Dokl. Akad. Nauk, 135 (1960) 535-537.

[64] SCHMIDT, J., *Beiträge zur Filtertheorie II*, Math. Nachr., 10 (1953) 197-232.

[65] SHANIN, N.A., *On special extensions of topological spaces*, Dokl. URSS, 38 (1943) 3-6, 110-113 and 154-156.

[66] SHARMA, P.L. & W.N. HUNSAKER, *Subcategories of Near*, preprint.

[67] SMIRNOV, YU. M., *On proximity spaces*, Math. Sbornik, 31 (73) (1952) 543-574.

[68] SMIRNOV, YU. M., *On completeness of proximity spaces*, Dokl. Akad. Nauk SSSR, 88 (1953) 761-764.

[69] STEINER, A.K. & E.F. STEINER, *Binding spaces: a unified completion and extension theory*, Fund. Math., 76 (1972) 43-61.

[70] STEINER, A.K. & E.F. STEINER, *On semi-uniformities*, Fund. Math., 83 (1973) 47-58.

[71] STEINER, A.K. & E.F. STEINER, *Countability and semi-uniformities*, General Topology and Appl. 3 (1973) 249-252.

[72] STEINER, E.F., *The relation between quasi-proximities and topological spaces*, Math. Ann., 155 (1964) 194-195.

[73] STEINER, E.F., *Wallman spaces and compactifications*, Fund. Math., 61 (1968) 295-304.

[74] STONE, A.H., *Paracompactness and product spaces*, Bull. Amer. Math. Soc., 54 (1948) 977-982.

[75] STONE, A.H., *Universal spaces for some metrizable uniformities*, Quart. J. Math., 11 (1960) 105-115.

[75a] SUZUKI, J., *On the metrization and the completion of a space with respect to a uniformity*, Proc. Japan Acad. 27 (1951) 219-223.

[76] TERWILLIGER, W.L., *On contiguity spaces*, thesis, Washington State Univ., 1965.

[77] THRON, W.J., *Proximity structures and grills*, Math. Ann., 206 (1973) 35-62.

[78] THRON, W.J., *On a problem of F. Riesz concerning proximity structures*, Proc. Amer. Math. Soc. 40 (1973) 323-326.

[79] TUKEY, J.W., *Convergence and uniformity in topology*, Ann. of Math. Studies 2, Amer. Math. Soc., Princeton, 1940.

[80] WARRACK, B.D. & S.A. NAIMPALLY, *Clusters and ultrafilters*, Publ. Inst. Math., 8 (1968) 100-101.

[81] WARREN, R.H., *Proximities, Lodato proximities and proximities of Čech*, thesis, Univ. of Colorado, Boulder, 1971.

[82] WEIL, A., *Sur les espaces à structure uniforme et sur la topologie générale*, Hermann, Paris, 1938.

MATHEMATICAL CENTRE TRACTS 52, 1974, 123-140

COMPONENT PROPERTIES AND FACTORIZATIONS

G.E. STRECKER *)

Dedicated to the memory of my great teacher and friend Johannes de Groot

INTRODUCTION

It is often useful in topology to be able to represent a given map f as a factorization f = hg where g is the "ultimate" map of a certain sort, and h is an "ultimate" map of a complementary sort. Typical examples are the factorization of any map into a quotient map followed by a one-to-one map, the factorization of any map between compact Hausdorff spaces into a monotone map followed by a light map, and the factorization of any map between completely regular spaces into a compact extendible dense map followed by a perfect map. This last factorization was shown to exist by HERRLICH [5] who also helped to explain the close connection between such factorizations and topological extensions and completions.

In this paper we will focus our attention on factorizations of the first two types mentioned above, i.e., those arising from some sort of connectedness property - or more precisely component subcategory of topological spaces. The classical (monotone, light) factorization theorem for maps between compact metric spaces was first proved by EILENBERG [4] and later improved and refined by WHYBURN [15], BAUER [2], PONOMAREV [12], MICHAEL [10] and others. A good account of the development of the theory and its current status can be found in a recent paper of MCAULEY [11]. Below we will show that for any component subcategory A there are naturally occurring unique (A-submonotone quotient, A-superlight)-factorizations. In

---

*) Kansas State University, Manhattan, Kansas, USA.

the case that A is connected spaces, the factorization is distinct from the classical one - even for compact Hausdorff spaces. Furthermore like the factorization recently discovered by COLLINS [3] it exists for all maps between topological spaces. In addition, by applying the general results concerning factorizations given in section 1 of the paper, it is shown that the submonotone quotient maps and the superlight maps have very useful cocompleteness and completeness properties, respectively.

1. PRELIMINARIES AND GENERAL FACTORIZATION THEOREM

In this section we establish some terminology and give a general factorization theorem (1.5) that will be useful in the sequel. All categorical terminology and notation will be that of [6]. Furthermore we will assume that all subcategories are both full and isomorphism-closed.

Recall that a subcategory $\mathcal{B}$ of a category $\mathcal{C}$ is called an *(epi)-reflective subcategory* of $\mathcal{C}$ provided that for each $\mathcal{C}$-object X there is a $\mathcal{B}$-object $\hat{X}$ and an (epi)morphism $r: X \to \hat{X}$ such that for any $\mathcal{B}$-object Y and any morphism $f: X \to Y$, there exists a unique morphism $\hat{f}: \hat{X} \to Y$ such that $f = \hat{f}r$. Dually, $\mathcal{B}$ is *(mono)coreflective* in $\mathcal{C}$ provided that for each $\mathcal{C}$-object X there is a $\mathcal{B}$-object $\check{X}$ and a (mono)morphism $m: \check{X} \to X$ such that for any $\mathcal{B}$-object Y and any morphism $f: Y \to X$, there exists a unique morphism $\check{f}: Y \to \check{X}$ such that $f = m\check{f}$. It is well-known (see [7], [8] and [9]) that the epireflective subcategories of *Top* (resp. *Haus*) are precisely those that are productive and (closed) hereditary, and that their (mono)coreflective subcategories are precisely those that are closed under the formation of coproducts (i.e., disjoint topological unions) and quotients. Some of the more recent proofs of these facts as well as general investigations into the characterizations of (co)reflections have shown their intimate connection with factorization and diagonalization theories.

1.1. <u>DEFINITION</u>. Let G, H and K be classes of morphisms in a category $\mathcal{C}$.

(i) $\Lambda(K) = \{h \mid$ for all s,t and g with $g \in K$ and $tg = hs$, there exists a d such that $dg = s$ and $hd = t\}$.

(ii) $\mathrm{T}(K) = \Lambda^{op}(K) = \{g \mid$ for all s,t and h with $h \in K$ and $tg = hs$, there exists a d such that $dg = s$ and $hd = t\}$.

(iii) $\mathcal{C}$ is said to have (G,H)-*diagonalizations* provided that $H \subseteq \Lambda(G)$, or, equivalently $G \subseteq T(H)$; i.e., iff whenever there is a commutative square $tg = hs$, with $g \in G$ and $h \in H$, then there exists a d such that the triangles in the square

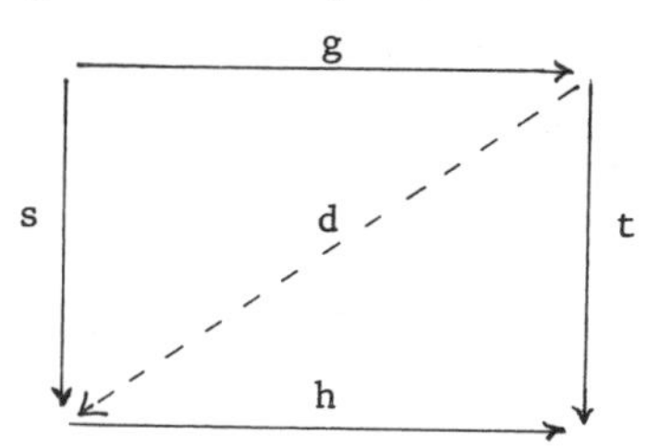

commute.

(iv) C is said to have *(G,H)-factorizations* provided that every morphism f in C can be expressed as a composition $f = hg$ where $g \in G$ and $h \in H$.

(v) C is said to have *unique (G,H)-factorizations* provided that it has (G,H)-factorizations and whenever $hg = f = h'g'$ are each (G,H)-factorizations, there exists an isomorphism k such that $kg = g'$ and $h'k = h$.

1.2. DEFINITION. G is called *right-cancellative* (resp. *self right-cancellative)* iff $hf \in G$ implies $h \in G$ (resp. $hf \in G$ and $f \in G$ implies $h \in G$). The dual notions are *left-cancellative* (resp. *self left-cancellative*).

1.3. PROPOSITION. *Suppose that C has (G,H)-diagonalizations and one of the following holds:*

(1) $G \subseteq$ {*C-epimorphisms*},

(2) $H \subseteq$ {*C-monomorphisms*},

(3) $G \cap H \subseteq$ {*C-isomorphisms*}, *G is self right-cancellative, and H is self left-cancellative.*

Then any (G,H)-factorization in C is unique.

PROOF. Suppose that $hg = f = h'g'$ are each (G,H)-factorizations of f. By the diagonalization property there are d and d' such that

$$dg = g', \; d'g' = g, \; h'd = h \text{ and } hd' = h'.$$

If (1) holds, then since epimorphisms are right-cancellative, d is an an epimorphism and $d'dg = d'g' = 1g$, so that, since g is an epimorphism, $d'd = 1$. Thus d is a section and an epimorphism, hence an isomorphism.

If (2) holds, the same result follows by a dual proof.

If (3) holds, then by the cancellativity conditions $d \in G \cap H$, so that by hypothesis d is an isomorphism. □

1.4. PROPOSITION. *If C has (G,H)-diagonalizations and (G,H)-factorizations, $G \cap H \subseteq$ {C-isomorphisms}, and G is closed under composition with isomorphisms and self right-cancellative, then G is closed under compositions.*

PROOF. Given $g_2 g_1$, where $g_i \in G$, take a (G,H)-factorization $g_2 g_1 = hg$. By the diagonalization property there is some d such that $dg_1 = g$ and $hd = g_2$. Applying self right-cancellation twice, we have $h \in G$. Thus h is an isomorphism, so that $hg \in G$ □

1.5. THEOREM. *Suppose that G and H are classes of morphisms in a category C where $G \cap H$ = {C-isomorphisms}, and G is self right-cancellative. Consider the following statements:*

(1) *C has (G,H)-diagonalizations and (G,H)-factorizations, G and H are each closed under composition with isomorphisms, and H is left-cancellative.*
(2) *C has unique (G,H)-factorizations, G and H are each closed under composition, and H is left-cancellative.*
(3) $\Lambda(G) = H$, $T(H) \supset G$, *C has (G,H)-factorizations and G is closed under composition.*
(4) $\Lambda(G) = H$ *and* $T(H) = G$.
(5) $T\Lambda(G) = G$ *and* $\Lambda T(H) = H$, *and either* $\Lambda T \Lambda(G) = H$ *or* $T\Lambda T(H) = G$.
(6) *G is closed under the formation of compositions, pushouts, multiple pushouts, and coproducts; and* $H = \Lambda(G)$ *is closed under the formation of compositions, pullbacks, multiple pullbacks, and products.*
(7) *G is closed under the formation of compositions, pushouts, and multiple pushouts; and* $H = \Lambda(G)$.

(i) *Always* (1) ⇔ (2) ⇒ (3) *and* (4) ⇔ (5) ⇒ (6) ⇒ (7).

(ii) *If $G \subseteq$ {C-epimorphisms} then* (3) ⇒ (4); (7) *implies that H is closed under the formation of inverse limits of inverse spectra; if furthermore C has a terminal object, T, then* (1) *implies that the (full) subcategory B with precisely those objects, X, such that each map* $X \to T$ *is in H, is epireflective in C, and epireflections are obtained by taking (G,H)-factorizations of terminal maps.*

(iii) *If $G \subseteq$ {C-epimorphisms} and C has multiple pushouts and is G-co-well-powered, then all seven statements are equivalent.*

PROOF.

(i) (1) ⇒ (2). Uniqueness of factorizations follows from propositon 1.3 and closure under compositions follows from proposition 1.4 and its dual.

(2) ⇒ (1). We need only show that C has (G,H)-diagonalizations. Let $sg = hr$ where $g \in G$ and $h \in H$. If $r = h'g'$ and $s = h''g''$ are (G,H)-factorizations of r and s, then by the hypotheses of (2) there exists an isomorphism k such that $h'kg''g = r$ and $hh'kg'' = s$. Thus $h'kg''$ is the required diagonal morphism.

(2) ⇒ (3). By the proof above, we have (G,H)-diagonalizations. Thus $\Lambda(G) \supseteq$ and $T(H) \supseteq G$. Let $f \in \Lambda(G)$ and let $f = hg$ be its (G,H)-factorization. By the definition of Λ, there is some d such that $dg = 1$ and $fd = h$. Using the cancellativity conditions of G and H, we have $d \in G \cap H$, so that d is an isomorphism. Hence $hd^{-1} = f \in H$. Thus $\Lambda(G) \subseteq H$.

(4) ⇒ (5) and (6) ⇒ (7). Trivial.

(5) ⇒ (4). Immediate from the fact that $\Lambda T \Lambda = \Lambda$ and $T \Lambda T = T$.

(5) ⇒ (6). This follows from [14; Proposition 2.6 and its dual].

(ii) The implication from (7) follows from the reference as above.

(3) ⇒ (4). Let $f \in T(\underline{H})$ and let $f = hg$ be its (G,H)-factorization. By the definition of T, there is some d such that $df = g$ and $hd = 1$. Since g is an epimorphism, d must be an epimorphism and a section; hence an isomorphism. Hence $d^{-1}g =$ $= f \in G$. Thus $T(H) \subseteq G$.

The implication from (1) follows by taking as reflection morphisms all G-factors of (G,H)-factorizations of maps to the terminal object. If $g: X \to \hat{X}$ is such a morphism and $f: X \to Y$ where $Y \to T$ is in H, then by the diagonalization property, there is some d such that $dg = f$. Uniqueness follows from the fact that g is an epimorphism.

(iii) By (i) and (ii), we need only show that (7) ⇒ (2). But this follows from [14, Theorem 2.8 and Proposition 2.6(2)]. □

1.6. EXAMPLES.

If $C = Top$, G = {final maps}, and H = {bijective maps} then the main hypotheses for theorem 1.5 hold and (1) can be easily verified. But G is also right-cancellative so by part (i) and its dual, statements (2) through (7) also hold. Thus G and H uniquely determine each other and each is closed under many types of constructions. If in Top, G = {quotient maps} and H = {injective maps} or G = {surjective maps} and H = {embeddings}, then all of the hypotheses of the theorem hold as well as (1). Similarly for $C = Haus$, G = {dense maps}, and H = {closed embeddings}, for C = = completely regular spaces, G = {compact extendible dense maps} and H = = {perfect maps}, and for C = T_1-spaces, G = {monotone quotient maps}, and H = {light maps}. Thus by statement (6) of the theorem, light maps and perfect maps are preserved by pullbacks in these categories. Using this and the epireflectors {T_1-spaces} $\to$ {completely regular spaces} $\to$ {compact Hausdorff spaces} one obtains an easy proof of MICHAEL's result [10] that the category of completely regular spaces and perfect maps has unique (monotone quotient, light)-factorizations in its own right. Notice also that if "H is left-cancellative" is weakened to "H is self left-cancellative", in (1) and (2) of theorem 1.5, then (1) and (2) are still equivalent. This is exemplified by the case where $C = Top$, G = {dense maps}, and H = {closed embeddings}.

2. COMPONENT SUBCATEGORIES

In this section we further develop the notion of "component subcategory" given in [8] (a natural generalization of the notion of connectedness) and establish certain diagonalization and factorization properties that each component subcategory gives rise to. Throughout the remainder of the paper, we will assume that A is a subcategory of Top. "Space" will mean topological space and "map" will mean continuous function.

2.1. DEFINITION. A collection $\mathcal{C}$ of subsets of a set will be called

(1) *centered* iff $\cap\mathcal{C} \neq \emptyset$.

(2) *chained* iff for any $A,B \in \mathcal{C}$ there exists a finite subfamily $C_1, C_2, \ldots, C_n$ of $\mathcal{C}$ such that $C_1 = A$, $C_n = B$ and $C_i \cap C_{i+1} = \emptyset$, $i=1,\ldots,n-1$.

2.2. DEFINITION. An A-*component* of a topological space X is a maximal subspace of X belonging to A.

2.3. PROPOSITION. (See [8]). *If every singleton space belongs to* A, *then the following are equivalent:*

(1) *For every space* X, *the set of all* A-*components of* X *forms a disjoint cover* X.
(2) *For every space* X, *the property that the collection of all non-empty* A-*subspaces of* X *is chained, implies that* X *is in* A.
(3) *For every space* X, *the union of every centered collection of* A-*subspaces of* X *is in* A.

2.4. DEFINITION. A will be called a *component subcategory of* Top provided that the following three conditions hold:

(1) If D is a discrete space, then $D \in A$ if and only if D is a singleton.
(2) The (equivalent) conditions of proposition 2.3 are valid for A.
(3) A is *map invariant*, i.e., if $f: X \to Y$ is a surjective map and $X \in A$, then $Y \in A$.

Throughout the remainder of the paper we will assume that A *is a component subcategory of* Top.

One obtains examples by letting A be e.g., all singleton spaces, or all connected spaces, or all pathwise connected spaces.

2.5. PROPOSITION. *For any topological space* X, *the following are equivalent:*

(1) *Each* $x \in X$ *has a neighborhood base consisting of subspaces in* A.
(2) *Each* A-*component of each open subspace of* X *is open in* X.

PROOF. (1) $\Rightarrow$ (2). Let C be an A-component of $U = U^0 \subset X$, and let $x \in C$. By (1) there is an A-space B such that $x \in B^0 \subset B \subset U$. By 2.3 (3), $B \cup C \in A$ so that by maximality $B \subset C$. Hence C is open.

(2) $\Rightarrow$ (1). Take as an open base all A-components of open sets. □

2.6. DEFINITION. Any topological space satisfying the equivalent conditions of proposition 2.5 will be called a locally A-space.

2.7. PROPOSITION. *The locally* A-*spaces form a (mono)coreflective subcategory of Top.*

PROOF. We need only show that locally A-spaces are preserved by coproducts and quotients. The former is immediate. To see the latter, suppose that $f: X \to Y$ is a quotient map, X is locally A, U is open in Y, C is an A-component of U, $x \in f^{-1}[C]$ and B is the A-component of x in $f^{-1}[U]$. By 2.5(2) B is open and since A is a component subcategory f[B] is in A and contained in C. Thus $x \in B \subseteq f^{-1}[C]$ so that $f^{-1}[C]$ is open. Since f is a quotient map, C is open, so that Y is locally A. □

Although by the above proposition, locally A-spaces constitute a well-behaved category -e.g., one that is complete and cocomplete and for which all colimits can be formed by forming them in *Top*- it is sometimes too restrictive. For example, it need not even contain the A-spaces. Next we will consider a subcategory of *Top* that "minimally" contains both the A-spaces and the locally A-spaces and is (mono)coreflective in *Top*.

2.8. PROPOSITION. *For any space* X, *the following are equivalent:*

(1) *Each* $x \in X$ *has a neighborhood belonging to* A.

(2) *Each* A*-component of* X *is an open subset of* X.

(3) *Each* A*-component of* X *is a closed and open subset of* X.

(4) *The topology of* X *is generated by* A *in the sense that a subset,* B*, of* X *is closed in* X *if and only if for each* A*-subspace* C *of* X*,* $B \cap C$ *is closed in* C.

(5) X *belongs to the smallest coreflective subcategory of* Top *that contains* A.

(6) X *is the disjoint union of its* A*-components.*

(7) X *is a disjoint union of spaces in* A.

(8) X *has the property that its nonempty simultaneously closed and open* A*-subspaces are precisely its* A*-components.*

PROOF. The equivalence of (1),(4),(5) and (7) follows from [8, Theorem 17].

(1) ⇒ (2). Immediate.

(2) ⇒ (3). The complement of any A-component is the union of all other A-components, which is open.

(3) ⇒ (6). Immediate.

(6) ⇒ (8). Let B be a nonempty closed and open A-subspace and C be its A-component. Then B and C-B are both closed and open in C. Let D be the discrete space {0,1} and $f: C \to D$ be defined by $f(x) = 0$ if $x \in B$; 1 if $x \in C-B$. Since A is a component subca-

tegory, $f[C] = \{0\}$, so that $C-B = \emptyset$.

(8) ⇒ (7). Immediate. □

2.9. DEFINITION. Any topological space satisfying the equivalent conditions of proposition 2.8 will be called a *weak locally* A*-space*.

2.10. PROPOSITION. *The weak locally* A*-spaces form a (mono)coreflective subcategory of* Top.

PROOF. Immediate from proposition 2.8 (5). □

2.11. DEFINITION. A map $f: X \to Y$ is called:

(1) A*-monotone* provided that $f^{-1}(y) \in A$ for each $y \in Y$.

(2) A*-submonotone* provided that $f^{-1}(y)$ is contained in some A-component of X.

(3) A*-light* provided that $f^{-1}(y)$ (as a subspace of X) has A-components that are singletons.

(4) A*-superlight* provided that $f^{-1}(y)$ meets each A-component of X in at most a singleton.

If A = {connected spaces}, then the prefix "A-" will usually be deleted. A space will be called *totally non* A provided that its A-components are singletons.

The notions of monotone and light map have been useful to topologists for many years. A-monotone and A-light are straightforward generalizations of them. Clearly A-submonotone is more general than A-monotone and A-superlight is more special than A-light. In [16] WHYBURN discusses the desirability of maps that preserve connectedness "both forward and backward", and shows that monotone hereditarily quotient maps do this. The next proposition shows that submonotone quotient maps are somewhat well-behaved in this respect, in particular if one's attention is focussed only on the maximal connected sets.

2.12. THEOREM. *Let* $f: X \to Y$ *be continuous. Then for the statements below:*

(i) (1) ⇔ (2) ⇔ (3) ⇔ (4) ⇔ (5) ⇔ (6), (6) ⇒ (7), *and* (7) ⇔ (8).

(ii) *If* f *is a quotient map and either* A = *{connected spaces} or* X *and* Y *are weak locally* A*-spaces, then all eight statements are equivalent.*

(1) *For each* A-*component* C *of* Y, $f^{-1}[C]$ *is empty or is an* A-*component of* X.
(2) *For each* A-*component* C *of* Y, $f^{-1}[C]$ *is empty or belongs to* A.
(3) *For each* A-*component* C *of* Y, $f^{-1}[C]$ *is contained in an* A-*subspace of* X.
(4) *For each* A-*component* C *of* Y, $f^{-1}[C]$ *is contained in an* A-*component of* X.
(5) *For each* A-*subspace* B *of* Y, $f^{-1}[B]$ *is contained in an* A-*subspace of* X.
(6) *For each* A-*subspace* B *of* Y, $f^{-1}[B]$ *is contained in an* A-*component of* X.
(7) *For each* $y \in Y$, $f^{-1}(y)$ *is contained in an* A-*subspace of* X.
(8) f *is* A-*submonotone*.

PROOF.

(i) (1) ⇒ (2), (2) ⇒ (3), (3) ⇒ (4), (5) ⇒ (6), and (7) ⇔ (8) are trivial.

(4) ⇒ (5). Clearly $B \subseteq C$, an A-component. Thus $f^{-1}[B] \subseteq f^{-1}[C] \in A$.

(6) ⇒ (1). $f^{-1}[C]$ is contained in some A-component B. If $x \in f^{-1}[C]$, then $f(x) \in C \cap f[B]$, so that by 2.3(3) and 2.4(3) $f[B] \subseteq C$. Hence $B \subseteq f^{-1}[C]$, so $B = f^{-1}[C]$.

(6) ⇒ (7). Immediate since each point is contained in an A-component (2.3(1)).

(ii) By part (i) we need only show that (8) ⇒ (1). Let C be an A-component of Y, and consider $f^{-1}[C]$.

Case I: A = {connected spaces}.

If $f^{-1}[C]$ is nonempty and disconnected, then there are closed nonempty disjoints subsets H and K such that $H \cup K = f^{-1}[C]$. For each $y \in C$, $f^{-1}(y) \subseteq A_y$ a component of X. Thus $A_y \subseteq H$ or $A_y \subseteq K$. If $\hat{H} = \{y \in C \mid A_y \subseteq H\}$ and $\hat{K} = \{y \in C \mid A_y \subseteq K\}$, then $f^{-1}[\hat{H}] = H$ and $f^{-1}[\hat{K}] = K$. Since f is a quotient map $\hat{H}$ and $\hat{K}$ must be closed, and hence form a partition of C.

Case II: X and Y are weak locally A.

If $f^{-1}[C] = 0$, let A be an A-component of X that meets $f^{-1}[C]$. Since A is component subcategory, it follows that $f[A] \subseteq C$; and since f is A-submonotone, $A = f^{-1}f[A]$. But A is closed and open in X (2.8) so that since f is a quotient map f[A] is closed and open in Y, (and also belongs to A (2.4(3))). Thus f[A] is an A-component of Y (2.8). But $f[A] \cap C \neq \emptyset$, so $f[A] = C$. Thus $A = f^{-1}[C]$. □

The following two examples show that neither of the hypotheses: "f is a quotient map" or "X and Y are weak locally A-spaces" can be deleted from 2.12(ii). In each case f is A-submonotone, but inverse images of A-components are not in A.

2.13. EXAMPLE. $X = [0,1] \cup (2,3]$, $Y = [0,2]$ and $f: X \to Y$ is defined by $f(x) = x$ if $x \in [0,1]$, $f(x) = x-1$ if $x \in (2,3]$. X and Y are weak locally connected and f is a surjective map.

2.14. EXAMPLE. $X = \{0\} \times [0,1] \cup \{(x, \sin \frac{1}{x}) \mid 0 < x \leq 1\}$, $Y = [0,1]$, $f: X \to Y$ is the first projection, and A = {pathwise connected spaces}. $Y \in A$ and f is a quotient map.

2.15. THEOREM. *Top has (A-monotone quotient, A-light)-diagonalizations and (A-submonotone quotient, A-superlight)-diagonalizations.*

PROOF. Consider the commutative square

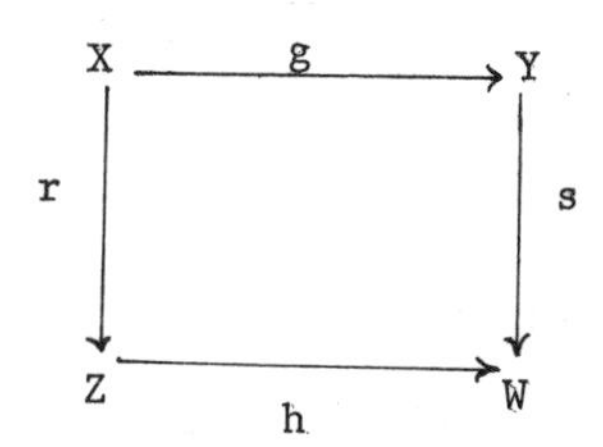

where g is A-monotone (resp. A-submonotone) quotient and h is A-light (resp. A-superlight). Let $y \in Y$. Then $\emptyset \neq g^{-1}(y) \in A$ (resp. is contained in an A-component of X). Thus $r[g^{-1}(y)] \in A$ (resp. is contained in an A-component of Z). But $r[g^{-1}(y)] \subset h^{-1}[s(y)]$ and $h^{-1}[s(y)]$ has singleton A-components (resp. meets each A-subspace of Z in at most a singleton). Call its nember z_y. Now $d: Y \to Z$ defined by $d(y) = z_y$ is a function, and for each $x \in X$, $dg(x) = z_{g(x)} \in r[g^{-1}(g(x))] = \{r(x)\}$. Thus $dg = r$. Since g is a quotient map, d is continuous and $hd = s$. □

2.16. COROLLARY. (WHYBURN [15]). *If a map has a (monotone quotient, light)-factorization, it must be unique.*

PROOF. Theorem 2.15 and proposition 1.3. □

2.17. THEOREM.

(1) *Top has unique (submonotone-quotient, superlight)-factorizations.*

(2) *The category of weak locally* A*-spaces has unique (*A*-submonotone quotient,* A*-superlight)-factorizations.*

PROOF. We need only show existence. Uniqueness will follow from proposition 1.3. Let the map $f\colon X \to Y$ be given and let Z be the collection of all non-empty intersections of fibers of f with A-components of X. Endow Z with the quotient topology induced by the natural (decomposition) map $\eta\colon X \to Z$. Define $h\colon Z \to Y$ by $h(f^{-1}(y) \cap C) = y$. Clearly h is a function, so that since η is a quotient map, and $h\eta = f$, h must be continuous. Also for any $f^{-1}(y) \cap C \in Z$,

$$\eta^{-1}(f^{-1}(y) \cap C) = f^{-1}(y) \cap C \subset C,$$

so that η is A-submonotone. If $y \in Y$ and $h^{-1}(y) \cap B \neq \emptyset$ for some A-component B of Z, then by 2.12(ii) $\eta^{-1}(B)$ is an A-component of X, so that

$$h^{-1}(y) \cap B = \{f^{-1}(y) \cap \eta^{-1}(B)\}$$

which is a singleton. Thus h is A-superlight. For part (2) Z is weak locally A since it is a quotient of a weak locally A-space (2.10). □

2.18. COROLLARY. *The category of locally* A*-spaces has unique (*A*-submonotone quotient,* A*-superlight)-factorizations.*

PROOF. Immediate from theorem 2.17 and proposition 2.7. □

Notice that if in theorem 2.17 A = *Top*, one obtains the usual unique (quotient, injective)-factorization for *Top*. Also both of theorems 2.15 and 2.17 fail to hold if the word "quotient" is deleted - or even changed to "surjective map". [If we let f be the map of example 2.13, then each of $f1$ and $1f$ is a ((sub)monotone surjective, (super)light)-factorization of f.] The following example shows that the hypothesis of theorem 2.17(2) that the spaces are weak locally A cannot be deleted.

2.19. EXAMPLE. Let X be the space of example 2.14, f be the map of X to the singleton space, T, and A be pathwise connected spaces. Then f has no (A-submonotone quotient, A-superlight)-factorization at all. Suppose that $f = hg$ is such a factorization. Let Z consist of the two path components of X and $\eta\colon X \to Z$ be the induced quotient map. By theorem 2.15 there is a map k such that $k\eta = g$. Since g is a quotient map, so is k, and since g is A-submonotone its codomain must have at least two points. Thus k is a homeomorphism, showing that h cannot be A-(super)light.

The unique ((A)-submonotone quotient, (A)-superlight)-factorizations guaranteed by theorem 2.17 are new and hopefully will become as useful to topologists as have been the classical (monotone, light)-factorizations. The following example shows that even for compact Hausdorff spaces, the (submonotone, superlight) and the (monotone, light) factorizations are different.

2.20. EXAMPLE. Let $X = [0,1] \times \{0,1\} \cup \{1\} \times [0,1]$, $Y = [0,1]$ and f be the "first projection" map from X to Y.

2.21. PROPOSITION. *Let G be the A-submonotone quotient maps and H be the A-superlight maps. Then*

(1) *G and H are each closed under composition with homeomorphisms.*
(2) *$f \in G \cap H$ if and only if f is a homeomorphism.*
(3) *G is self right-cancellative, but not right-cancellative.*
(4) *H is left-cancellative.*

PROOF. (1) and (2) are immediate from the definitions (2.11) and the fact that injective quotient maps are homeomorphisms.

(3). If $g = sr$ where g and r belong to G, then s is clearly a quotient map, and if $s^{-1}(y)$ is a FIBER of s, then $g^{-1}(y) = r^{-1}s^{-1}(y) \subseteq C$ where $C \in A$. Then $r[C] \in A$ and $r[C] \supseteq s^{-1}(y)$, since r is surjective. Hence G is self right-cancellative. To see that it isn't right-cancellative let $X \in A$, $r: X \to X \times \{0,1\}$ be an injection and s, g be terminal maps such that $g = sr$. Then g is A-submonotone quotient, but s isn't.

(4). Suppose $f = kh$ and $h^{-1}(y)$ meets two A-components of its domain. Then so will $f^{-1}(k(y))$. □

Theorems 2.15 and 2.17, corollary 2.18, and proposition 2.21 together with the fact that quotient maps are epimorphisms in any subcategory of *Top* establish that all of the hypotheses as well as statement (1) of theorem 1.5 hold whenever we let:

(I) C = *Top*, G = {submonotone quotient maps}, and H = {superlight maps},

or

(II) C = {weak locally A-spaces} or C = {locally A-spaces}, G = {A-submonotone quotient maps}, and H = {A-superlight maps}.

Some consequences of this are stated below. In the following statements we assume that either (I) or (II) holds.

2.22. PROPOSITION. *(A)-submonotone quotient and (A)-superlight maps determine each other; namely* $\Lambda\{$*(A)-submonotone quotient*$\}$ = *(A)-superlight and* $\mathrm{T}\{$*(A)-superlight*$\}$ = *(A)-submonotone.*

2.23. PROPOSITION. *(A)-submonotone quotient maps are closed under the formation of compositions, pushouts, multiple pushouts, and coproducts in Top.*

PROOF. Since C is coreflective in *Top*, the formation of the colimits in C is the same as their formation in *Top*. □

2.24. PROPOSITION. *(A)-superlight maps are closed under the formation of compositions, pullbacks, multiple pullbacks, products, and inverse limits of inverse spectra.*

N.B. If in the above proposition we are operating under hypotheses (II) it should be remembered that although C is complete, the formation of various limits such as pullbacks and products will, in general, be different from their construction in *Top*.

2.25. PROPOSITION. *The subcategory of all totally non A-spaces is epireflective in C.*

Notice that although the class *G* of all submonotone quotient maps has many nice properties, e.g.

(1) contains all homeomorphisms

(2) closed under composition

(3) closed under the formation of pullbacks, and

(4) closed under the formation of multiple pullbacks;

it nevertheless fails to be a "standard class" of epimorphisms in the sense of [13] or [14] because it is not left-cancellative w.r.t. epimorphisms.*)
To see this, consider f: $[0,2\pi) \to S^1$ defined by $f(x) = e^{ix}$. Then f is surjective and the first factor of a submonotone quotient map, but is not submonotone quotient. According to the results of [14] the smallest class of maps that contains *G*, has properties (1) through (4) above, and is left-cancellative w.r.t. epimorphisms, is the class of all surjective totally disconnected extendible maps.

3. COMBINATIONS OF FACTORIZATIONS

In this section we consider some ways of combining two types of factorizations into triple (G,K,H)-factorizations, i.e., representations of maps as compositions $f = hkg$, where $g \in G$, $k \in K$, and $h \in H$.

3.1. PROPOSITION. *If a category* C *has* (G,H)*-factorizations and* $(\hat{G},\hat{H})$*-factorizations and* H *and* $\hat{H}$ *are left-cancellative, then* C *has both* $(G,\hat{G}\cap H,\hat{H})$*-factorizations and* $(\hat{G},G\cap\hat{H},H)$*-factorizations.*

PROOF. Given f, let $f = hg$ be a (G,H)-factorization and let $h = \hat{h}\hat{g}$ be a $(\hat{G},\hat{H})$-factorization of h. Since H is left cancellative, $\hat{g} \in H$. Thus $\hat{h}\hat{g}g$ is a $(G,\hat{G}\cap H,\hat{H})$-factorization. The other factorization is obtained similarly. □

*) B is said to be *left-cancellative w.r.t epimorphisms* iff whenever $gf \in B$ and f is an epimorphism, f must be in B.

3.2. THEOREM. *The non-full subcategory* C *of* Top *consisting of all spaces, homeomorphisms, and maps with* T *codomain, has unique (monotone quotient, light submonotone quotient, superlight)-factorizations and (submonotone quotient, superlight monotone quotient, light)-factorizations that are not necessarily unique.*

PROOF. That maps in the category have unique (monotone quotient, light)-factorizations in Top is well-known (see e.g. [10]) and that they have unique (submonotone quotient, superlight)-factorizations in Top follows from theorem 2.17. Let $f: X \to Y$ be in C and let $X \xrightarrow{g} Z \xrightarrow{h} Y$ be its factorization of the first (resp. second) type. If f is a homeomorphism we can take $g = f = h$. If not, then Y is T_1 so that if $z \in Z$ then z is a component of $f^{-1}(y)$ (resp. the intersection of a component of X with $f^{-1}(y)$). Since both $f^{-1}(y)$ and components are closed, z considered as a subspace of X must be closed. But $z = g^{-1}(z)$ and g is a quotient map. Thus z must be closed in Z, so Z is T_1 and both g and h are in C. Applying proposition 3.1, the required triple factorizations are obtained. To show uniqueness suppose that $hkg = f = h'k'g'$ are each (monotone quotient, light submonotone quotient, superlight)-factorizations of f. Since every superlight map is light and light maps are closed under composition, kh and h'k' are light. Thus by the uniqueness of the (monotone quotient, light)-factorization (2.16) there is a homeomorphism d such that $dg = g'$ and $h'k'd = hk$. Now by the (submonotone quotient, superlight)-diagonalization property there is a $\hat{d}$ such that $\hat{d}k = k'd$ and $h'\hat{d} = h$. Since d is a homeomorphism, k'd is submonotone quotient so that $\hat{d}$ is also (2.21). By left-cancellativity of superlight maps $\hat{d}$ is superlight. Thus $\hat{d}$ is a homeomorphism. To see that (submonotone quotient, superlight monotone quotient, light)-factorizations are not necessarily unique, consider the map $f: X \to Y$ of example 2.20. If $hg = f = h'g'$ are its (monotone quotient, light)- and (submonotone quotient, superlight)-factorizations, resp. then $h1g = f = h'1g'$ are non-equivalent triple factorizations of f of the required types. □

Occasionally much can be gained by considering factorizations of a very restricted class of maps. The following theorem illustrates this.

3.3. THEOREM. *For the subcategory Haus of Top consisting of Hausdorff spaces, terminal maps have unique (compact extendible dense, perfect (sub)-monotone quotient, perfect (super)light)-factorizations,* $f = hgc$ *and the maps* gc *together with their codomains give the Banaschewski* [1] *zero-dimensional compact Hausdorff epireflection for Haus.*

PROOF. Let X be a Hausdorff space and $t: X \to T$ its terminal map. Let $c: X \to \beta X$ be the compact Hausdorff reflection of X and let hg be the ((sub)monotone quotient, (super)light)-factorization of the terminal map from βX. Denote the codomain of g by ζX. hg is perfect since βX is compact and g is perfect since perfect maps are left-cancellative. Since X and T are compact Hausdorff, so is ζX [12] Thus h is also perfect. Hence $t = hgc$ is a factorization of the required type. To show uniqueness suppose that $t = h'g'c'$ is also a factorization of the same type. Since perfect maps are closed under composition h'g' is perfect, so that Y is compact. Thus since each of c and c' is compact extendible, there are d and d' such that $dc = c'$ and $d'c' = c$. Since c and c' are dense it follows that d is a homeomorphism. Thus h'(g'd) is a ((sub)monotone, (super)light)-factorization of $\beta X \to T$. By the uniqueness of such factorizations (2.17) there is a homeomorphism k such that $kg = g'd$ and $h'k = h$. Thus

$$X \xrightarrow{c} \beta X \xrightarrow{g} \zeta X \xrightarrow{h} T$$

is the unique factorization of the required sort. Since h is light, its domain must have singleton components. Thus since ζX is compact Hausdorff, it is also zero-dimensional. Also $gc: X \to \zeta X$ is dense, thus an epimorphism in Haus. Now suppose that $f: X \to Y$ where Y is zero-dimensional compact

Hausdorff. Clearly there is a map $\hat{f}$: $\beta X \to Y$ such that $\hat{f}c = f$. But now by the (monotone quotient, light)-diagonalization property, there is some d: $\zeta X \to Y$ such that $dg = f$. Hence $d(gc) = f$. Since gc is dense, d is unique. Therefore $(gc, \zeta X)$ is the required epireflection for X. □

REFERENCES

[1] BANASCHEWSKI, B., *Über nulldimensionale Räume*, Math. Nachr., 13 (1955) 129-140.

[2] BAUER, H., *Verallgemeinerung eines Faktorisierungssatzes von G. Whyburn*, Arch. Math. (Basel), 10 (1959) 373-378.

[3] COLLINS, P.J., *Concordant mappings and the concordant-dissonant factorization of an arbitrary continuous function*, Proc. Amer. Math. Soc., 27 (1971) 587-591.

[4] EILENBERG, S., *Sur les transformations continues d'espaces métriques compacts*, Fund. Math., 22 (1934) 292-296.

[5] HERRLICH, H., *A generalization of perfect maps*, in: *General topology and its relations to modern analysis and algebra III*, (Proceedings of the Third Prague Topological Symposium, 1971), Academia Prague, 1972, pp. 187-191.

[6] HERRLICH, H. & G.E. STRECKER, *Category theory*, Allyn and Bacon, Boston, 1973.

[7] HERRLICH, H. & G.E. STRECKER, *Coreflective subcategories*, Trans. Amer. Math. Soc., 157 (1971) 205-225.

[8] HERRLICH, H. & G.E. STRECKER, *Coreflective subcategories in general topology*, Fund. Math., 73 (1972) 199-218.

[9] KENNISON, J.F., *Reflective functors in general topology and elsewhere*, Trans. Amer. Math. Soc., 118 (1965) 303-315.

[10] MICHAEL, E., *Cuts*, Acta Math., 111 (1964) 1-36.

[11] MCAULEY, L.F., *Some fundamental theorems and problems related to monotone mappings*, Proc. First Conf. on Monotone Mappings and Open Mappings (SUNY at Binghampton, Binghampton, N.Y., 1970), State Univ. of New York at Binghampton, N.Y., 1971 pp. 1-36.

[12] PONOMAREV, V.I., *On continuous decomposition of bicompacts*, Uspehi Mat. Nauk., 12 (1957) 335-340.

[13] STRECKER, G.E., *Epireflection operators vs. perfect morphisms and closed classes of epimorphisms*, Bull. Austral. Math. Soc., 7 (1972) 359-366.

[14] STRECKER, G.E., *On characterizations of perfect morphisms and epireflective hulls*, Proceedings of the Second International Pittsburgh Conference on General Topology, 1972, Springer-Verlag (to appear).

[15] WHYBURN, G.T., *Open and closed mappings*, Duke Math., J., 17 (1950) 69-74.

[16] WHYBURN, G.T., *Dynamic topology*, Amer. Math. Monthly, 77 (1970) 556-570.

MATHEMATICAL CENTRE TRACTS 52, 1974, 141-175

OPEN PROBLEMS IN INFINITE-DIMENSIONAL TOPOLOGY

R.D. ANDERSON & NELLY KROONENBERG *)

This problem list is a successor to earlier problem lists prepared following conferences in Ithaca (January 1969), Baton Rouge (December 1969), and Oberwolfach (September 1970). The Oberwolfach problem list was published as Mathematisch Centrum Report ZW 1/71. The current list includes problems suggested and discussed at a conference in Baton Rouge (October 1973). It is not, of course, a complete list of all open questions known to the conference participants but does include representative problems from the principal areas of current activity in the point-set topology of infinite-dimensional (I-D) spaces and manifolds known to the authors. Because of changing patterns of activity over the past few years, the problems on linear groups and the older problems on differential topology, included in the 1971 list, have been omitted. The interested reader is referred to the paper *Embeddings, Isotopy and Stability of Banach Manifolds*, Compositio Math., 24 (1972) 175-226, by DAVID ELWORTHY for a discussion of recent results in I-D differential topology. It is likely that a few of the problems listed below are inadequately worded, are trivial or are known. Because of many interrelationships, some aspects of various problems are listed under more than one heading below. See footnotes for results added in proof.

The following mathematicians (with addresses listed in the AMS-MAA combined membership list) are possible sources of continuing more recent information on many of the problems: R.D. ANDERSON, T.A. CHAPMAN, DOUGLAS W.

---

*) Louisiana State University, Baton Rouge, Louisiana 70803, USA.

CURTIS, ROSS GEOGHEGAN, R.M. SCHORI and JAMES E. WEST. The following are sources on certain types of problems. W.E. HAVER, R. HEISEY, J.E. KEESLING, N.S. KROONENBERG, W.K. MASON, W.E. TERRY, DAVID C. WILSON, and RAYMOND Y.T. WONG.

HENRYK TORUŃCZYK of the Mathematics Institute of the Polish Academy of Sciences in Warsaw and CZESLAW BESSAGA of the Mathematics Institute of the University of Warsaw are also knowledgeable about many of the problems and results in the area.

Over the past three years there has been a change in the direction of much of the research effort in I-D topology. Whereas many or most of the results prior to September 1970 had dealt with non-locally compact linear spaces and manifolds modelled on them -although using some results from the compact Hilbert cube- most of the more recent results have dealt with compact or locally compact infinite-dimensional spaces and manifolds modelled on them. There are big open problems of both types before us now and it is not sure where the next big thrusts will come.

Continuing problems are the obtaining of further usable general characterizations of Hilbert space ℓ_2 and the Hilbert cube Q. Manifolds modelled on ℓ_2 and Q have been characterized by homotopy type for ℓ_2-manifolds and simple homotopy type for Q-manifolds and effective representation theorems have been obtained. A characterization of ℓ_2 in terms of other linear spaces (all separable infinite-dimensional Fréchet spaces are homeomorphic) was obtained in 1966 from combined work of ANDERSON, KADEC, and BESSAGA & PEŁCZYNSKI. A characterization of any compact convex infinite-dimensional subset of ℓ_2 as homeomorphic to Q had been obtained in 1931 by KELLER and was extended by KLEE to such subsets of any Fréchet space. Characterizations of ℓ_2 and Q as products of factors other than lines or intervals have been the subject of much recent research and substantial partial results are known. Usable characterizations independent (or semi-independent) of linear or convex structure or of product structure are not yet known.

There have been three major sets of results in the past two years and in addition a new and useful proof technique. The three results have been:

(1) The characterization and representation theorems for Q-manifolds and their use in establishing the invariance of Whitehead torsion (CHAPMAN). This work has intimately related Q-manifold theory with homotopy theory and particularly simple-homotopy theory. It suggests that Q-manifolds may be the proper framework for reformulating and extending

various algebraic topological concepts or procedures since Q-manifolds don't have the dimensional limitations of finite-dimensional manifolds. Specifically, CHAPMAN has shown that every Q-manifold is triangulable, i.e., is the product of a locally finite polyhedron with Q and that two compact Q-manifolds are homeomorphic iff their polyhedral factors have the same simple homotopy type. CHAPMAN has extended this result to non-compact manifolds with the appropriate definition of infinite simple homotopy type. His techniques use surgery and a good bit of the finite-dimensional theory.

(2) The characterizations of the factors of ℓ_2 (and other linear spaces). Using functional analytic and topological methods, TORUŃCZYK has shown that a separable complete metric space X is an ℓ_2-factor, i.e., $X \times \ell_2 \cong \ell_2$, iff X is an absolute retract. He also shows that such a space X is a factor of some ℓ_2-manifold iff X is an ANR. He has comparable results for many other linear spaces. His results together with the earlier results of GEOGHEGAN that the space H(M) of all homeomorphisms of a finite-dimensional manifold M admits ℓ_2 as a factor, i.e., $H(M) \times \ell_2 \cong H(M)$, show that H(M) is an ℓ_2-manifold iff H(M) is an ANR (since $H(M) \times \ell_2$ will be an ℓ_2-manifold if H(M) is an ANR and $H(M) \times \ell_2$ will be homeomorphic to H(M) (GEOGHEGAN); and since every ℓ_2-manifold is an ANR and $H(M) \times \ell_2$ projects onto H(M), then H(M) must be an ANR). The TORUŃCZYK results are naturally related to the long standing question as to whether every compact metric AR is a Q-factor but his methods do not yield that result.

(3) Let X be a separable metric space and let 2^X be the space of all non-empty closed subsets of X with the Hausdorff metric. Let C(X) be the subset of 2^X consisting of the subcontinua of X. SCHORI & WEST had earlier proved that $2^I \cong Q$ and $2^\Gamma \cong Q$ where Γ is any non-degenerate connected finite graph and WEST had proved that $C(X) \cong Q$ for X any dendron with a dense set of branch points. Using these results and a delicate geometric argument, CURTIS & SCHORI proved that $2^X \cong Q$ iff X is a non-degenerate Peano continuum and that $C(X) \cong Q$ iff X is a non-degenerate Peano continuum containing no free arc. (The "only if" results were known earlier.)

In their proofs they used mapping cylinder theorems by WEST, e.g., if X and Y are Q-factors and f is a map of X into Y, then M_f, the mapping cylinder of f, is a Q-factor. They also used near-homeomorphisms, i.e., maps which are uniform limits of homeomorphisms. Recently, CHAPMAN has shown that any cell-like map of a Q-manifold onto a Q-manifold is a near-homeomorphism, a general result including many earlier special cases and applicable to the CURTIS-SCHORI argument. The mapping cylinder and near-homeomorphism techniques appear to be both powerful and useful.

It should be mentioned that there are three major areas of contact or potential contact of current research in infinite-dimensional topology with other areas of topology: the work of CHAPMAN with simple homotopy theory, the work of several people on spaces of homeomorphisms of finite-dimensional manifolds, and the involvement of many areas of infinite-dimensional topology with the theory of retracts. It seems likely that infinite-dimensional topology will become basic to the study of these other areas.

Following a list of notation, the problems are listed under the headings and with the letter designations below.

I.	PRODUCTS AND FACTORS	PF
II.	HYPERSPACES, DECOMPOSITIONS AND SHAPE OF COMPACTA	
	Hyperspaces	H
	Decompositions	D
	Shape of compacta	SC
III.	OTHER PROBLEMS ON Q AND Q-MANIFOLDS	
	Hilbert cube manifolds	QM
	Group actions	GA
	Compactifications	CMP
	Topological dynamics	TD
	Miscellaneous	MSQ
IV.	PROBLEMS ON LINEAR SPACES AND MANIFOLDS	
	Spaces of homeomorphisms and mappings	HS
	Characterization of ANR's	ANR
	Linear spaces	LS
	Lipschitz and uniformly continuous homeomorphisms	L-U
	ℓ_2-manifolds	M
	Compactifying s as the Hilbert cube	CSQ
	I-D topology in Euclidean spaces	E

NOTATION

1) Q = Hilbert cube = $I^\infty = [-1,1]^\infty$.
2) ℓ_2 = separable Hilbert space.
3) $s = (\mathring{I})^\infty = (-1,1)^\infty$ = countable infinite product of lines (is homeomorphic to ℓ_2). s is referred to as the *pseudo-interior* and $Q\backslash s$ as the *pseudo-boundary* of Q.
4) For X any space, let X^n be the n-fold product of X by itself and X^∞ or X^ω be the countable infinite product of X by itself. For X an infinite-dimensional coordinate space, let $X_f = \{(x_i)_i \in X \mid \text{for all but finitely many } i, x_i = 0\}$.
5) "$\sim$" = "has the same homotopy type as".
6) "$\cong$" = "is homeomorphic to".
7) Y is an *X-manifold* if Y is a paracompact Hausdorff space modelled on X, i.e., if Y admits an open cover by sets homeomorphic to open subsets of X. Q-manifolds are locally compact and metric and ℓ_2-manifolds are completely metrizable.
8) X is a *Q-factor* if $X \times Q$ is homeomorphic to Q. This is equivalent to the existence of a Y such that $X \times Y \cong Q$.
9) X is a *Q-manifold factor* if $X \times Q$ is a Q-manifold.
10) A closed subset K of an ANR space X is a *Z-set* in X if for every non-empty contractible open subset U of X, $U\backslash K$ is non-empty and contractible. An alternative definition, which is equivalent for Q-manifolds and ℓ_2-manifolds, reads: a closed subset K of an ANR space X is a Z-set in X if for every map $\varepsilon: X \to R^+$ there exists a map $f: X \to X\backslash K$ with for each $x \in X$, $d(f(x),x) < \varepsilon(x)$. A *σ-Z-set* is a countable union of Z-sets. Z-sets play an important role in infinite-dimensional topology.
11) An onto map $f: X \to Y$, where $X \cong Y$, is a *near-homeomorphism* if f is a uniform limit of homeomorphisms.
12) An onto map $f: X \to Y$ *stabilizes to a near-homeomorphism* if $f \times id_Q: X \times Q \to Y \times Q$ is a near-homeomorphism.
13) Let X be compact and let $f: X \to Y$ be any map; then the *mapping cylinder* M_f is the attachment space $X \times I \cup_{f_0} Y$ with attachment map $f_0: X \times \{0\} \to Y$ defined by $f_0(x,0) = f(x)$. Y is the *base* of M_f.
14) A space X is LC or *locally contractible* at a point $p \in X$ if for every neighborhood U of p there exists a neighborhood $V \subset U$ of p such that

V is contractible in U. A space X is LC^n (LC^∞) at $p \in X$ if for each neighborhood U of p and each $i \leq n$ (each $i < \infty$) there exists a neighborhood V of p such that every map $f: \partial I^{i+1} \to V$ can be extended to $\bar{f}: I^{i+1} \to U$. A space X is LC (LC^n, LC^∞) if X is LC (LC^n, LC^∞) at each of its points.

15) A map $f: X \to Y$, where X and Y are locally compact, is *proper* if the inverse of a compact set is compact.

16) A proper map f is CE, *cell-like* or *cellular*, if f is onto and point-inverses have trivial shape. For the notion of *shape* see section SC.

17) AR's and ANR's are understood to be AR's (ANR's) with respect to separable metric spaces (or compact metric spaces when appropriate).

18) I-D = infinite-dimensional.

19) fd = finite-dimensional.

20) PL = piecewise linear.

21) A subset M of a metric ANR X is said to have the (*finite-dimensional*) *compact absorption property* or to be an (*fd*) *cap-set for* X if $M = \bigcup_{i>0} M_i$ such that
   (i) for each $i > 0$, M_i is a (finite-dimensional) compactum which is a Z-set in X,
   (ii) for each $i > 0$, $M_i \subset M_{i+1}$, and
   (iii) for any (finite-dimensional) compact Z-set $K \subset X$, any open cover $\mathcal{U}$ of X and any positive integer m, there exists an integer $n > 0$ and a homeomorphism g of X onto X such that $g(K) \subset M_n$, $g|K \cap M_m = \mathrm{id}$ and g is limited by $\mathcal{U}$, i.e., for any $x \in X$ there exists a $U \in \mathcal{U}$ such that $x, g(x) \in U$.

   $Q \backslash s$ is a cap-set for Q and s_f is an fd cap-set for Q.

I. PRODUCTS AND FACTORS

One of the most important current problems in infinite-dimensional topology is whether every AR is a Q-factor (trivially all Q-factors are AR's). As pointed out below, a positive answer to this would solve the old problem of whether every compact metric ANR has finite homotopy type. TORUŃCZYK ([25],[26]) showed that every complete separable metric AR is an ℓ_2-factor and every complete separable metric ANR is an ℓ_2-manifold factor. However, his techniques are not applicable to the Hilbert cube case.

By various results of WEST the class of Q-factors is known to contain all compact contractible polyhedra and to possess the following two closure properties (cf. [27],[29]):

1) If $f: X \to Y$ is a map between Q-factors, then the mapping cylinder M_f is a Q-factor.
2) If X, Y and $X \cap Y$ are Q-factors, then $X \cup Y$ is a Q-factor.

CHAPMAN observed that it follows from TORUŃCZYK's results that the product of a locally compact ANR and the Hilbert cube has a basis of contractible open subsets. For let X be a locally compact ANR and let $(x,q) \in X \times Q$. By homogeneity of Q, we may assume that $q \in s$. Let 0 be a contractible open neighborhood of (x,q) in s, and let 0^* be any open subset of $X \times Q$ such that $0^* \cap s = 0$. We show that 0^* is homotopically trivial. Let $f: S^n \to 0^*$ be any map. Then there exist maps $\tilde{f}: S^n \to s$ which are arbitrarily close to f and hence homotopic to f and can therefore be supposed to map into 0^* and hence into $0 = 0^* \cap s$. Now $\tilde{f}$ can be extended to $\tilde{\tilde{f}}: I^{n+1} \to 0$. But then there exists also an extension $\bar{f}: I^{n+1} \to 0^*$ of f.

Using the above, CHAPMAN observed that a positive solution of the AR-problem would imply that every locally compact ANR is a Q-manifold factor and therefore, by triangulability of Q-manifolds, has the homotopy type of a locally finite simplicial complex. We only give a simpler argument for the compact case. Let X be a compact ANR. Then the cone of X is an AR and, by assumption, a Q-factor. But then $X \times [0,1) \times Q$ is homeomorphic to an open subset of Q and thus is a Q-manifold. Hence $X \times [0,1] \times Q$ is a compact Q-manifold and by CHAPMAN's characterization has the homotopy type of a finite complex. Besides the AR-problem, we list various weaker versions of it, some related questions and problems and some techniques which might be helpful.

PF 1) If X is a compact metric AR, is $X \times Q \cong Q$?

In trying to solve PF 1 one encounters the problem that an AR can show pathologies like the singularity of MAZURKIEWICZ, that is, it might not be a local AR. There is ground for hope that such pathologies disappear upon multiplication by finitely many or even one interval. The remark above implies that the product of a compact AR and the Hilbert cube has a basis of contractible open sets. However, we would like to obtain a stronger result:

PF 2) If X is a compact AR, does $X \times Q$ (or $X \times I^n$ for some n) admit arbitrarily small brick decompositions? For a definition of brick decomposition, see [2], p.178 on condition Γ. This is probably true for the example in [2], pp.152-156, with $n = 1$.

An onto map $f: X \to Y$ between compact ANR's is called a *fine homotopy equivalence* if for any ε there is a map $g: Y \to X$ such that $f \circ g$ is ε-homotopic to id_Y and $g \circ f$ is homotopic to id_X by a homotopy $F: X \times I \to X$ such that the paths in $f \circ F$ of points in X have diameter less than ε. For a map f between compact ANR's it is straightforward to prove that (f is a near-homeomorphism) $\Rightarrow$ (f is a fine homotopy equivalence) $\Rightarrow$ (f is cellular). In some special cases there are converse implications: CHAPMAN has shown that if $f: X \to Y$ is a cellular map between Q-manifold factors then f stabilizes to a near-homeomorphism. HAVER has recently shown that cellular maps between locally compact ANR's are fine homotopy equivalences, extending a finite-dimensional result of LACHER.

PF 3a) Is there a cell-like map $f: Q \to X$ for X a compact metric AR? (By HAVER's result f will be a fine homotopy equivalence.) What about the case in which X is finite-dimensional? CHAPMAN has claimed that an affirmative answer would imply finiteness of homotopy types of compact metric ANR's, which is a long-standing unsolved problem.

PF 3b) If $f: Q \to X$ is a fine homotopy equivalence onto an AR-space X then is X a Q-factor? CURTIS observed that X is a Z-set in the mapping cylinder M_f (where X is identified with the base of M_f) iff f is a fine homotopy equivalence. According to WEST it is almost certain that $M_f \cong Q$. (WEST also expects to be able to show that M_f is a Q-manifold if X is a compact ANR.) See also problem PF 5.

Let X and Y be compact metric spaces. A continuous surjection $f: X \to Y$ is *tiltable* if for each $\varepsilon > 0$ there exists a homeomorphism $h: X \to X$ such that 1) $d(f \circ h, f) < \varepsilon$ and 2) for $d(x,x') > \varepsilon$ with $x,x' \in X$, $f \circ h(x) \neq$ $\neq f \circ h(x')$.

<u>THEOREM</u>: $f: X \to Y$ *is tiltable iff* f *is a near-homeomorphism* (*and hence* $X \cong Y$).

One can show the only-if part by inductively constructing a sequence $(h_n: X \to X)_n$ such that $\lim_{n\to\infty} f \circ h_n \circ \ldots \circ h_1$ is a homeomorphism ε-close to f. The proof of this and the converse is fairly straightforward.

<u>TILTING LEMMA</u> (cf. [29]). *Let* X, Y *and* $X \cap Y$ *be* Q-*factors and let* $Z = (X \times I) \cup (Y \times \{0\})$. *Then* $(X \cap Y) \times \{0\}$ *is a* Z-*set in* $X \times I$ *and hence it is known that* Z *is a* Q-*factor. If* $p: Z \to X \cup Y$ *is the natural projection then* $p \times id: Z \times Q \to (X \cup Y) \times Q$ *is tiltable and hence* $X \cup Y$ *is also a* Q *factor.*

Possible further applications of the notion of tiltability are:

PF 4a) Let A, X and Y be Q-factors where $A \subset X$ and let $f: A \to Y$ be any map. Then is $X \cup_f Y$ a Q-factor? It is known that if A is a Z-set in X, then $X \cup_f Y$ is a Q-factor.

By the above, PF 4a can be reduced to the following tiltability problem:

PF 4b) Let A, X and Y be Q-factors where $A \subset X$ and let $f: A \to Y$ be any map. Then $A \times \{0\}$ is a Z-set in $X \times I$ and hence $(X \times I) \cup_{f_0} Y$ is a Q-factor where $f_0: A \times \{0\} \to Y$ is defined by $f_0(x,0) = f(x)$. Let $p: (X \times I) \cup_{f_0} Y \to X \cup_f Y$ be the natural projection. Then is $p \times id: [(X \times I) \cup_{f_0} Y] \times Q \to [X \cup_f Y] \times Q$ tiltable? If so, then $X \cup_f Y$ is a Q-factor.

PF 5) In view of PF 3a and 3b the following application is of special interest: If $f: Q \to X$ is a fine homotopy equivalence from Q onto an AR-space X and M_f is the mapping cylinder of f and $c: M_f \to X$ is the collapse to the base, is $c \times id: M_f \times Q \to X \times Q$ tiltable? If so, then X is a Q-factor, according to WEST's claim of PF 3b.

PF 6) Is there some way to build up the class of factors of Q (or at least a large subclass of them) from the class of contractible finite complexes or other known factors? In the last few years several closure properties of the class of Q-factors have been shown. The combination of BROWN's Inverse Limit Theorem (cf. [3]) and near-homeomorphism and mapping-cylinder techniques as outlined in SCHORI & WEST [23] has produced important results. It would be very interesting to find techniques for approximating spaces "from the outside": if A is embedded as a closed subset in X and A is the intersection of a family $\{A_i\}_i$ of closed subsets of X, what conditions on the family $\{A_i\}_i$, e.g. maps $f_i: A_i \to A_{i+1}$ with certain properties, would warrant which conclusions on A?

PF 7) Let Y_1 and Y_2 be Q-factors. Is there a map $f: Y_1 \to Y_2$ such that $f \times id: Y_1 \times Q \to Y_2 \times Q$ is a near-homeomorphism? (By CHAPMAN's assertion, it is sufficient that f be cellular.) Are there integers n_1, n_2 and an f' such that $f' \times id_Q: (Y_1 \times I^{n_1}) \times Q \to (Y_2 \times I^{n_2}) \times Q$ is a near-homeomorphism?

PF 8) Under what conditions on X and Y is it true that if $X \times Y$ is a Q-manifold then $X \times Q$ is?

One can consider the following special cases:

a) X and Y compact and Y a cone (or contractible),

b) the answer is yes if X and Y are compact and contractible, since in this case both X and Y are Q-factors.

PF 9) Is every countable infinite product of topologically complete separable metric AR's with infinitely many non-compact factors homeomorphic to ℓ_2? Suppose each contains a closed copy of the real line.

PF 10) Let $\underline{m}$ be an infinite cardinal. Let D_m be a discrete space of cardinality $\underline{m}$. By an *$\underline{m}$-spider* $S^{\underline{m}}$ we mean the "fan" $(D_m \times [0,1])/(D_m \times \{0\})$ endowed with the "streetcar metric" $d((x,t),(y,\bar{s})) = t+s$ if $x \neq y$ and $d((x,t),(x,s)) = |t-s|$. An *$\underline{m}$-porcupine* $P^{\underline{m}}$ is the product of countably many copies of $S^{\underline{m}}$. Is $P^{\aleph_0} \cong \ell_2$? More generally, if m is infinite, then does there exist a Hilbert space H such that $P^{\underline{m}} \cong H$? WEST has shown that for any infinite $\underline{m}$ we have $S^{\underline{m}} \times H \cong P^{\underline{m}} \times H \cong H$ for some Hilbert space H.

PF 11) Let X be a topologically complete separable metric space.

a) Does $X \times (0,1) \cong s$ imply $X \cong s$?

b) Does $X \times Q \cong s$ imply $X \cong s$?

c) Does $X \times X \cong s$ imply $X \cong s$?

d) Does $X \times Y \cong s$ imply $X \cong s$, where Y is some factor of Q?

As noted elsewhere, shrinking wild arcs in Q presumably produce counterexamples in the compact (Q) cases comparable to a) and c). But since there are no wild compacta in s, the questions for s appear rather interesting.

II. HYPERSPACES, DECOMPOSITIONS AND SHAPE OF COMPACTA

II-H *Hyperspaces*

By 2^X, where X is metric, we denote the space of all non-empty compact subsets of X; by C(X) the space of all non-empty compact connected subsets, both endowed with the Hausdorff metric. In CURTIS & SCHORI [9], it is shown that $2^X \cong Q$ iff X is a non-degenerate Peano continuum and $C(X) \cong Q$ iff X is a non-degenerate Peano continuum without free arcs. (Note that $C(I) \cong I^2$.) As the first result in this direction, SCHORI & WEST [23] showed that $2^I \cong Q$. Next the case where X is a connected finite graph was solved and finally the general case was solved by approximating a Peano continuum X by finite graphs and employing inverse-limit and near-homeomorphism and mapping-cylinder techniques.

In an attempt to find subsets of hyperspaces which reflect the structure of the original space more closely we might consider the collection of "small" subsets. Note that (for X a Peano continuum) 2^X is contractible to the point $X \in 2^X$. By restricting the size of the subsets, we can hopefully avoid losing the homotopy structure of X.

H 1) Let X be a non-degenerate compact ANR. Does there exist a suitable notion of smallness such that the collection of "small" closed non-empty subsets of X is homeomorphic to $X \times Q$? Specifically, does there exist a metric (presumably convex) on X and an $\varepsilon > 0$ such that $2^X_\varepsilon =$ $= \{A \in 2^X | \text{diameter}(A) \leq \varepsilon\} \cong X \times Q$? In particular, is this true if X is a manifold? The answer is yes if X is an interval or $X \cong S^1$.

H 2) Let X be a non-degenerate compact contractible ANR. Does there exist a metric such that $2^X_\varepsilon \cong Q$ for all positive ε?

H 3) Let X be a non-degenerate Peano continuum. Does there exist a metric on X such that 2^X_ε is an ANR for all $\varepsilon > 0$? (This might be true for every convex metric.) Does there exist a metric on X such that $2^X_\varepsilon \cong 2^X_\varepsilon \times Q$? If, moreover, X is contractible, does there exist a metric such that $2^X_\varepsilon \cong Q$ for every $\varepsilon > 0$? It might be helpful to first consider the case where X is a compact connected complex.

H 4) Let K be a non-degenerate compact connected complex and K' a barycentric subdivision. Let $2^{st(K)} = \{A \in 2^K \mid A$ is contained in the closed star (with respect to K') of some vertex of K'$\}$. Is $2^{st(K)} \cong K \times Q$?[1)]

Below are some questions concerning s me naturally defined subsets of 2^X or $C(X)$.

H 5) Let X be a non-degenerate Peano continuum and let $A \subset 2^X$. Is $2^X(A) = \{B \in 2^X \mid A \cap B \neq \emptyset\}$ a Q-factor? If so, is $2^X(A) \cong Q$?

CURTIS & SCHORI have shown that the set of all closed sets containing a given proper non-empty closed subset of X is Q.

H 6) A closed subcollection $\mathcal{A}$ of 2^X, where X is a non-degenerate Peano continuum, is called a *growth-hyperspace* if for any $B \in 2^X$, $B \in \mathcal{A}$ whenever for some $A \in \mathcal{A}$, $B \supset A$ and every component of B meets A. KELLEY [17] showed that $\mathcal{A}$ is an AR. Is $\mathcal{A}$ a Q-factor? If so, under what condition is $\mathcal{A}$ homeomorphic to Q?

H 7) KROONENBERG [19] showed that $\{A \in 2^I \mid A$ zero-dimensional$\}$ and $\{A \in 2^I \mid A$ is a topological Cantor set$\}$ are topological pseudo-interiors for $2^I \cong Q$. It seems reasonable that the same is true for any connected finite graph instead of I.

H 8) Is the collection of finite subsets of I an fd cap set for 2^I? See also LS 9.

H 9) GEOGHEGAN & SUMMERHILL [12] (see section E) found finite-dimensional analogues for several infinite-dimensional notions and results, e.g. they defined (strong) Z_m-sets in E^n. Is $\{K \in 2^{I^n} \mid K$ is a (strong) Z_m-set$\}$ a pseudo-interior for 2^{I^n} for suitable m? And is $\{K \in C(I^n) \mid K$ is a (strong) Z_m-set$\}$ a pseudo-interior for $C(I^n)$? In KROONENBERG [19], it is shown that $\{K \in 2^Q \mid K$ is a Z-set$\}$ is a topological pseudo-interior for 2^Q and that $\{K \in C(Q) \mid K$ is a Z-set$\}$ is a pseudo-interior for $C(Q)$.

II-D *Decompositions*

The following problems deal with the images of Q under strictly cell-like mappings, i.e., mappings of Q onto compact metric spaces with all point-inverses being Z-sets of trivial shape. The basic problem is to identify conditions under which the image must be homeomorphic to Q. Since it is not assumed in general that the image space is a Q-manifold and there exist many examples of images of Q different from Q under maps where the point-inverses are of trivial shape but are not Z-sets (for example, Q/α for α a wild arc or a cut slice), the hypothesis of the point-inverses being Z-sets is a natural one.

Two results are known. By a simple modification of Eaton's argument that there exist "dog-bone" decompositions for each Euclidean space, it can be shown that there exists a "dog-bone" decomposition of Q, i.e., a map $f: Q \overset{\text{onto}}{\to} X$ such that $X \ncong Q$ and for each $x \in X$, $f^{-1}(x)$ is a point or a Z-set arc with the image of the union of the non-degenerate point-inverses under f being a topological Cantor set in Q. The union of the non-degenerate elements does not lie in a Z-set or even in a σ-Z-set. By an argument of ANDERSON, it can be shown that for any strictly cell-like mapping $f: Q \to X$ such that (1) the union of the non-degenerate point-inverses lies in a Z-set in Q, and (2) the image of the union of the non-degenerate point-inverses under f is finite-dimensional, then $X \cong Q$. As a corollary of this result and Chapman's characterization of the shape of compacta (cf. [8]) (sh X = sh Y iff $Q\backslash X \cong Q\backslash Y$ when X and Y are Z-sets in Q), it follows that if $f: X \to Y$ is a cell-like map of any compactum X onto a compactum Y with the image of the union of the non-degenerate point-inverses under f finite-dimensional, then sh X = sh Y.

Several specific open questions about decompositions of Q remain. In the statements below let f be a strictly cell-like map of Q onto a compactum X.

D 1) If the union of the non-degenerate point-inverses under f lies in a Z-set, is $X \cong Q$? (In other words, can we eliminate the finite-dimensional condition in ANDERSON's theorem above? If so, then all cell-like maps of compacta would preserve shape.)[3)]

D 2) If the union of the non-degenerate point-inverses lies in a countable union of Z-sets, is $X \cong Q$?

D 3) More specifically, if the set of non-degenerate point-inverses is countable, is $X \cong Q$? (This is known if the union of the non-degenerate point-inverses is a G_δ.)

D 4) If the union of the non-degenerate elements lies in s, is $X \cong Q$?

Problems like D 2 and D 4 are also interesting with the added restriction that the non-degenerate elements be arcs or n-cells or copies of Q.

D 5) Under what conditions is X a Q factor? We may assume that f be only cell-like, not strictly cell-like. And note that a cell-like map of a Q-factor induces a cell-like map of Q.

II-SC *Shape of compacta*

BORSUK introduced the concept of shape as a generalization of the concept of homotopy type and CHAPMAN's characterization cited in II-D above put the shape of compacta in the category of homeomorphism of complements. CHAPMAN also proved a finite-dimensional analogue of this theorem. The following problems deal with questions of shape that have come up in I-D topology.

SC 1) Suppose $A \subset Q$ is closed and has trivial shape. Is Q/A a Q factor? Remark: If A is a Z-set, then $Q/A \cong Q$. If A is a wild arc in Q (e.g. contains a Wong Cantor set), then $Q/A \not\cong Q$ (since $Q \setminus A$ is not 1-ULC) but it is known by CHAPMAN & BRYANT (unpublished) that for A an arc, $Q/A \times I \cong Q$, and it is almost certainly true that $Q/A \times Q/A \cong Q$.

SC 2) What characteristics of the embeddings distinguish AR's from other compacta of trivial shape when embedded as Z-sets in Q?

SC 3) If X and Y are compact Q-manifolds and $f: X \to A$ and $g: Y \to A$ are cellular mappings onto a compactum A, then is $X \cong Y$?

SC 4) By CHAPMAN's theorem above, two polyhedra P_1 and P_2 which are embedded as Z-sets in Q have the same homotopy type iff their complements in Q are homeomorphic. Can simple homotopy type be characterized in a similar way, e.g. by putting additional restrictions on the homeomorphisms which map $Q \setminus P_1$ onto $Q \setminus P_2$?

III. OTHER PROBLEMS ON Q AND Q-MANIFOLDS

III-QM *Hilbert cube manifolds*

The two major problems on Q-manifolds, triangulability and classification (by infinite simple homotopy type) have been solved by CHAPMAN (cf. [5],[6]). Many techniques for PL manifolds can be adapted for Q-manifolds and are usually simpler in the I-D case.

QM 1) Give a locally flat embedding of codimension 3 of one Q-manifold into another which does not have a normal bundle. Finite dimensional examples exist. In [7] CHAPMAN showed that an arbitrary-codimensional embedding of Q itself in a Q-manifold is flat, which result is false of course, even in codimension 1, when we replace Q by an arbitrary Q-manifold.

QM 2) Let X be a non-compact contractible Q-manifold. Does Q contain a Z-set K such that $Q\setminus K \cong X$? More generally, what are conditions on Q manifolds X and Y of the same homotopy type and with Y compact and X not such that Y contains a Z-set K so that $Y\setminus K \cong X$?

QM 3) Let X be a compact connected Q-manifold. Show that if $\pi_1(X) = 0$ and $h: X \to X$ is a homeomorphism homotopic to the identity, then h is ambient isotopic to the identity. Recently CHAPMAN found, using finite-dimensional results of HATCHER and WAGONER a counter-example for the non-simply connected case where $X = S^1 \times Q$.[4)]

QM 4) Let X be a compact Q-manifold, and $\mathcal{U}$ a finite open cover of X by contractible open subsets such that intersections of subcollections of $\mathcal{U}$ are either empty or contractible. Is X homeomorphic to $N(\mathcal{U}) \times Q$? Here $N(\mathcal{U})$ denotes the nerve of $\mathcal{U}$.

QM 5) (ENGULFING) Let X be a connected Q-manifold and let K and L be compact Z-sets in M. Suppose $L \subset U$, where U is open and $\pi_k(X,U) = 0$ for all $k \geq 0$. Does there exist an ambient isotopy $(h_t)_t: X \times I \to X$ such that $h_0 = id_X$, $h_t|_L = id_L$ for all t and $h_1(U) \supset K$? <u>Remark</u>: This is known to be true when $L = \emptyset$.

III-GA *Group actions*

It is known by WEST [30] that all compact metric groups can operate on ℓ_2 with an arbitrary closed set as the set of fixed points. It is a routine application of covering space theory to show that all fixed point free periodic homeomorphisms of prime period p on ℓ_2 are equivalent. It appears that a study of group actions on Q or Q-manifolds should be much more interesting. As this report goes to press, WEST has just shown that every two involutions of Q with a single fixed point are equivalent, i.e., are conjugates of each other. His result extends earlier partial results of WONG. Clearly, periodic actions on Q-factors can be used to induce various periodic actions on Q but it is not known whether such actions are, in fact, different from canonical ones.

GA 1) For what prime $p > 2$ are every two period p homeomorphisms of Q with exactly one fixed point equivalent? A similar question about actions of non-prime period can be posed. No counterexamples are yet known.[5)]

GA 2) Let $f: Q \to Q$ be a homeomorphism of Q onto itself with exactly one fixed point and with f of prime period p. Must f be trivial at x, i.e., are there arbitrarily small contractible neighborhoods of x which are invariant under f? WONG has shown that if f and g are period p homeomorphisms of Q with exactly one fixed point and are trivial at that point then f is equivalent to g.[5)]

The concept of triviality can be extended to a periodic homeomorphism fixed on an arbitrary contractible closed set.

If $m: Y \to Y$ is a map, let $\phi(m)$ denote the set of fixed points of m.

GA 3) Suppose $f,g: Q \times [0,1] \to Q \times [0,1]$ are periodic level-preserving homeomorphisms of period p having fixed point sets $\phi(f) = x \times [0,1] = \phi(g)$ for some point $x \in X$. Is f equivalent to g by means of a level-preserving homeomorphism $h: Q \times [0,1] \to Q \times [0,1]$?

GA 4) What if we assume in addition that both f and g are trivial at $x \times [0,1]$?

If the above questions have affirmative answers, we may consider replacing $[0,1]$ by $[0,1]^n$ or a polyhedron.

GA 5) Let K be a Z-set in Q which is homeomorphic to $[0,1]^n$. Suppose $f,g\colon Q \to Q$ are period p homeomorphisms such that $\phi(f) = K = \phi(g)$ and both f and g are trivial at K. Is f equivalent to g?

In the following let M denote a Q-manifold and let K denote a subset of M which is either empty or consists of a single point. We would like to know when two Z_p-actions on M are equivalent. In particular we ask:

GA 6) Suppose $f,g\colon M \to M$ are period p homeomorphisms satisfying (1) $\phi(f) = K = \phi(g)$, (2) both f and g are trivial at K, (3) f is properly homotopic to g. Is f equivalent to g?[6)]

III-CMP *Compactifications*

Consider the general problem: under what conditions a compact space X, which contains an open dense subset Y which is a Q-manifold, is itself either a Q-manifold or a Q-manifold factor. Cases of special interest are those where X is a mapping cylinder and where X\Y is an ANR and a Z-set in X (the general problem needs some such strong conditions). In this section a closed subset A of X is a Z-set in X if for all $\varepsilon > 0$ there is a map $f\colon X \to X\backslash A$ with $d(f,id_X) < \varepsilon$. In WEST [28] it is shown that if, moreover, X and X\Y are Q-factors and if X\Y is a Z-set in X, then $X \cong Q$. In the mapping cylinder case West is fairly positive that $M_f \cong Q$ if f is a fine homotopy equivalence of Q onto an AR, and that M_f is a Q-manifold if f is a fine homotopy equivalence from a Q-manifold onto an ANR. See also PF 3 and PF 5.

As to the question when X is a Q-factor we have the mapping cylinder theorem (cf. [27]) which says that the mapping cylinder of a map between Q-factors is a Q-factor.

CMP 1) Let X be a compact AR and $A \subset X$ be a Z-set in X and an AR. Suppose X\A is homeomorphic to $Q \times [0,1)$. Is $X \cong Q$ or is X a Q-factor?

CMP 2) CHAPMAN showed that if X is a non-compact Q-manifold which is 1-LC at infinity and which has finitely generated homology $H_*(X)$ then a compactum can be added to X to obtain a compact Q-manifold. When can this compactum be prescribed to be a compact polyhedron? See also ANR 3B.

Another general question one can ask is: when is the one-point compactification of a Q-manifold or Q-manifold factor again a Q-manifold factor?

CMP 3) If K is a finite-dimensional one-ended (i.e., any compact subset is contained in a larger compact subset which has a connected complement) locally finite simplicial complex, find conditions under which the one-point compactification of K is a Q-manifold factor.

CMP 4) Dropping the finite-dimensionality restriction in CMP 3 and using CHAPMAN's triangulation theorem (cf. [5]) we are dealing with the question as to when the one-point compactification of an arbitrary one-ended Q-manifold is a Q-manifold factor.

CMP 5) For which one-ended $K(Z_2,1)$ Q-manifolds M (for a definition of $K(Z_2,1)$, see [24], p.424) is the one-point compactification of M a Q-factor, if it is an AR at all? Let M be $(Q\setminus\{0\})/\alpha$, the orbit space of the involution α which maps x onto -x. Then Q/α is the one-point compactification of M; W. BARIT and R.M. SCHORI have observed that Q/α is a Q-factor. Moreover, it is easily seen that M is a $K(Z_2,1)$ Q-manifold which is one-ended. Not all one-ended $K(Z_2,1)$ spaces have the same proper homotopy type, though.

III-TD *Topological dynamics*

There has so far been practically no study of flows on Hilbert cube manifolds but many natural questions arise. Since $S^1 \times Q$ is homeomorphic to $([0,1] \times Q)/R$ for any homeomorphic identification R of $\{0\} \times Q$ with $\{1\} \times Q$, any discrete flow on Q can be canonically imbedded in a continuous flow on $S^1 \times Q$. Questions of the existence of minimal sets and of various types of flows such as expansive flows have not yet been studied beyond fairly obvious examples. It is not hard to show that Q itself admits a regularly almost periodic homeomorphism which is not periodic. Also as a countable infinite product of itself, Q admits a shift homeomorphism.

We list two special problems as representative of the much wider class of open problems.

TD 1) Is $S^1 \times Q$ a minimal set, i.e., does $S^1 \times Q$ admit a discrete flow with all orbits being dense?

TD 2) Does Q admit an expansive flow, i.e., is there a homeomorphism

$h: Q \overset{onto}{\to} Q$ and a number $\varepsilon > 0$ such that for each $(x,y) \in Q \times Q$, $x \neq y$, there is an n, $-\infty < n < \infty$, for which $d(f^n(x), f^n(y)) > \varepsilon$?

III-MSQ *Miscellaneous*

Characterization of Q (MSQ 1-1")

MSQ 1) Are the one-point set and Q the only homogeneous contractible metrizable compacta?

MSQ 1') Let X be compact metric, homogeneous and homeomorphic to its own cone K(X). Is X homeomorphic to Q?

Note: By a theorem of SCHORI [22], $K(Y) \times I \cong KK(Y)$ for any compact Hausdorff space Y. Therefore $X \cong X \times I$. If we can prove that the projection map $p: X \times I \to X$ is either tiltable (see chapter I) or a near-homeomorphism, then by an inverse-limit argument it follows that $X \times Q \cong X$. Furthermore, DE GROOT observed that X is locally homogeneous, i.e., every point $x \in X$ has arbitrarily small neighborhoods O such that for any two points $y,z \in O$, y can be mapped onto z by an autohomeomorphism of X that is the identity outside O; and KROONENBERG observed that X is n-point order-preserving homogeneous for any n. A possible counterexample might be obtained in the following way: SCHORI showed that $K(Y) \times Q$ is homeomorphic to its own cone for every compact metric space Y. However, homogeneity and local contractibility at the cone point rule out spaces $K(Y) \times Q$ for Y a space like the Cantor set or the universal curve.

MSQ 1") We can pose a problem similar to MSQ 1' about ℓ_2. If X is homogeneous, complete metric and not locally compact and $X \cong K(X)$ (where an appropriate metric definition of cone is used), then is $X \cong \ell_2$?

Unions of Hilbert cubes and Q-factors (MSQ 2-3)

WEST [29] showed that the union of two Hilbert cube factors whose intersection is a Hilbert cube factor must be a Hilbert cube factor. An analogous statement might be true for Hilbert cubes.

MSQ 2a) Suppose Q_1, Q_2 and $Q_1 \cap Q_2$ are all homeomorphic to Q. Is $Q_1 \cup Q_2$ homeomorphic to Q? This problem has been open for several years and has been attacked by several people.

We have the following partial result by WONG & KROONENBERG [32]: if we are in the situation of MSQ 2a and moreover we know that $Q_1 \cap Q_2$ is a Z-set in Q_1 and contains an fd cap set which is a σ-Z-set in Q_2, then $Q_1 \cup Q_2 \cong Q$. This is proved by first showing that the fd cap set can be replaced by a cap set and next applying an inverse-limit argument.

MSQ 2b) Suppose $A \subset Q$ and $A \cong Q$. Does A contain an fd cap set which is a σ-Z-set in Q? If so, then $Q_1 \cup Q_2$ is homeomorphic to Q if Q_1, Q_2 and $Q_1 \cap Q_2$ are also homeomorphic to Q and if moreover $Q_1 \cap Q_2$ is a Z-set in Q_1. KROONENBERG [20] proved that every closed finite-dimensional subset of Q which has a 1-ULC complement and in particular every closed finite-dimensional subset which has deficiency 1, is a Z-set in Q. Therefore the answer to MSQ 2b is yes if A has deficiency 1.

MSQ 2c) Suppose Q_1, Q_2 and $Q_1 \cap Q_2$ are all homeomorphic to Q, and suppose $Q_1 \cap Q_2$ contains an fd cap set which is a σ-Z-set both in Q_1 and in Q_2. Is $Q_1 \cup Q_2$ homeomorphic to Q?

MSQ 2d) Does every sub-Hilbert cube A in Q contain an n-cell or copy of Q which is a Z-set in Q? The result is known only in dimension 1: using the characterization of finite-dimensional Z-sets cited under MSQ 2b, KROONENBERG observed that the collection of arcs which are Z-sets both in A and in Q is a dense G_δ-subset in the collection A^I of all paths in A.

MSQ 3) Under what conditions is $X = Y \cup W$ a Q-manifold when both Y and W are Q-manifolds? What if both Y and W are Hilbert cubes? It is not a necessary condition that the intersection is a Q-manifold (e.g. let γ be a wild arc in Q, then $Y = ([-1,0] \times Q)/(\{0\} \times \gamma)$ and $W = ([0,1] \times Q)/(\{0\} \times \gamma)$ are Hilbert cubes whose union is a Hilbert cube but whose intersection is not a Hilbert cube), but it will be very hard to prove anything without such a condition.

MSQ 4) Does every arc, or more generally every n-cell in Q which is not a Z-set contain a topological Cantor set which is not a Z-set? If there is a counterexample for an arc then there exists an arc in Q whose 0-dimensional subsets are exactly its Z-set subsets. It should be noted that any cut-slice of Q, e.g. $\{(x_i) \in Q | x_1 = \frac{1}{2}\}$ is a sub-cube of Q all of whose closed finite-dimensional subsets are Z-sets in Q. Therefore the question is false for arbitrary non-Z-sets.

IV. PROBLEMS ON LINEAR SPACES AND MANIFOLDS

IV-HS *Spaces of homeomorphisms and mappings*

Let M be a compact manifold; then H(M) denotes the space of homeomorphisms on M and $H_\partial(M)$ denotes the subspace of H(M) consisting of those h which are the identity on the boundary ∂M (in case $\partial M = \emptyset$, $H_\partial(M) = H(M)$). It is known (ANDERSON [1]) and easy to show that the space $H_\partial(I)$ is homeomorphic to s (or ℓ_2). Recently much work has been done on spaces of homeomorphisms on n-manifolds ($n > 1$). Currently the main research efforts are concentrated on finite-dimensional, and especially on combinatorial manifolds and among them on I^n in particular. For a manifold with boundary we mainly consider $H_\partial(M)$, because this space is somewhat more accessible than H(M).

The two major steps done thus far are:

i) (GEOGHEGAN). For every manifold M of finite positive dimension, H(M) has an ℓ_2-factor, i.e., $H(M) \times \ell_2 \cong H(M)$. The same is true for $H_\partial(M)$. These are special cases of GEOGHEGAN [10], Theorem 2.7.

ii) (TORUŃCZYK [26], Theorem 4.2). For every ANR X, $X \times F$ is an F-manifold for some linear space F of the same density-character as X. For X a separable metric ANR he has (Theorem 4.5):
   a) If X is complete then $X \times \ell_2$ is an ℓ_2-manifold.
   b) If X is the countable union of closed compact sets then $X \times \ell_2 \times \ell_2^f$ is an $\ell_2 \times \ell_2^f$-manifold.
   c) If X is the countable union of locally compact locally finite-dimensional sets then $X \times \ell_2^f$ is an ℓ_2^f-manifold.
   d) If X is σ-compact then $X \times Q \times \ell_2^f$ is a $Q \times \ell_2^f$-manifold.

   In all cases, the manifold is embeddable as an open subset in the model space.

Combining i) and ii) a), in order to show that H(M) or $H_\partial(M)$ is an ℓ_2-manifold we merely have to show that it is an ANR, since it is easily seen to be topologically complete. LUKE & MASON [21] showed that $H_\partial(M)$ is an

ANR if M is a compact 2-manifold. See section ANR for possible ways of proving that a space is an ANR, especially problem ANR 3.

In view of the methods suggested there and also because of their independent interest, we can study spaces of special kinds of homeomorphisms. Consider PLH(M), the space of piecewise-linear autohomeomorphisms of a combinatorial manifold M, and $PLH_\partial(M)$, the space of all $h \in PLH(M)$ which are the identity on ∂M. It is not known in general when $PLH_\partial(M)$ is dense in $H_\partial(M)$ or when the inclusion is a homotopy equivalence. As a consequence of the effort of several authors, finally explicitly stated by KEESLING & WILSON [16], it is proved that PLH(M) is an ℓ_2^f-manifold. The same is true for $\overline{PLH}(M)$, the set of PL maps $f: M \to M$ which can be approximated by PL homeomorphisms on M (see HAVER [15] for references and a discussion of the material involved). Another subspace of H(M) which conceivably could play the role of a dense subspace in H(M) in problems ANR 2 and 3 is LIP(M), the set of Lipschitz-homeomorphisms in H(M), which is easily seen to be σ-compact. Virtually no work is done yet in this direction. For a discussion of Lipschitz-homeomorphisms, see section L-U.

HS 1) Is $H_\partial(M)$ an ANR for M an n-manifold ($n > 2$) or a Q-manifold? As pointed out above, this would imply that $H_\partial(M)$ is an ℓ_2-manifold. See also ANR 2,3. Recall that ČERNAVSKII [4] and KIRBY & EDWARDS have shown that $H_\partial(M)$ is locally contractible for M a compact n-manifold. For M = Q, WONG's techniques [31] show that H(Q) is contractible and locally contractible, as observed by RENZ and others.

HS 2) For which manifolds M is $H_\partial(M)\backslash PLH_\partial(M)$ homotopy-negligible in every open subset of $H_\partial(M)$? It is reported that SIEBENMANN has shown that the answer is yes for $M = I^n$ and $n \neq 4$. KIRBY & SIEBENMANN have shown that $H(S^2 \times S^3)$ has a component containing no PL homeomorphisms (see KIRBY [18]). So we might better ask the same question about the components of $H_\partial(M)$ and $PLH_\partial(M)$ containing id_M. Together with a positive answer to ANR 3, and using HAVER's result cited under ii) in section ANR, this would show that the homeomorphism space under consideration would be an ℓ_2-manifold. Furthermore we can ask similar questions about H(M) and PLH(M).

HS 3) Is $H_\partial(M)\backslash LIP_\partial(M)$ homotopy-negligible in every open subset of $H_\partial(M)$? For a discussion, see section L-U and the beginning of this section.

HS 4) Let K be a closed subset of $H_\partial(I^n)$ such that for every integer m, every $\varepsilon > 0$ and every map $g: I^m \to H_\partial(I^n)$ there exists a map $h: I^m \to H_\partial(I^n)\setminus K$ such that $d(h,g) < \varepsilon$. Is K a Z-set in $H_\partial(I^n)$, i.e., are there arbitrarily small maps $f: H_\partial(I^n) \to H_\partial(I^n)\setminus K$? According to MASON, this would imply that $H_\partial(I^n)$ is homeomorphic to ℓ_2.

HS 5) Let $\overline{H(M)}$ denote the closure of H(M) in the space of mappings on a compact manifold M.

a) Can the elements of $\overline{H(M)}$ be canonically approximated by homeomorphisms, or, more formally, does there exist for every $\varepsilon > 0$ a map $h: \overline{H(M)} \to H(M)$ such that $d(h,id) < \varepsilon$?

b) Is $\overline{H(M)}$ an ANR, and hence an ℓ_2-manifold? According to HAVER, this would imply that H(M) is an ℓ_2-manifold. He has shown that $\overline{H(M)}$ is homogeneous.

HS 6) Compute homotopy groups of H(M). This is done for 2-manifolds by M.-E. HAMSTROM, but for higher-dimensional manifolds, there are virtually no known results.

For mapping spaces we have the following results: for two metric spaces X and Y, where X is compact, let C(X,Y) be the space of continuous functions from X to Y. If moreover both are polyhedra, let PL(X,Y) be the space of piecewise-linear maps from X onto Y.

THEOREM (GEOGHEGAN, [10],[11]). *Let* K *and* L *be two simplicial complexes,* K *finite and* L *countable and locally finite. Then* $(C(|K|,|L|),PL(|K|,|L|))$ *is an* (ℓ_2,ℓ_2^f)*-manifold pair, provided* $|K|$ *and all components of* $|L|$ *are positive-dimensional.*

A relative version of this theorem is also valid. In particular, $C(|K|,|L|)$ is an ℓ_2-manifold and $PL(|K|,|L|)$ is an ℓ_2^f-manifold.

HS 7) Is $C(X,|L|)$ an ℓ_2-manifold, where X is a non-discrete or positive-dimensional compact metric space and $|L|$ a countable locally finite polyhedron, all of whose components are positive-dimensional?

Note. Write X as an inverse limit of compact polyhedra

$$|X_0| \leftarrow |X_1| \leftarrow |X_2| \cdots$$

and apply the contravariant functor $C(-,|L|)$ to this sequence. Then we get

$$C(|X_0|,|L|) \to C(|X_1|,|L|) \to C(|X_2|,|L|) \to \cdots$$

and it is not difficult to show that $C(|X|,|L|)$ is homeomorphic to $\varinjlim C(|X_k|,|L|)$. So the problem is reduced to showing that this direct limit is an ℓ_2-manifold. However, direct limits are not easy to work with.

HS 8) Under what usable conditions is a direct limit of ℓ_2-manifolds an ℓ_2-manifold?

HS 9) Let M be a compact metric n-manifold. Is the space $RE(M) = \{f: M \to M \mid f \text{ is a retraction}\}$ an ℓ_2-manifold?

IV-ANR *Characterization of ANR's*

The result of TORUŃCZYK (cf. [26], Theorem 4.2), that ANR's are factors of a linear space of the same density character (see section HS) has given new significance to the question of finding further characterizations of ANR's, especially in connection with problems on homeomorphism spaces. In view of those applications, our interest is not limited to the compact case, but extends to arbitrary separable metric ANR's.

For closure properties of the class of ANR's the reader is referred to [2], Chapters IV and V. We mention the following sufficient conditions for a space to be an ANR:

i) If X is compact metric, finite-dimensional and locally contractible (or only LC^n, where $n = \dim(X)$), then X is an ANR.

ii) (HAVER [14]). If X is a locally contractible metric space that can be written as a countable union of finite-dimensional compacta then X is an ANR.

iii) (HANNER [13]; DOWKER). A metric space X is an ANR iff for every open cover $\mathcal{U}$ of X there exists a locally finite polyhedron P that $\mathcal{U}$-dominates X. (P $\mathcal{U}$-dominates X if there exist maps $f: X \to P$ and $g: P \to X$ and a homotopy $H: X \times I \to X$ such that $H_0 = id_X$, $H_1 = g \circ F$ and for all $x \in X$ $H(\{x\} \times I)$ is contained in some $U \in \mathcal{U}$).

ANR 1) Find new useful characterizations of ANR's.

In view of applications to homeomorphism spaces, we are especially interested in the following situation:

ANR 2) Let (X,X_0) be a pair of metric spaces where X_0 is a dense subset of X and an ANR. Find conditions on (X,X_0) under which X is an ANR.

TORUŃCZYK made the following suggestion:

ANR 3) Let X be LC^∞ or otherwise locally contractible and let $X_0 \subset X$ be an ANR such that $X \setminus X_0$ is homotopy-negligible in every open subset of X (a subset K of a space Y is homotopy-negligible in Y if the inclusion $Y \setminus K \subset Y$ is a homotopy equivalence). Is X an ANR? What if

A) X is a completely metrizable topological group and X_0 is an ℓ_2-manifold and/or a topological group, or

B) X is compact and X_0 is a Q-manifold? This general problem is also considered under section CMP on compactifications and in PF 3.

Remark. Taking products with an appropriate normed linear space (see the introduction to section HS under ii) we may assume in most cases that X_0 is a manifold modelled on such a space. TORUŃCZYK claims that every subset of X which is an ANR is contained in a G_δ which is also an ANR. Thus if X is complete then we can assume that X_0 is an ℓ_2-manifold.

Applications. a) Let Y be a separable metric linear space and let Y_0 be the linear hull of a countable dense subset. By ii) Y_0 is an ANR and it is easily seen that $Y \setminus Y_0$ is homotopy-negligible in Y. Therefore a positive answer to ANR 3 would imply that every separable metric linear space is an ANR (it is known that every locally convex linear metric space is an ANR).

b) Let M_f be the mapping cyliner of a finite homotopy equivalence $f: Q \overset{onto}{\to} Y$. If we set $X = M_f$ and $X_0 = M_f \setminus Y$ then we are in case ANR 3B. Note that in PF 3 we assume that Y is an AR or ANR. A positive answer to ANR 3B would give us that X and hence Y is an AR. What if f is only assumed cellular?

c) Let $X = H_\partial(I^n)$ and $X_0 = PLH_\partial(I^n)$ where $n \neq 4$ and $H_\partial(I^n)$ and $PLH_\partial(I^n)$ are defined as in section HS. Applying the remark we can find a subset X_0 such that $PLH_\partial(I^n) \subset X_0$ and $X_0 \times \ell_2$ is an ℓ_2-manifold. Moreover, TORUŃCZYK informed the authors that SIEBENMANN had claimed that $H_\partial(I^n) \setminus PLH_\partial(I^n)$ is strongly homotopy negligible in I^n if $n \neq 4$. Therefore a positive answer to ANR 3A would show that $H(I^n)$ is an ANR and therefore an ℓ_2-manifold.

Remark. TORUŃCZYK claims that if X is an ANR and X_0 is a subset of X such that $X \setminus X_0$ is homotopy-negligible in every open subset of X then X_0 is an ANR.

IV-LS *Linear spaces*

In a sense, infinite-dimensional topology originated with problems posed by FRÉCHET and by BANACH concerning the topological as distinct from the linear and topological structure of linear spaces. While almost all of the originally posed problems have been solved, several intriguing open questions exist. BESSAGA, PEŁCZYNSKI and TORUŃCZYK are probably the best sources concerning such problems. We first list problems concerning separable spaces.

LS 1) Is every I-D separable normed space homeomorphic to some pre-Hilbert space, i.e., to a linear subspace (not necessarily closed) of a Hilbert space?

LS 2) Let X be an I-D separable pre-Hilbert space. Is $X \times R \cong X$? $X \times X \cong X$? $X_f^\omega \cong X$ or $X^\omega \cong X$? The answers are probably negative for the added condition of uniform homeomorphisms.

LS 3) If a σ-compact separable normed space contains a topological copy of Q, is it homeomorphic to $\{x \in \ell_2 \mid \sum i^2 \cdot x_i^2 < \infty\}$?

LS 4) Identify classes of subsets of ℓ_2 which are all homeomorphic to Q. The result should be more general than the Keller characterization of all I-D compact convex subsets of ℓ_2 as homeomorphic to Q. For example, as a starter, is the union of two arbitrary Keller cubes which intersect in a cube homeomorphic to Q? See also MSQ 2c. It is easy to construct an fd cap set in the intersection which is a σ-Z-set in both cubes.

LS 5) Let E be a locally convex linear metric space and let X be a non-complete retract of E. Is $X \times E^\omega \cong E^\omega$? It is known by TORUŃCZYK that $X \times E^\omega \times \ell_2^f \cong E^\omega \times \ell_2^f$ and that if X is complete, then $X \times E^\omega \cong E^\omega$.

Some problems on non-separable spaces are the following.

LS 6) Let $\{X_n\}_{n\geq 1}$ be Banach spaces of the same density character $\underline{m}$, $\underline{m} > \aleph_0$. Is $\prod_{n\geq 1} X_n$ homeomorphic to a Hilbert space?

LS 7) Is every I-D Banach space homeomorphic to some Hilbert space?

LS 8) For every I-D Banach space E is $E \cong E^{\omega}$? (The result is known for Hilbert spaces.) A positive answer to this question would extend the domain of many theorems on non-separable spaces and manifolds which suppose $E \cong E^{\omega}$.

LS 9) Prove or give a counterexample. Let K be a countable simplicial complex, let $|K|$ be its geometric realization (in the sense of SPANIER [24], Chapter III), and for any metric d on $|K|$ denote the resulting metric space by $|K|_d$. Assume that the topology of $|K|_d$ induces the usual topology on all simplexes of K and that the "open" star of every point in $|K|_d$ is an open set. Then $|K|_d$ is an ℓ_2^f-manifold if and only if every simplex is a Z-set.

Remark: If there is a counterexample one would wish to know what further hypotheses on d are necessary.

LS 10) The most general theorems concerning the classification of C^{∞} Banach (separable) manifolds seem to be in ELWORTHY's paper [Comp. Math., 24 (1972) 175-226]. Can one give an adequate treatment of C^{∞}-manifolds, perhaps restricting the permissible models more than ELWORTHY does, based on the methods of C^{∞} finite-dimensional topology and C^0 infinite-dimensional topology? GEOGHEGAN and RIVAUD can prove by such methods that open subsets of ℓ_2 are ℓ_2-stable in the C^{∞} sense. They hope to do more. They make use of the property of S^1, the unit "sphere" of ℓ_2 (which is diffeomorphic to ℓ_2), that the topology inherited from ℓ_2 coincides with the product topology, i.e., a sequence of points in S^1 converges iff it converges coordinatewise.

IV- L-U *Lipschitz and uniformly continuous homeomorphisms*

There has been almost no recent organized successful study of Lipschitz or uniformly continuous homeomorphisms between linear spaces or of linear spaces onto subsets of themselves. The questions L-U 4 to L-U 10 listed below appear naturally interesting in themselves, but it is difficult to assess the eventual possibilities of the study implicitly proposed. The problems L-U 1-3 are of a different sort since they propose a possible use of Lipschitz homeomorphisms in studying the spaces of all homeomorphisms of a manifold.

Let X,Y be metric spaces. A map f of X into Y is *Lipschitz* if there is a $K > 0$ such that $d(f(x),f(y)) \leq K \cdot d(x,y)$, for all x,y. We say that f is a *Lipschitz homeomorphism* or *isomorphism* of X onto Y if f is 1-1, onto and both f and f^{-1} are Lipschitz maps.

A map $f: X \to Y$ is *uniformly continuous* if for each $\varepsilon > 0$ there is a $\delta > 0$ such that $d(x,y) < \delta$ implies $d(f(x),f(y)) < \varepsilon$. A homeomorphism f is a *uniform homeomorphism* if both f and f^{-1} are uniformly continuous.

F denotes a topological vector space. Let $LIP(M) = \{f \in H(M)$: f is Lipschitz$\}$ for a manifold with suitable metric, e.g. combinatorial.

L-U 1) Is $LIP_\partial(I^n)$ a cap set in $H_\partial(I^n)$?

L-U 2) Does there exist, for each $\varepsilon > 0$, a map $f: H_\partial(I^n) \to LIP_\partial(I^n)$ such that $d(f,Id) < \varepsilon$?

The same problems can be posed for LIP(M) or for the orientation preserving homeomorphisms of LIP(M) if the manifold M has a suitable metric.

L-U 3) Is LIP(M) an ANR (or even locally contractible)?

L-U 4) Let K_1, K_2 be homeomorphic Z-sets in F. For a given homeomorphism h of K_1 onto K_2, does there exist a homeomorphism u of F onto itself such that the induced map $h_* = uhu^{-1}$ of $u(K_1)$ onto $u(K_2)$ is a Lipschitz isomorphism? WONG has shown that the answer is yes when $F = \ell_p$ for $1 \leq p < \infty$.

L-U 5) Let K_1, K_2 be Z-sets in ℓ_2 and let f be a Lipschitz isomorphism of K_1 onto K_2. Can f be extended to a Lipschitz isomorphism of ℓ_2 onto itself? This is known to be true when K_1 is compact.

L-U 6) Does a homeomorphism h between two compact subsets of F always extend to a uniform homeomorphism H of F onto itself?

L-U 7) a) If two Banach spaces are uniformly homeomorphic, are they then isomorphic? (True if one is a Hilbert space.)

b) Is the following subgroup G of the additive group of $L_2[0,1]$ uniformly homeomorphic to $L_2[0,1]$? G consists of all L_2-functions which have integers as values for almost all x in [0,1].

L-U 8) Is every separable metric space uniformly homeomorphic to some subset of c_0 (where c_0 is the space of sequences convergent to zero with the supremum norm)?

L-U 9) Are the unit balls in c_0 and $C[0,1]$ uniformly homeomorphic?

L-U 10) What about the concept of "boundary" in uniform topology?

a) Does there exist a uniform homeomorphism of the closed unit ball in ℓ_2 onto itself such that 0 is mapped to a point on the boundary?

b) Is a closed half-space of ℓ_2 uniformly homeomorphic to ℓ_2?

c) Is the closed unit ball in ℓ_2 uniformly homeomorphic to the set $\{x \mid r_1 \leq \|x\| \leq r_2\}$, $r_2 > r_1$?

IV-M ℓ_2-*manifolds*

Except for work on the space of homeomorphisms problem there has been little recent activity on manifolds modelled on ℓ_2 or other linear spaces. Basic characterization and representation theorems were obtained several years ago except in the general non-separable Banach space category which depends on the problem as to whether $E = E^{\omega}$ (see LS 8). The following questions are open. The questions in M 2 are related to various ANR problems. Questions concerning ℓ_2-manifolds can obviously be generalized to manifolds modelled on other linear spaces.

M 1) For M a separable ℓ_2-manifold, can every homeomorphism of M onto itself be approximated by diffeomorphisms? BURGHELEA and HENDERSON have proved that such homeomorphisms are isotopic to diffeomorphisms.

M 2) Let X be a topologically complete separable metric space.

(i) If X is an ANR, $Y \subset X$ is dense in X, and Y is an ℓ_2-manifold, under what conditions can we conclude that X is an ℓ_2-manifold?

(ii) If X is an ANR, Y is an ℓ_2-manifold, and Y is open and dense in X, under what conditions can we conclude that X is an ℓ_2-manifold?

(iii) Let M be an ℓ_2-manifold, and suppose that $X \subset M$ is the closure of an open set Y. Under what conditions can we conclude that X is an ℓ_2-manifold?

HENDERSON has observed relative to (i), for example, that if Z-sets are strongly negligible in X and if $X \backslash Y$ is a countable union of

Z-sets, then $X \cong Y$. However, it seems difficult to verify these conditions in many naturally arising cases.

In the following three problems we assume K and M to be ℓ_2-manifolds and K to be a closed subset of M. Then K is said to have *local deficiency* n *at a point* p if there exist an open set U with $p \in U$ and a homeomorphism h of $(-1,1)^n \times \ell_2$ onto U such that $h(\{0\} \times \ell_2) = K \cap U$. If K has local deficiency n at every point of K, then we say that K has local deficiency n. Let $R \subset K$ be such that (a) R consists of a single point, (b) R is compact, or (c) R is a Z-set in M and a Z-set in K.

M 3) If K has local deficiency 1 at every point of $K \backslash R$, does K have local deficiency 1 for cases (a), (b) and (c) above?

M 4) For $n > 1$, under what conditions does local deficiency n at every point of $K \backslash R$ imply that K has local deficiency n for cases (a), (b) and (c) above? KUIPER has given examples for $n = 2$ where R is a single point, an arbitrary n-cell, or a copy of ℓ_2, such that K does not have local deficiency 2. The examples involve knots. For $n > 2$ no examples are known.

M 5) For $n > 1$, does local deficiency n imply the existence of a neighborhood U of K such that U is the total space of a fibre bundle over K with fibre $(-1,1)^n$?

M 6) Let M and K be ℓ_2-manifolds with $K \subset M$ and K a Z-set in M. Then K may be considered as a "boundary" of M, i.e., for any $p \in K$ there exists an open set U in M with $p \in U$ and a homeomorphism h of U onto $\ell_2 \times (0,1]$ such that $h(K \cap U) = \ell_2 \times \{1\}$. Under what conditions on the pair (M,K) does there exist a homeomorphism h of M into ℓ_2 such that the topological boundary of h(M) in ℓ_2 is h(K)? It is known that if the identity map of K into M induces a homotopy equivalence of K and M, then the embedding is possible.

M 7) Let A be a closed subset of the ℓ_2-manifold M such that for each closed $B \subset A$, $M \backslash B \cong M$. Must A be a Z-set in M?

M 8) Let $\xi: E \to B$ be a fibre bundle over a paracompact space B with fibre F an ℓ_2-manifold. Suppose K is a closed subset of E such that $K \cap \xi^{-1}(b)$ is a Z-set in each $\xi^{-1}(b)$. Is there a fibre-preserving homeomorphism of $E\backslash K$ onto E?

M 9) Is a locally contractible complete separable metric topological group which is not locally compact an ℓ_2-manifold?

M 10) If G is a separable metric topological group which is the countable union of compact finite-dimensional subsets and not locally compact, then is G an ℓ_2^f-manifold?

M 11) Classify the connected ℓ_2-manifolds which support topological group structures. Are these the spaces of trivial loops of locally finite polyhedra?

Note. No Q-manifold supports a topological group structure.

IV-CSQ *Compactifying* s *as the Hilbert cube*

Problems CSQ 1-4 below are concerned with compactifications of s as Q. These questions arose several years ago but have not been studied recently.

CSQ 1) Let $s \subset N \subset Q$. What are necessary and sufficient conditions that $s \cong N$? It is obvious that N must be a G_δ-subset of Q and it is known that if $Q\backslash N$ contains an fd cap-set, then $N \cong s$. Is this condition necessary? For the existence of a homeomorphism $h: Q \to Q$ with $h(s) = N$, it is necessary and sufficient that N be a G_δ-subset of Q and that $Q\backslash N$ contain a cap-set.

CSQ 2) In CSQ 1 assume that $Q\backslash N$ is a dense (in Q) countable union of disjoint finite-dimensional cubes (or disjoint Hilbert cubes) σ_i with σ_i a cube in an endslice and slightly smaller than the endslice. Such an N can have the property (or must have the property) that every compact subset of N is a Z-set in N. If it could be shown that every Z-set in N is strongly negligible in N, then $N \cong s$ and we would have an example showing that $Q\backslash N$ need not contain an fd cap-set.

CSQ 3) Let f be a homeomorphism of s onto a dense subset of Q. Is there a map g of Q onto Q such that $g|s$ is a homeomorphism of s onto f(s)? (This is known true for $Q\backslash f(s) \cong s_f$). If $Q\backslash f(s)$ is homogeneous, what other conditions guarantee that $Q\backslash f(s)$ is homeomorphic to $Q\backslash s$ or s_f?

CSQ 4) If h is a homeomorphism of s onto itself, is there a homeomorphism $g: s \to s$ such that ghg^{-1} can be extended to a homeomorphism of Q? WONG has shown that if K is a Z-set in s and h is a homeomorphism of K onto K, then there is a homeomorphism $g: s \to s$ such that $ghg^{-1}|g(K)$ can be extended to a homeomorphism of Q which takes s onto itself.

IV-E *I-D topology in Euclidean spaces*

In GEOGHEGAN & SUMMERHILL [12] several I-D concepts are adapted for Euclidean spaces. They gave an axiomatization for pseudo-boundaries relative to a family of subsets of a complete metric space X. Let, for U an open subset of X and $\varepsilon: U \to \mathbb{R}^+$ a continuous function, $V_U(\varepsilon)$ denote the collection of autohomeomorphisms h of X which are the identity outside U and such that for all $x \in U$, $d(x,h(x)) < \varepsilon(x)$. A subset B of X is a pseudo-boundary for a family $\mathcal{S}$ of subsets of X if $B \in \mathcal{S}$ and B possesses the following absorption property: for every $S \in \mathcal{S}$, every open $U \subset X$ and $\varepsilon: U \to R^+$ there exists an $h \in V_U(\varepsilon)$ such that $h(S \cap U) \subset B \cap U$. Notice that this differs from our definition of cap set. Under certain conditions on $\mathcal{S}$, pseudo-boundaries are topologically invariant, i.e., if h is an autohomeomorphism on X then h(B) is a pseudo-boundary if B is. Moreover, pseudo-boundaries are unique in the following strong sense: suppose B and B' are pseudo-boundaries for $\mathcal{S}$, then for every open $U \subset X$ and $\varepsilon: U \to R^+$ there is an $h \in V_U(\varepsilon)$ such that $h(U \cap B) = U \cap B'$ ([12], Theorem 2.5). In the I-D case cap-sets are the pseudo-boundaries for the family of countable unions of Z-sets and fd cap-sets are the pseudo-boundaries for the family of countable unions of fd Z-sets.

In the Euclidean case the role of $\mathcal{S}$ is played either by $\mathcal{M}_n^k$, the family of countable unions of strong Z_{n-k-2}-sets in E^n (for $k \leq n-3$ this is the family of "tame" $\leq$ k-dimensional subsets of E^n) or by $\mathcal{P}_n^k$, the family of countable unions of "tame" polyhedra in E^n of dimension not higher than k. In explicit constructions are given for their respective k-dimensional pseudo-boundaries B_n^k and $\tilde{B}_n^k$. Their complements P_n^{n-k-1} and $\tilde{P}_n^{n-k-1}$ in E^n are (n-k-1)-dimensional.

E 1) For which pairs (n,k) is $P_n^{n-k-1} \cong \tilde{P}_n^{n-k-1}$? In the I-D case the complement of a cap-set and the complement of an fd cap-set are both homeomorphic to ℓ_2. It is felt that the sets B_n^k correspond to cap-sets and $\tilde{B}_n^k$ to fd cap-sets.

E 2) For which triples (n,m,k) is $P_m^k \cong P_n^k$ or $\tilde{P}_m^k \cong \tilde{P}_n^k$? No results are known.

A subset Y of a metric space X is *strongly negligible in* X if for each open U in X and $\varepsilon: U \to \mathbb{R}^+$ there is an $h \in V_U(\varepsilon)$ such that $h(X) \cap (U \cap Y) = \emptyset$.

<u>THEOREM</u>. *If* $k \geq \frac{n-1}{2}$ *then* σ*-compact subsets of* P_n^{n-k-1} *are strongly negligible in* P_n^{n-k-1}*, and if* $k \leq \frac{n-1}{2}$ *then compact subsets of* B_n^k *are strongly negligible in* B_n^k*. If* $k \geq \frac{n-1}{2}$ *and* $n \neq 4$ *then subsets of* $\tilde{P}_n^{n-k-1}$ *which are countable unions of tame (in* E^n*) polyhedra are strongly negligible in* $\tilde{P}_n^{n-k-1}$*, and if* $k \leq \frac{n-1}{2}$ *and* $n \neq 4$ *then compact subsets of* $\tilde{B}_n^k$ *are strongly negligible in* $\tilde{B}_n^k$*.*

E 3) What arbitrary compact subsets of $\tilde{P}_n^{n-k-1}$ are negligible for $\tilde{P}_n^{n-k-1}$?

E 4) Let $h: E^n \to E^n$ be a homeomorphism. Then $h(B_n^k)$ is a pseudo-boundary for M_n^k. Therefore for every open U in E^n and $\varepsilon: U \to R^+$ there exists a $g \in V_U(\varepsilon)$ such that $g(B_n^k \cap U) = h(B_n^k) \cap U$. Does there exist a g such that for *all* $k \leq n$, $g(B_n^k \cap U) = h(B_n^k) \cap U$? Similarly for $\tilde{B}_n^k$.

REFERENCES

[1] ANDERSON, R.D., *Spaces of homeomorphisms of finite graphs*, (preprint).

[2] BORSUK, K., *Theory of retracts*, Polska Akad. Nauk, Warsaw, 1967.

[3] BROWN, M., *Some applications of an approximation theorem for inverse limits*, Proc. Amer. Math. Soc., <u>11</u> (1960) 478-483.

[4] ČERNAVSKII, A.V., *Local contractibility of the homeomorphism group of a manifold*, Soviet Math. Dokl., <u>9</u> (1968) 1171-1174.

[5] CHAPMAN, T.A., *All Hilbert cube manifolds are triangulable*, (in preparation).

[6] CHAPMAN, T.A., *Classification of Hilbert cube manifolds and infinite simple homotopy types*, (preprint).

[7] CHAPMAN, T.A., *Locally flat embeddings of Hilbert cubes are flat*, (preprint).

[8] CHAPMAN, T.A., *On some applications of infinite-dimensional manifolds to the theory of shape*, to appear in Fund. Math.

[9] CURTIS, D.W. & R.M. SCHORI, 2^X *and* C(X) *are homeomorphic to the Hilbert cube*, (preprint).

[10] GEOGHEGAN, ROSS, *On spaces of homeomorphisms, embeddings and functions, I*, Topology, 11 (1972) 159-177.

[11] GEOGHEGAN, ROSS, *On spaces of homeomorphisms, embeddings and functions, II The piecewise linear case*, to appear in Proc. London Math. Soc.

[12] GEOGHEGAN, ROSS & R. RICHARD SUMMERHILL, *Pseudo-boundaries and pseudo-interiors in Euclidean spaces and topological manifolds*, (preprint).

[13] HANNER, O., *Some theorems on absolute neighborhood retracts*, Ark. Math. Svenska Vetensk. Akad., 1 (1951) 389-408.

[14] HAVER, W.E., *Locally contractible spaces that are absolute neighborhood retracts*, to appear in Proc. Amer. Math. Soc.

[15] HAVER, W.E., *The closure of the space of homeomorphisms on a manifold-The piecewise linear case*, (preprint).

[16] KEESLING, J. & D. WILSON, *The group of* PL-*homeomorphisms of a compact* PL-*manifold is an* ℓ_2^f-*manifold*, to appear.

[17] KELLEY, J.L., *Hyperspaces of a continuum*, Trans. Amer. Math. Soc., 52 (1942) 22-36.

[18] KIRBY, R.C., *Lectures on triangulations of manifolds*, University of California, Los Angeles, 1969.

[19] KROONENBERG, N., *Pseudo-interiors of hyperspaces*, (preprint).

[20] KROONENBERG, N., *Characterization of finite-dimensional* Z-*sets*, to appear in Proc. Amer. Math. Soc.

[21] LUKE, R. & W.K. MASON, *The space of homeomorphisms on a compact two-manifold is an absolute neighborhood retract*, Trans. Amer. Math. Soc., 164 (1972) 275-285.

[22] SCHORI, R.M., *Hyperspaces and symmetric products of topological spaces*, Fund. Math., 63 (1968) 77-88.

[23] SCHORI, R. & J.E. WEST, 2^I *is homeomorphic to the Hilbert cube*, Bull. Amer. Math. Soc., 78 (1972) 402-406.

[24] SPANIER, H., *Algebraic topology*, McGraw-Hill, New York, 1966.

[25] TORUŃCZYK, H., *Compact absolute retracts as factors of the Hilbert space*, to appear in Fund. Math.

[26] TORUŃCZYK, H., *Absolute retracts as factors of normed linear spaces*, (preprint).

[27] WEST, J.E., *Mapping cylinders of Hilbert cube factors*, General Topology and Appl., 1 (1971) 111-125.

[28] WEST, J.E., *The subcontinua of a dendron form a Hilbert cube factor*, Proc. Amer. Math. Soc., 36 (1972) 603-609.

[29] WEST, J.E., *Sums of Hilbert cube factors*, (preprint).

[30] WEST, J.E., *On fixed points of transformation groups*, Louisiana State University, 1966, (dissertation).

[31] WONG, R.Y.T., *On homeomorphisms of certain infinite-dimensional spaces*, Trans. Amer. Math. Soc., 128 (1967) 148-154.

[32] WONG, R.Y.T. & N. KROONENBERG, *Unions of Hilbert cubes*, (preprint).

ADDED IN PROOF

1) (H 4) Recently CURTIS & SCHORI have obtained an affirmative answer for a modified version of st(K).

2) (H 5) Recently CURTIS & SCHORI proved that $\{B \in 2^X \mid A \cap B \neq \emptyset\}$ is homeomorphic to Q.

3) (D 1) X is homeomorphic to the mapping cylinder M_f, where the base is homeomorphic to X. Thus if X is an AR, then X is homeomorphic to Q (see PF 3B).

4) (QM 3) This is recently proved to be the case by CHAPMAN.

5) (GA 1,2) Solved affirmatively by WEST for all finite group actions with only one common fixed point, with only the identity having more than one fixed point.

6) (GA 6) Trivially false by Lens space theory: there are homotopic fixed point free periodic homeomorphisms on S^3 whose orbit spaces have different simple homotopy type, and are therefore not equivalent, even when crossed with id_Q.

OTHER TITLES IN THE
SERIES MATHEMATICAL CENTRE TRACTS

A leaflet containing an order-form and abstracts of all publications mentioned below is available at the Mathematical Centre, 2e Boerhaavestraat 49, Amsterdam-1005, The Netherlands. Orders should be sent to the same address.

MCT 1 T. VAN DER WALT, *Fixed and almost fixed points*, 1963.

MCT 2 A.R. BLOEMENA, *Sampling from a graph*, 1964.

MCT 3 G. DE LEVE, *Generalized Markovian decision processes, part I: Model and method*, 1964.

MCT 4 G. DE LEVE, *Generalized Markovian decision processes, part II: Probabilistic background*, 1964.

MCT 5 G. DE LEVE, H.C. TIJMS & P.J. WEEDA, *Generalized Markovian decision processes, Applications*, 1970.

MCT 6 M.A. MAURICE, *Compact ordered spaces*, 1964.

MCT 7 W.R. VAN ZWET, *Convex transformations of random variables*, 1964.

MCT 8 J.A. ZONNEVELD, *Automatic numerical integration*, 1964.

MCT 9 P.C. BAAYEN, *Universal morphisms*, 1964.

MCT 10 E.M. DE JAGER, *Applications of distributions in mathematical physics*, 1964.

MCT 11 A.B. PAALMAN-DE MIRANDA, *Topological semigroups*, 1964.

MCT 12 J.A.TH.M. VAN BERCKEL, H. BRANDT CORSTIUS, R.J. MOKKEN & A. VAN WIJNGAARDEN, *Formal properties of newspaper Dutch*, 1965.

MCT 13 H.A. LAUWERIER, *Asymptotic expansions*, 1966, out of print; replaced by MCT 54.

MCT 14 H.A. LAUWERIER, *Calculus of variations in mathematical physics*, 1966.

MCT 15 R. DOORNBOS, *Slippage tests*, 1966.

MCT 16 J.W. DE BAKKER, *Formal definition of programming languages with an application to the definition of ALGOL 60*, 1967.

MCT 17 R.P. VAN DE RIET, *Formula manipulation in ALGOL 60, part 1*, 1968.

MCT 18 R.P. VAN DE RIET, *Formula manipulation in ALGOL 60, part 2*, 1968.

MCT 19 J. VAN DER SLOT, *Some properties related to compactness*, 1968.

MCT 20 P.J. VAN DER HOUWEN, *Finite difference methods for solving partial differential equations*, 1968.

MCT 21 E. WATTEL, *The compactness operator in set theory and topology*, 1968.

MCT 22 T.J. DEKKER, *ALGOL 60 procedures in numerical algebra, part 1*, 1968.

MCT 23 T.J. DEKKER & W. HOFFMANN, *ALGOL 60 procedures in numerical algebra, part 2*, 1968.

MCT 24 J.W. DE BAKKER, *Recursive procedures*, 1971.

MCT 25 E.R. PAERL, *Representations of the Lorentz group and projective geometry*, 1969.

MCT 26 EUROPEAN MEETING 1968, *Selected statistical papers, part I*, 1968.

MCT 27 EUROPEAN MEETING 1968, *Selected statistical papers, part II*, 1969.

MCT 28 J. OOSTERHOFF, *Combination of one-sided statistical tests*, 1969.

MCT 29 J. VERHOEFF, *Error detecting decimal codes*, 1969.

MCT 30 H. BRANDT CORSTIUS, *Excercises in computational linguistics*, 1970.

MCT 31 W. MOLENAAR, *Approximations to the Poisson, binomial and hypergeometric distribution functions*, 1970.

MCT 32 L. DE HAAN, *On regular variation and its application to the weak convergence of sample extremes*, 1970.

MCT 33 F.W. STEUTEL, *Preservation of infinite divisibility under mixing and related topics*, 1970.

MCT 34 I. JUHASZ a.o., *Cardinal functions in topology*, 1971.

MCT 35 M.H. VAN EMDEN, *An analysis of complexity*, 1971.

MCT 36 J. GRASMAN, *On the birth of boundary layers*, 1971.

MCT 37 G.A. BLAAUW a.o., *MC-25 Informatica Symposium*, 1971.

MCT 38 W.A. VERLOREN VAN THEMAAT, *Automatic analysis of Dutch compound words*, 1971.

MCT 39 H. BAVINCK, *Jacobi series and approximation*, 1972.

MCT 40 H.C. TIJMS, *Analysis of (s,S) inventory models*, 1972.

MCT 41 A. VERBEEK, *Superextensions of topological spaces*, 1972.

MCT 42 W. VERVAAT, *Success epochs in Bernoulli trials (with applications in number theory)*, 1972.

MCT 43 F.H. RUYMGAART, *Asymptotic theory of rank tests for independence*, 1973.

MCT 44 H. BART, *Meromorphic operator valued functions*, 1973.

MCT 45 A.A. BALKEMA, *Monotone transformations and limit laws*, 1973.

MCT 46 R.P. VAN DE RIET, *ABC ALGOL, A portable language for formula manipulation systems, part 1: The language*, 1973.

MCT 47 R.P. VAN DE RIET, *ABC ALGOL, A portable language for formula manipulation systems, part 2: The compiler*, 1973.

MCT 48 F.E.J. KRUSEMAN ARETZ, P.J.W. TEN HAGEN & H.L. OUDSHOORN, *An ALGOL 60 compiler in ALGOL 60, Text of the MC-compiler for the EL-X8*, 1973.

MCT 49 H. KOK, *Connected orderable spaces*, 1974.

* MCT 50 A. VAN WIJNGAARDEN, B.J. MAILLOUX, J.E.L. PECK, C.H.A. KOSTER, M. SINTZOFF, C.H. LINDSEY, L.G.L.T. MEERTENS & R.G. FISKER (eds.), *Revised report on the algorithmic language ALGOL 68*.

MCT 51 A. HORDIJK, *Dynamic programming and Markov potential theory*, 1974.

MCT 52 P.C. BAAYEN (ed.), *Topological structures*.

MCT 53 M.J. FABER, *Metrizability in generalized ordered spaces*, 1974.

MCT 54 H.A. LAUWERIER, *Asymptotic analysis, part 1*.

MCT 55 M. HALL JR. & J.H. VAN LINT (eds.), *Combinatorics, part 1: Theory of designs, finite geometry and coding theory*.

MCT 56 M. HALL JR. & J.H. VAN LINT (eds.), *Combinatorics, part 2: Graph theory; foundations, partitions and combinatorial geometry*.

MCT 57 M. HALL JR. & J.H. VAN LINT (eds.), *Combinatorics, part 3: Combinatorial group theory*.

MCT 58 W. ALBERS, *Asymptotic expansions and the deficiency concept in statistics*.

A star (*) before the number means "to appear".